W9-AXA-361

TOWARD A
CHRISTIAN ECONOMIC ETHIC

Stewardship and Social Power

Prentiss L. Pemberton
and Daniel Rush Finn

WINSTON PRESS

To Leota Pemberton
and Nita Jo Rush

Cover design: Terry Dugan

Printed in the United States of America

Library of Congress Catalog Card Number: 83-25409

ISBN: 0-86683-876-7

5 4 3 2 1

Winston Press, Inc.
430 Oak Grove
Minneapolis, Minnesota 55403

Contents

Preface iv

Chapter 1: Christianity and Economic Life: Overcoming
the Sense of Powerlessness 1

Part One
History of the Christian Economic Ethic

Chapter 2: Biblical, Patristic, and Medieval Resources
for a Christian Economic Ethic 26

Chapter 3: Luther and Calvin: Ethical Dilemmas of the
Commercial Revolution 53

Chapter 4: Lockean Liberalism: A Radical Shift from the
Biblical Economic Ethic 67

Chapter 5: New Challenges to the Christian Economic
Ethic: Revolutions Within Revolutions 83

Part Two
Toward an Effective
Christian Economic Ethic Today

Chapter 6: Beginning an Ethical Assessment of Economic
Analysis 116

Chapter 7: Social Justice and Economic Efficiency 139

Chapter 8: Empowering Justice in Economic Life 167

Chapter 9: Empowerment Through Small Disciplined
Communities 204

Notes 240

Index 252

Preface

Over the past twenty years Christians in the United States and their official church bodies have become far more attentive to public issues. This is not to say that there was a time when Christians were not involved *at all,* but that in recent years many groups of believers have asked themselves just what their faith implies for the public life of the nation and the world.

Of all the dimensions of public life that pose difficulties for morally sensitive people, economics is for most Christians the most difficult to understand and respond to. Of course, there is no *purely* economic issue, since every such issue is thoroughly entwined with social, political, and cultural elements. This truth makes the strengths of our economic system even stronger, as they are clearly rooted in our individual and collective lives in all their depth and variety. This truth is especially important for us to remember as we address the fundamental flaws in our economic system. For it is naive to assume that the only task before us is to solve our economic problems. Sinfulness permeates all of human life, and we must keep in mind that evil permeates all dimensions of our lives.

Still, it is useful to "take on" economic life by itself to analyze it in detail, to understand better its dynamics, and to make clear the relation between individual economic actions and the economy as a whole. In this book we will be doing just that in light of the demands of Christian faith. While we will not be examining all of economic science nor all of Christian ethics, we will be investigating each of these areas in our efforts to assist Christians who want to live more responsibly within the national and international economy.

In doing so, we will be relying on some of the insights of sociology concerning power and the internal operations of groups. This will allow the reader to understand better how social change comes about and how small groups of committed Christians can help bring about more just economic and social structures in their local situation and even in the nation as a whole. Employing social sciences such as sociology and economics entails the use of some language that may be foreign to many readers. Since technical language can be a barrier, we apologize in advance for the difficulties this may cause. Yet because the insights provided by social science are so important to understanding society, we have provided clear and straightforward explanations for these terms and have relied on them to sharpen the analysis of our economic life today. The need for greater economic justice in our society is so great that each of us needs to make an integrating effort such as this.

It is a fundamental conviction of Christian belief that any follower of Christ should live a life of both affirmation and critique. Believers need to affirm what is good and to critique what is not. In most of our daily life the affirmation and the critique take place in small groups, in the local organizations, in the local worshiping community. Less frequently, though regularly, it occurs in the public realm. The increased attention that Christians have been showing to public issues in recent years has most often been in the form of criticizing the current pattern of events. This has upset many people, so that some individuals and congregations have dissented from the positions taken by their church authorities. These same people often have a sense that the churches have become all too negative, all too quick to criticize or condemn the activities of the nation.

This is, however, a misreading. It only *seems* to be accurate because for so many years the Christian churches were so reluctant to engage in any critique at all. If anything, Christianity in the United States has most often affirmed all that the nation has stood for. Civic ceremonies on any national holiday illustrate this; so do the lessons for children taught at nearly every Sunday school or church school around the country. Yet many who

uncritically "baptize" American ways judge Christians who seek
justice to be ungrateful, unaffirming of what is good about life
here. This reaction is illustrated by those who reply to justice
efforts with "Don't you realize that if you were in Russia you'd be
jailed for such statements?" Such a reply reveals a defensiveness
and an un-Christian attachment to the status quo. Still, it reminds
us to be critical of sinfulness in social, economic, and political
structures of every society, even if we have a *particular* responsibility to alter those structures in our own nation.

We would like to thank a number of people who have been very
helpful to us as we prepared this book. We are grateful to
colleagues and students, too numerous to name, who have
challenged and taught us as we studied and struggled together in
facing our respective missions. St. John's University has provided
support in many ways, including a MacPherson grant for study
and travel. Ann Pilon spent many long hours typing the man-
uscript. Michael Yates worked hard on the index. Richard
Broholm of the Center for the Ministry of the Laity and Joseph
Friedrich and several others on the faculty at St. John's University
and the College of St. Benedict have made helpful suggestions.
We are grateful to Judson Press for permission to reprint Chapter
5, which appeared originally in *In the Great Tradition: In Honor of
Winthrop Hudson,* Joseph D. Ban and Paul R. DeKar, eds. (Valley
Forge, Pa.: Judson Press, 1982). All scripture quotes are taken
from the *Revised Standard Version Common Bible,* copyright ©
1973 by the Division of Christian Education of the National
Council of the Churches of Christ in the U.S.A. Used by
permission.

1

Christianity and Economic Life: Overcoming the Sense of Powerlessness

It is high time that all of us who claim to be Christians take a second look at just what Christian faith requires of us in regard to our economic values and commitments. We all too often presume that being a good Christian in all areas of life is either simple and straightforward (and that we do fairly well at it) or that it is so difficult and demanding that no one of us could possible live up to the standards set for us (and that it is naive to try to do so). Taking either of these positions leads to serious failings. We must see the ways in which both of them are true at the same time. It is a fundamental premise of this book that we have not really lived up to the demands that Christ places upon us in economic life, but that there are some clearly defined steps we can and must take to empower the Christian economic ethic in our lives.

We know, of course, that one of the clearest demands that Jesus articulated was for his followers to be on the side of the poor and the downtrodden.

We know, in addition, that being on the side of the downtrodden means fulfilling responsibly our obligations to all who are economically unsuccessful. It means living in accord with what Jesus was saying in his dramatic parable of the final judgment in Matthew 25. Here he announced that the Son of man will return as the king who will mete out judgment in his kingdom. Then comes the startling announcement that the judge sitting on his cosmic throne identifies himself with all suffering, rejected, exploited persons. When, therefore, the disciples have provided food and drink for the hungry and thirsty; when they have welcomed the stranger, clothed the naked, visited the sick, called upon those in prison; when they have ministered to the "least of these"—his brothers and sisters—they have likewise ministered to him.

And while we must share the goods we possess, we know, too, that our Christian faith requires that we work responsibly to help produce the goods and services that are required to sustain human life—our life and that of others. And we must do so in an ethically responsible manner: with honesty, fairness, common courtesy. Both what gets done and the way it is done are important.

Living according to the Christian economic ethic entails still another obligation that has been seen clearly only in recent centuries. Since the beginning of history, persons have sought to help one another but sometimes in piecemeal, tragic, even superstitious ways. Then, in the rapid change that occurred during the sixteenth through the nineteenth centuries, they began glimpsing possible new ways to organize human assistance. This new vision was part of the more general sense that people came to: that habitual patterns of human action could be changed, that social structures were not eternally fixed. And this in turn was related to the wider development of invention. Many new inventions began to change the face of human life, but more importantly, as one commentator put it, humans invented how to invent! The mindset of people slowly began to shift. Rather than taking the current situation for granted, they began to assume that things could be improved—whether through science and engineering, through national political change, or through discussion and decision in a small local organization.

This remarkable historical development opened up unheard of possibilities for developing more humane and ethically founded social structures. Whereas in earlier times the Christian economic ethic was either primarily personal (in the sense of individual) or else was limited to obligations *within* the churches, the driving force of that ethic could now be channeled to humanize economic life more generally. Unfortunately, just when the churches could have helped to structure this beneficial change, too often they failed to do so. It was precisely during the sixteenth through the nineteenth centuries, especially during the Lockean era, that the prophetic biblical word became overwhelmed by a secular and less humane formulation of what human life is and could be. We hope that during the remainder of the twentieth century we may rediscover the imperative for new and sound moral structures. If we are to build such structures, we must do nothing less than gain a new vision of what it means to be a twentieth-century good Samaritan.

Let us concede that we are no longer good Samaritans if, for example, we visit those sick with malaria but do not help to structure community health programs to deal with the mosquitoes that spread the disease. We are no longer good Samaritans if we complain about big government with its bloated bureaucracies and behind-the-scenes pressure groups but do not also help to structure more nonpartisan, general-interest lobbies that work resolutely to reduce inefficiency and secrecy in what should be public areas of government. Are we in the churches—to become quite specific—aware of crucial structural differences between the oil lobby and the Common Cause lobby: differences in what they expect of their members in closed or open ways, in how they decide to support or oppose certain policies, and in the goals they strive to obtain? The oil lobby is expected to seek special advantage for its member corporations, while the goal of the nonpartisan Common Cause lobby is to promote policies that serve the well-being of public causes and programs. This is not to say that one is always wrong and the other always right, but that there is a pivotal difference. Have we in the churches really thought through what will be required of us if we are to structure new efficiency and fairness?

This all means, in other words, that twentieth-century good Samaritans must marshal a new kind of power—power to build counter-structures that effectively challenge unjust social structures. Even as we organize power to move against special-interest organizations, our Christian motivation must stem from care for, not from hostility to, our opponents. Our goal must be to

structure not pain and divisiveness, but new health and together-
ness for all people.

The United States:
In Need of a Sound Economic Ethic

Compared with most of the world, our nation is extremely
wealthy. It is true, of course, that the United States some time
ago was surpassed as the nation with the greatest wealth per
person (technically put as "per capita gross national product"). We
now rank approximately fourteenth on the list (behind Belgium,
Denmark, France, West Germany, Luxembourg, Norway, Swe-
den, Switzerland, and a number of other nations). Still, there is no
question that U.S. citizens enjoy a standard of living that far
surpasses that of most other people on this planet.

By contrast, the most severe economic problems are found
not in the United States but in the nations of the Third World.
Bangladesh, for example, is a nation with an area about the size of
Wisconsin and a population of eighty million people, half of whom
consume less than the 1500 calories per day considered to be the
minimum survival level.[1] In Latin America, Africa, and Asia a
billion people go hungry in agricultural areas where the best farm
land is used to produce "cash crops" for export to the United
States and Europe. In the face of such problems, the economic
difficulties of U.S. citizens are relatively small.

So it might seem that any inquiry into the demands of a
Christian economic ethic would have to begin with the problems
and challenges faced in the Third World. But this would not be the
best way to proceed. We do not mean to make light of the
extremely harsh, inhumane, and even violent conditions faced by
the poor and oppressed in the rest of the world. Rather, the
difficulty with centering on the Third World is that while all agree
that fundamental economic structures need to be changed, the
proposed solutions vary tremendously. In particular, advocates of
a free market system claim that the hope of the poor in the

developing countries is to move more and more toward an economic system like ours in the United States, while critics of the free market system claim that developing countries must move to more worker ownership of firms, planning of growth, and greater control of large multinational corporations operating in those countries.

This difference appears very clearly in recent writings of two Christian theologians addressing the demands of the Christian economic ethic. Liberation theologian Gustavo Gutiérrez has argued that the poverty of Latin America is directly related to the influence of multinational firms and the international economic system. He sees the need for common people to liberate themselves from the economic oppression in which they find themselves.[2] On the other hand, North American theologian Michael Novak argues that Latin America suffered from poverty long before multinationals were formed and that it is exactly the capitalist spirit and the investment capital of multinationals that will be the only salvation for poor nations. Novak sees the temptation of planning and control to be a trap that would lead Third World nations to totalitarian socialism.[3]

The debate between these two positions is crucially important, but it is our judgment that it will not and cannot be resolved until we have answered this question about the economic problems experienced in the United States: Are the structures of economic life in the United States fundamentally sound, or do they need some basic change? If thoughtful North Americans conclude that our own system requires significant change, then any proposal for assisting the Third World will have to entail some serious challenge to the way our nation and American multinational firms operate in the international economic arena.

Hence this book will concentrate on the operation of the economic structures in the U.S. economy. This could have the unintended negative effect of leading the reader to think that the problems of the rest of the world are unimportant or can be ignored in assessing our moral responsibilities in the economic realm. Nothing could be farther from the truth. We center on the United States because those who argue against employing the

Christian economic ethic to transform national and world economic structures generally presume that in the United States
economic life is already structured as it ought to be. It is not.

The single most important fact pointing to the faulty structuring of our economy is something that many Americans do not
realize: One out of every six citizens of this nation lives with
serious deprivation.

It is part of our upbringing to be convinced that we live in the
wealthiest nation on earth, where anyone who wants to can "get
ahead." The United States has the most productive industrial
system in the world, and Americans benefit from this system in
an unprecedented way. But because such a large portion of our
people do *not* participate in this wealth, our self-image as a nation
is not accurate. Because most of us do *not* see the millions of poor
in the country, we have never even questioned our illusion of
universal prosperity.

Let us introduce a special category of economically "successful" individuals—those who achieve career employment
within a context of Christian commitment. It is to this group that
this book is primarily addressed. Even as we link "success,"
career employment, and biblical commitment, we need to alert
ourselves to the moral threat in career success. All too often in
the past, Christians (and others, of course) have ranked their
own personal success over the obligations they owe to others
who are less well treated in the system.

Indeed, we introduce the idea of a Christian sense of "career
success" with considerable hesitancy. Other religious terms such
as "vocation" or "calling" would be preferable in many ways. We
concede that there is a very real danger in linking career success
to the obligations of biblical commitment. Yet as we will make
clear in Chapter 9, biblical commitment must be empowered to
inspire and discipline career success within small communities of
biblical disciples.

The term "successful careers" here refers to positions or jobs
where persons find at least basic satisfactions in their employment, where their pay provides for at least a decent standard of
living, where fringe benefits are perquisites to the job, where

most workers feel sufficient confidence in future benefits, advances, and promotions to be reasonably committed to their firms or organizations, and where employees feel some respect for their employers. We stress that these factors, plus others that could be cited, are not all essential to career success for every worker. But at least some of them and often all of them will be operative in the process of achieving a career.

Money can become a positive means for successfully achieving personal and institutional goals. For individuals, money opens to us the procurement of life's necessities and the privilege of acquiring and enjoying the arts, literature, and many other enriching areas of human life. Institutionally, money opens to us resources with which to support many organizations and causes. But these very opportunities are some of the pressures that must be faced and controlled by biblical commitment. Indeed, the question of how successful individuals can live responsibly looms large in deliberations about the Christian economic ethic in the United States.

We now turn to those who fail to achieve career employment. Just as a well-paying position is a sign of *success,* failure to attain career work and larger incomes becomes a mark of *unsuccess.* Some 46 million United States citizens (including dependents) are locked out of career employment and locked into menial, dead-end jobs or into sheer joblessness.

These unsuccessful persons tend to be judged utterly unqualified to move into career employment in our economic system. Even in the best of economic times, it is for them an act of futility to check the many employment opportunities cited in the Sunday *New York Times,* even though those pages offer attractive, high-paying professional or union careers. Who among these impoverished unsuccessful can hope to become "software engineers" or "financial engineering analysts"?

Robert K. Merton, the late distinguished sociologist at Columbia University, has probed this money-success-unsuccess theme. He begins, ". . . although 'success' has of course been diversely defined in American culture . . . no other definition 'enjoys such universal favor in America as that which equates success with making money.'"[4] Merton points out that there is a "comparatively marked emphasis on the moral obligation as well as the factual possibility of striving for monetary success and of achieving it."[5]

Merton warns, finally, that the assumption that acquiring a larger income is a major key to success cannot but downgrade the impoverished to unsuccess and failure. This leads to a subsidiary theme which Merton develops and which we will later see is rooted in the individualistic mindset that Americans, both rich and poor, tend to hold. All too often, people presume that

> success or failure are results wholly of personal qualities, that he who fails has only himself to blame, for the corollary of the concept of the self-made man is the self-unmade man. . . . Failure represents a double defeat: the manifest defeat of remaining far behind in the race for success and the implicit defeat of not having the capacities and moral stamina needed for success.
>
> The moral mandate to achieve success thus exerts pressure to succeed, by fair means if possible and by foul means if necessary.[6]

The link between economic failure, unemployment, and crime has been voluminously documented. The "unsuccess" of the welfare system visits the tragedy of parents upon their children into future generations. The parents, locked into the frustrations of this poverty cycle, often are simply unable to provide the example, education, and training that might boost their children into successful careers.

How did we reach this figure of forty-six million unsuccessful Americans? We begin with the U.S. government's definition of the poverty level. This level is based on an "economy food plan"—a minimal diet—drawn up by the Department of Agriculture in 1961. Since a 1955 food-consumption survey had indicated that most families of three or more persons spend about one-third of their income on food, the poverty level for these families was set at three times the money cost of the economy food plan. Each year this is adjusted for inflation, and as a result the dollar amount of "the poverty level" has been rising each year—although because of inflation, these rising dollar amounts are able to buy only exactly as much as the lower amounts could in earlier years. That is, in "real," uninflated dollars, the poverty level stays the same, year after year.

Because the poverty level is such a minimal standard of living, the government also began keeping records about families whose incomes were below 125% of the poverty level. This income level still represents a minimal standard of living and significant deprivation, and so it is a more helpful way of measuring just how many Americans are living in economic hardship.

The following table shows that in 1982 there were about forty-six million Americans living below 125% of the poverty level. We have chosen the year 1982 because it is far enough distant in time to allow for a wide range of relevant statistics in many comparable areas. As the table and even more recent data indicate, the number of people suffering in poverty has increased since then.

AMERICANS AND THE POVERTY LEVEL[7]

Year	Millions below poverty level	% below poverty level	Millions below 125% of poverty level	% below 125% of poverty level
1959	39.5	22.4%	54.8	31.1%
1969	24.1	12.1%	34.7	17.4%
1979	25.3	11.7%	35.1	15.8%
1980	29.3	13.0%	40.7	18.1%
1981	31.8	14.0%	43.7	19.3%
1982	34.4	15.0%	46.5	20.3%

The National Advisory Council on Economic Opportunity made an annual report to the President and Congress in October

1980. This updated information concerning the poverty syndrome should alert all of us to changing nuances within this ongoing problem. Arthur I. Blaustein, Chairperson of the Council, warned of several disturbing developments:[8]

• Some are promoting the "glib" view that "growth in the private economy" is the best means to fight poverty. "Such growth has ceased to 'trickle down' to the poor."

• Federal programs such as welfare and food stamps as well as anti-poverty programs are responsible for virtually all of the reduction of 11 million people in the population of poor people since 1964. Let us remind ourselves that that reduction came mostly in the 1960s. Note, in the above table, that there is no improvement from the 1960s to the 1980s in the percentages of Americans below the poverty level or below 125% of the poverty level.

• There is a "frightening pattern" in the shifting makeup of the poverty population, with increasing portions being women, youth, and minorities "who are beyond the reach of most of the benefits of private sector growth."

• Inflation has raised the poverty level for a non-farm family of four from $2973 in 1959, to $8414 in 1980. (For 1983, the number was about $10,000.)[9]

Those left behind in our economy have neither the power nor the numbers to demand and obtain their fair share in the politico-economic arena, if the successful ignore or oppose them. The above table reveals that all was not well with United States economy throughout the seventies, so far as improving the economic situation of the 46 million impoverished was concerned. In the face of overall economic growth in real, non-inflated dollars from $1.07 trillion in 1970 to $1.38 trillion in 1978, there was no real reduction in the numbers or percentages of the locked-out and seriously deprived. Here is clear evidence that the growing prosperity of the majority was not trickling down to the destitute. The inability of our economy to include these economically unsuccessful indicates that it is dangerously skewed. The impoverished are never able to become active participants in producing and consuming, saving, and investing—a serious loss to the national economy.

Today's large minority of indigent persons is all too often neglected by the successful majority. This confronts the nation with both an economic and a moral crisis that is, in many ways, more ominous than the calamitous Great Depression of the thirties. Indeed, many can well remember how urgently almost everyone recognized, by the time of the bank crisis in 1933, that the nation was teetering on the very brink of total disaster. More than one-third of the labor force was unemployed, and all banks were suddenly closed from March 6 through March 9, 1933, by the newly elected president, Franklin D. Roosevelt. Emergency action was imperative. Today, however, one sixth of the nation's people—the locked-out and the seriously deprived—all too often are swept under the rug of public indifference.

We economically advantaged need to awaken to the present plight of so many millions. We must realize that the 46 million of the nation's economic unsuccessful in 1982 were equal, roughly, to the total combined population of Florida, Georgia, South Carolina, West Virginia, Washington, D.C., Delaware, New Jersey, and Pennsylvania. Is not this host of needy persons too many to be ignored or brushed aside with patronizing, inadequate handouts? How can we begin to tear down the wall that is partitioning off the 46 million unsuccessful from the rest of America?

As we recognize the urgency of this question, we can also see that many other aspects of economic life need our attention. The United States needs a sound energy policy, one that will ensure adequate supplies without irresponsible depletion of resources. Local communities want and need more control over the large firms that affect communal life so drastically when factories move to regions with lower labor costs. Older Americans hear apprehensively public debate over cuts in Social Security, for many the only source of retirement income. More and more Federal money is spent on weapons systems of immense destructiveness while funds for education and research in non-military areas are reduced severely. U.S. leaders decry the violation of national sovereignty in Central America when Cuban arms are shipped across national borders, yet the United States secretly funds right-wing military operations aiming to overthrow socialist governments in the region.

It should be clear that the United States is not the only nation where fundamental changes in policies and structures are needed. The Christian ethic places demands on every nation and critiques the evils inherent in each economic and political system. It is a gross misunderstanding of the Christian message to think that any criticism of the United States is equivalent to a defense of, say, life in the Soviet Union. In fact, the Christian ethic is fundamentally opposed to much that the U.S.S.R. stands for in the world: the jailing of dissidents, the denial of free speech and assembly, the invasion of neighboring states—the list goes on.

The point here is that no matter how bad things are in the Soviet Union or elsewhere, Americans have the obligation to improve life at home. The bumper sticker that reads "America, Love It or Leave It" indicates a flagrantly irresponsible attitude. It makes sacred a mere human institution that, like all human endeavors, is flawed by sin. Thus in this book we will be examining our economic system in the United States in the light of the Christian economic ethic. Similar examinations of life in the U.S.S.R., Great Britain, China, West Germany, and every other nation are important, but this small volume cannot include them within its scope. Instead we will focus on some of those issues that silhouette the character of economic life in the United States: for example, poverty, energy policy, government regulation, and the character of American firms.

These and many more issues are in the news daily. What should we do about them? What *can* we do about them? We will turn to several of these problems in later chapters, but for now we must realize that whatever answer Christians develop will have to deal creatively with the moral structures of society.

The Christian Economic Ethic
and Reformative Structural Power

In the face of problems as severe and persistent as the ones we have just reviewed, the crucial question for us all is this: Can committed Christians exert reformative structural power to alter our economic life in the United States in accord with more fully human values? We are in the realm of social ethics when we ask this inescapable question. To develop careful answers to this question, and to any question involving social ethical issues, we need first to recognize the important difference between individual action and structured action.

Individual action is almost self-explanatory. It entails doing something as an individual—a citizen voting in an election, or an individual feeding a hungry person—without organizing these actions with others into ongoing patterns of action designed to shape future policies or social structures.

Structured action occurs when members of any group *expect or require one another to enact certain ongoing patterns of behavior.* Individuals cannot initiate and carry out structured action on their own. Participation in a group is needed for structured action to come about. The whole point to a structured action is that it is not just a matter of whim on the part of the individual. Even important decisions, which are by no means a matter of whim, do not entail structured action unless the person who makes the decision is significantly influenced by an expectation or a requirement arising from a group with which that person identifies.

For example, a woman who has recently retired from a job she has held many years comes to feel that she now has time to do some volunteer work in service to others. She wants to visit elderly shut-ins who are often lonely and feel cut off from the rest of the community. If this woman decides simply to visit one or more elderly people on her own, she is involved in individual action—though certainly individual action that is quite commendable. But if she decides to become part of the social service project her congregation is engaged in, she participates as a group where she influences and is influenced by group expectations about the importance of such service to elderly persons. What actually goes on between her and any elderly shut-in she visits may not appear different from what would happen if she were not part of the wider group (though discussion with others making similar visits will probably give her some insight that will help her). By becoming a part of the group and identifying with it, however, her own resolve is likely to become stronger, and her convictions are likely to reaffirm and strengthen the commitment of the others. In fact, if the group actually works at it, this mutual raising of expectations can deepen the accountability of all to live in accord with the gospel demand to visit the sick.

Another important element of the definition of structured action is that it can be either expected or required. The most strictly structured actions in any society are those required by law. We must each pay income taxes; if we do not, the laws of the land (which we have approved through our representatives in Congress) stipulate serious penalties. Most of us, of course, pay our taxes not just because we might be put in jail if we don't. Most of us would pay our fair share even if the penalty were less severe, and many would continue to pay even if there were no penalty at all for not doing so. However, since we recognize that some sort of equitable taxation is necessary to accomplish public goals, we do *require* payment under pain of severe penalty. Other kinds of actions may be required, but not in so exacting a way. When a club or other voluntary organization imposes obligations through rules, the penalty is not so severe, but the idea is that some things are required rather than voluntary for members of the group. Thus, even with the realm of "required" action there is a range of seriousness.

When we turn to behavior that is "expected" rather than required, we find an even greater range of possibilities. A very loosely defined group will often have some very "soft" expectations of one another. In an adult education course in cooking or woodworking, for example, participants may feel some expectation to attend even if they do not feel like it on a particular evening, but usually the sense is a very weak one. At a corporate office, on the other hand, employees may feel a very strong expectation that they should attend the office Christmas party whether they want to or not. There may be no explicit rule about attending—it is not "required"—but the expectation is a powerful one. What this means is that while there may be no explicitly stated penalty for not attending, there are indeed some costs in a more informal sense. Co-workers may question that person's willingness to associate with them. The boss may begin to doubt that employee's "commitment" to the firm.

Employees might still go to the party because they expect to have a good time, and people may still go to the adult education class because they want to learn, but there are additional motivations embedded in the groups' expectations of group members. Returning to our earlier example, once the retired woman joins the church group, she does not then visit elderly people only because it is expected of her. No, she still *wants* to do so. But her wanting to visit the elderly is strengthened by the additional expectation that shapes her commitment.

One obvious difference in these examples is that while the office employees probably have no control over the expectation to attend the Christmas party, the woman did decide to allow the group to expect certain things of her. In both cases, group expectations or "norms" have their influence, but in the latter the group was more self-conscious about them. This is a crucial element in social ethics. The group must give careful attention to the expectations that prevail among its members. In fact, in many groups—Christian or otherwise—expectations are in force that are not healthy and that do not further the goals that both the individuals and the group hold dear. For instance, in some groups there is the unstated expectation that no one will openly and strongly disagree with anyone else. This pushes disagreements below the surface, prevents the members' group from dealing with an issue, and blocks any action regardless of how important it is to the group.

Christian social ethics requires that we be clear and conscious about the norms that prevail in group life. We must move to take responsibility for them. We must address them with conscientious intentions and must ensure that the expectations and requirements in social life are in accord with just ultimate values. Kurt Baier aptly summarizes a healthy moral point-of-view as follows: "(O)ne is not egotistical, one is doing things on principle, one is willing to universalize one's principle, and in doing so one considers the good of everyone alike."[10] The choice as to which particular values should be incorporated into our common economic life will be addressed in detail in Chapters 2 through 8. If either conscientious intentions or just values are missing from consideration, the power inherent in group expectations can and will be marshaled for destructive purposes rather than for healthier communal and individual life.

We can, however, affect social structures if we are careful to begin with conscientious intentions as we work toward just ultimate values and if we are equally careful to develop additional expectations appropriate to the current situation. We must stress how important it is to improve group expectations in a *realistic* way. If we are not careful to estimate what the group is ready for and what would be an unrealistic dream, we might be trying to push ourselves as a group to a level of commitment that is absolutely unobtainable at this time. Then the members would either ignore the new expectation or, if pushed too hard by group leaders, simply withdraw. For example, the members of that church social concern project may be ready to raise their expectations of one another to spend two afternoons each week in visiting the elderly, and a discussion of this norm may solidify and strengthen such a resolve in each member of the group. However, for group leaders to expect members to spend four afternoons each week may simply be unrealistic.

What we are aiming for, then, is to develop norms—whether expected or required—that will be actually operative in the life of a group. If such norms are carefully devised, the group will in fact marshal the power to enact actual change. As we have seen, this power may be either the force of expectation or requirement, but it will bring about concrete change in the actions or policies of the group.

Figure 1 summarizes this understanding of communal life.

FIGURE 1
Building Sound Moral Structures

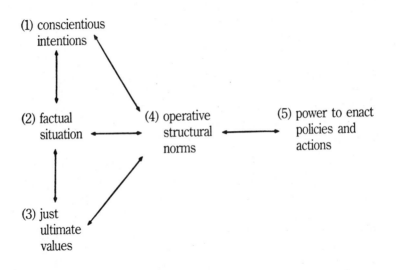

Here is the interactive process for building sound moral structures. The double-arrow lines indicate back-and-forth interactions. We isolate each of the above five ethical factors on the chart, but all of them are in dynamic exchange; one's inner conscientious intentions are always shaped and structured by foundational ultimate values, and vice versa. Indeed, a sound moral structure can disentangle the biblical economic ethic from foolish dependence upon either powerless abstract ideals (mere talk about love and justice) or powerless unstructured individual actions.

By beginning with conscientious intentions we can build a sounder moral structure in the economic realm if we develop operative structural norms that aim at ultimately just values in light of the current situation. When this is done well, the power to enact concrete actions and social policies is created and exercised.

We have seen several examples on the scale of relatively small groups. We now turn to a more dramatic and historic example: the Montgomery bus boycott, a crucial event in the struggle of black Americans for civil rights.

On December 1, 1955, Mrs. Rosa Parks was riding on a bus in Montgomery, Alabama. Tired from her hard work, she refused to yield her seat to a white male when all seats were filled. She refused even though she knew full well that a Montgomery legal ordinance required blacks to sit behind whites, or, if all seats were filled, to stand up and surrender their seats to whites. On that historical day, however, Mrs. Parks simply refused to kowtow to this senseless injustice and humiliation. She was, of course, arrested as a lawbreaker. But quickly her challenge to a tradition that segregated and discriminated against blacks as second-class citizens triggered the beginning of the long Montgomery bus boycott.

Mrs. Parks telephoned Mr. E. D. Nixon to report her arrest, and he called others to meet and face this new crisis: Ralph D. Abernathy, W. E. Powell, Martin Luther King, Jr., and other ministers and lay persons. They immediately began organizing the Montgomery Improvement Association, which provided leadership for the boycott. Dr. King was elected its first president. Later he led in organizing the Southern Christian Leadership Conference (SCLC) in Atlanta, and this conference became an affiliate of the Montgomery Improvement Association.

The Montgomery movement continued to focus upon the bus boycott. The bus company suffered a costly decrease in riders. Finally, after 381 tense, sometimes violent days and nights, the U.S. Supreme Court declared the bus segregation law unconstitutional. The black boycott had won a significant victory.

Ever since slavery was introduced in this tormented nation, there had been, across the South primarily, many individuals and small bands of blacks (sometimes supported by a few whites) who defied and rebelled against these dehumanizing legal structures and customs. But it was not until after December 1, 1955, that blacks took the lead in organizing a massive, continuing set of voluntary structures which created radically new expectations that anti-racists should and could stand against white bigots.

The Montgomery Improvement Association and the SCLC took the lead in building an intentional black-white community for racial justice, with black churches often at the forefront. Sound new moral-political structures were created in Montgomery and across the South during 1955-56. How did all this come about?

By referring to Figure 1 we can illustrate how the building of this new community developed. A sound new moral structure began to arise from inner, critical moral consciences (1) from roots in the ultimate values of the gospel (3) and of a long-suffering black community (2). The factual signs of black impoverishment and denigration in the South confronted them empirically (2). Indeed, Mrs. Parks' action triggered a new operative structural norm concerning what blacks should expect of one another (4). New policies called blacks to a "walk for freedom" (5). The black community began to put into practice the new operative norm concerning their refusal to ride the buses. Then the civil rights movement enlarged the norms to challenge other forms of segregated and discriminating public accommodations and other areas of religious, political, and economic injustice.

The Crucial Issue of Power in Operative Norms

In the light of these historical achievements in race relations—many of them brought about during the Montgomery bus boycott—we need to ferret out what is surely one of the most critical problems in this field, the problem of *social power*.

How often in ethical discussions we affirm what *ought* to be, yet seem helpless to determine what *will* be! If a church person is affirming moral values before a legislative committee in reference to some current issue, sooner or later this Christian spokesperson is likely to be asked, "How many 'troops' can you call into action?" Such a question is intended to expose the powerlessness of idealists who lack actual political power. This realization should bring us face to face with a crucial question: Will our building of a sound normative structure *empower* us to enact what ought to happen in concrete areas of policy and social action? A second question that calls for a careful answer is, What empowered the blacks of Montgomery to refuse bus rides until the existing legal structure of bus services was dismantled?

We submit that the answer is not in piecemeal individual action—there had been much of that during past centuries. The breakthrough came when thousands of people were quickened by a fresh vision of the present and future power they could marshal by means of new, voluntarily expected norms or patterns to defy the law, for the sake of a higher, more just law. They intuitively sensed that in between weak, unstructured individual action and coercively unjust laws that required discriminatory bus seating, there was a new operative and normative guideline that could lead to new policies for acceptable bus seating.

After their consciences were motivated to "walk for freedom," *after* they deepened their ultimate values, and *before* the unjust law was dismantled, the thousands of protestors had become a voluntary, disciplined, nonviolent, powerful movement for restructuring social life. Their discovery has much to teach us about effecting social change.

Sociologists point us to the heart of how this moral and voluntarily expected power can freely generate social change. Voluntary expectations always rest upon norms or patterned structures. Thus, during the frequent Montgomery rallies, Dr. King and others exhorted those attending to feel that this was their opportunity to volunteer to share in the walk for freedom. But why did so many volunteer, and why did they expect others to volunteer?

The first answer is that voluntarily expected norms may be only abstractly held in the mind (in which case they lack the power to trigger action) or they may be fully *operative*. "An 'operative' norm is one that is not merely entertained in the mind but is considered worthy of following in actual behavior; thus, one feels that one ought to conform to it."[11] Note how the power arising from an operative norm is doubly oriented: (1) acting according to such a norm is not an unpleasant duty; rather, it is "worthy" of being followed in actual behavior; (b) it depends upon an inner sense of duty to motivate public conformity. Thus, in Montgomery, participants became convinced that they were walking to achieve a future freedom for their grandchildren, which made walking preferable to riding buses during their present deprivations. New behavior (not riding buses) was definitely expected by large numbers of blacks.

In the light of this interpretation of operative norms, we can now briefly note definite ways in which such norms become effective in restructuring public policies and actions. There are, in other words, *four tests* that sound operative norms must pass if they are to generate the indispensable moral and political power to form new effective policies.

1. Vital operative norms need to *focus upon specific, easily interpreted, transformative policies.*
The manifest goal of the Montgomery Improvement Association and the SCLC focused upon changing the existing traditions and laws with regard to bus seating. Many other goals were latent in this protest, some of them profound and ultimate. Blacks and whites knew that deeply inculcated segregating and discriminating patterns were at stake. But note especially that this focus upon one clear-cut issue of bus seating kept the cause so simple that an eight-year-old could understand and act for greater justice and freedom.

2. Vital operative norms need to *connect their simply-interpreted policies with transformative values.*
This need is already glimpsed in our point on focus. One radical issue at stake (radical in the sense of penetrating down to the

roots) was: Are blacks full, or second-class, human beings and citizens? Significantly, the leaders of the Movement continuously linked pragmatic bus seating with creative biblical and human values.

3. Vital operative norms need to be built upon the awareness that nonviolent, deep-level social change in democracies can occur *when large numbers of persons bring about small degrees of radical policy change.*

When personal income-tax payers authorize the federal government to allocate one dollar of their tax payment to the political party of their choice, presidential campaigns are financed publicly and made more equitable. When large numbers of people are involved, small degrees of focused change can generate accumulated power. Hence the issue of bus seating becomes a wisely chosen policy.

Bus seating was not so extremist that only a few persons would risk all. Rather, it was a reasonable goal that eliminated only one of many symbols of blacks' second-class life. Indeed, changing bus seating was, by itself, a minor action. Yet winning this particular protest could point toward a major victory. The general rule here is that persons who are striving to build sound new moral structures must pay careful attention to strategies whereby large numbers of persons can effect small degrees of social change.

4. Those who are building operative norms need to appreciate and *enact social power* in order to effect greater social justice and efficiency.

Power is the capacity to bring about an intended result. Power in social relations can be exerted by influence, by persuasion, by being able to provide rewards or to impose deprivations, or by using various kinds of coercion—e.g., physical or legal threat, or outright violence.[12]

Martin Luther King, Jr., and other black leaders had been challenging white racism by exercising the nonviolent direct power of influence and persuasion. Then, when Mrs. Parks refused to give up her seat to a white man, the decision by those black leaders was to launch a bus boycott. This, in turn, went beyond influential and persuasive power, although they continued to do everything possible to persuade everyone involved to avoid hatred and violent tactics.

Obviously, the commitment to the economic boycott on this large scale required moving into a new degree of power—*reward/deprivation*. Many blacks deprived themselves of their means of transportation, and the bus company was deprived of much-needed revenue. In spite of these responsible efforts, some of those resisting the "march for freedom" resorted to shootings and other terroristic acts—coercive violence.

Eventually, the Movement's disciplined use of power, and the consequent national protest against the city of Montgomery, resulted in the bus segregation law being appealed to the U.S. Supreme Court and being declared unconstitutional. Here an effective use of power became decisive. The careful yet inspired use of operative structural norms resulted in a more just society—obviously not in every possible way, but in some very crucial ones.

A Brief Summary of This Chapter and a Look Ahead

We have completed our introduction to the economic plight of this nation and the need to bring about structural change. The successful and the unsuccessful are before us. We are in position to perceive the tragic results that occur when the successful majority lacks a sound moral structure. The moral consciences of such a majority often do not nurture a genuinely critical moral point of view toward themselves and others. Their bumper stickers may read "I'm against poverty, I work." They often have a deep prejudice against the unsuccessful. They do not consider the "good of everyone alike." Weakness of moral conscience develops because they have failed to join their inner intentions with sound ultimate values. Furthermore, they seldom face the U.S. economic situation as it is. Self-sufficient achievers move into

desirable career jobs and fail to recognize how an existing network of operative norms assists them in attaining economic
success and condemns the unsuccessful to economic and personal failure. Thus the poor in these United States are too often
downgraded and forgotten.

We have also endeavored to develop an ethical method with
which to build sound moral structures. Operative norms are
essential in creating the power to build structured moral action.
They focus upon limited, concrete policies that can readily be
linked with ultimate values. Such norms can activate large numbers of people to bring about small degrees of radical policy
change by means of influential, persuasive, and reward-depriva-
tional power.

We are now ready to move into Part One, which centers upon
our interpretation of the biblical economic ethic in its various
historical settings, from early Old Testament times to the modern era. Chapter 2 develops an extended historical exposition of
the Judeo-Christian economic ethic. Our work will concentrate
upon the Christian development of this biblical ethic. [13]

Chapter 3 traces the beginning of the decline of the authority
of the biblical economic ethic, as the Protestant Reformation
failed to integrate it into the Commercial Revolution. Chapter 4
chronicles the sweeping rejection of the biblical economic ethic
during the roughly one century of Lockean Liberalism,
1680-1760. To conclude Part One, Chapter 5 brings us into the
disarray in Western economics, politics, and ethics that developed during the Industrial and Cybernetic/Nuclear Revolutions,
from 1760 into the present and immediate future.

PART ONE
History of the
Christian Economic Ethic

2

Biblical, Patristic, and Medieval Resources for a Christian Economic Ethic

To any thoughtful person who listens to the debates about how to treat our economic problems, it becomes immediately evident that many of our goals are in conflict. In addition, the means proposed to accomplish those various goals are often incompatible. Among the conflicting aims held by many Americans are low inflation and low unemployment, a high standard of living and the conservation of our natural resources, inexpensive staples like coffee and bananas and yet a responsible relationship with Third World nations, freedom from a stranglehold by OPEC and freedom to use our *own* economic might throughout the world. The list of conflicts goes on.

How should a Christian respond? By just ignoring the problem? Of course not. By making one's own self-interest the ultimate standard? That would be worse. By simply accepting the positions put forth by this political leader or that columnist? Obviously not. Rather, the believer ought first to look to the basic elements of Christian faith in beginning to answer such pressing economic questions. In order to do just that, we will in this chapter investigate the roots of a Christian economic ethic in the scriptures and will examine how that ethic was developed within Christianity through the patristic and medieval eras. This is perhaps the most fundamental way in which the Christian is a "radical"—in the original sense of "one who goes to the roots." Unless we ground ourselves in the development of the Christian perspective on economic matters, we may be able to call the positions we take *our* positions, but we ought not call them Christian.

The Biblical Roots of a Christian Economic Ethic

A major assumption underlying this work is that wherever biblical religion exists—Hebraic or Christian—it provides theological and moral resources for a sound economic life. (This is not to argue, however, that these religions have always utilized these resources effectively.) This constructive biblical economic ethic is founded upon faith's vision of God as the creator and possessor of all creation. This relationship of all persons and things to the Lord is central to every conclusion entailed by a biblical approach to economic life.

Crucial to the Old Testament vision of economic life is the fact that Israel was a people of God, a community. Hebraic religion was not primarily a one-to-one relation with God. Rather, God's action created a people of his own, and each Israelite related to the Lord as a member of that people. Thus, the very understanding of the human person was not that he or she was first an individual who then decided to be related to neighbor and to God. Instead, the person was essentially a part of a community within which he or she lived in relationship with God and others. When the prophets insist on justice for widows, orphans, and the poor, this is not merely a duty imposed by God or the nation. It is a natural outgrowth of the fact that each Israelite's own person is wrapped up in the other members of the people of God. Because each individual's identity is inextricably rooted in the covenant between Israel and the Lord, no individual can live a righteous and full life without addressing the needs of all of God's people. As John R. Donahue has put it, "The doing of justice is not the application of religious faith, but its substance."[1] The true worship of God cannot be separated from actions of justice within the human community.

As we emphasize the centrality of community in the Old Testament understanding of the individual person, another theme running parallel to this one also needs to be accentuated. This sense of community at the same time represents a breaking away from the exclusiveness that usually characterized tribal groups or clans in cultures based on extended families. This is most clearly seen in the frequency with which the scriptures affirmed the place of foreigners ("sojourners") within the Hebrew community.

> When a stranger sojourns with you in your land, you shall not do him wrong. The stranger who sojourns with you shall be to you as the native among you, and you shall love him as yourself; for you were strangers in the land of Egypt: I am the Lord your God.
>
> (Lev. 19:33-34)

Similarly, the people of Israel are directed to extend to the sojourner the same legal justice (Deut. 1:16-17 and Num. 15:16) and economic assistance (Deut. 10:17-19) as must be shown to the widows and orphans who were full members of the community from birth. The fact that the Old Testament views the person as communal as well as individual does *not* imply a degradation of all persons outside the community itself.

With regard to the question of property ownership, we should note that when initiating a covenant with Israel, God authorizes persons to acquire material goods so long as they fulfill their covenant obligations to use them justly and to share them charitably. In Deuteronomy God warns Israel:

> "Beware lest you say in your heart, 'My power and the might of my hand have gotten me this wealth.' You shall remember the LORD your God, for it is he who gives you power to get wealth; that he may confirm his covenant which he swore to your fathers, as at this day."
>
> (Deut. 8:17-18)

Here is a stern warning to God's people that their power to get wealth belongs within their covenantal obligations to the creator, who entrusts wealth to them.

The New Testament carries on and extends the insights of the Hebrew scriptures into economic life, but there was one point at which New Testament Christianity introduced new elements in its approach to wealth and property. Jesus was proclaiming a radical new age, already at hand and yet still coming—the age of God's kingdom on earth. Jesus, concerned primarily for new life in this kingdom, cautioned against the dangers of wealth. The first disciples he sent forth to preach the kingdom were told:

> "Take nothing for your journey, no staff, nor bag, nor bread, nor money; and do not have two tunics."
>
> (Lk. 9:3)

At the same time, however, Jesus made no effort to organize radical action against the wealthy. And although he challenged the rich young man to sell all and give to the poor, he did not command all disciples to do so.

Paul, the dominant missionary force after Jesus, accentuated this attitude toward economic interests.

> I have learned, in whatever state I am, to be content. . . . I have learned the secret of facing plenty and hunger, abundance and want.
>
> (Phil. 4:11-12)

In the first letter of Timothy we read:

> If we have food and clothing, with these we shall be content. But those who desire to be rich fall into temptation, into a snare, into many senseless and hurtful desires that plunge men into ruin and destruction. For the love of money is the root of all evils.
>
> (1 Tim. 6:8-10)

The author of Hebrews emphasized the same theme:

> Keep your life free from love of money, and be content with what you have.
>
> (Heb. 13:5)

These exhortations indicate how seriously the early Christians alerted themselves to the warning Jesus gave in Luke:

> "Sell your possessions, and give alms; provide yourselves with purses that do not grow old, with a treasure in the heavens that

does not fail, where no thief approaches and no moth destroys.
For where your treasure is, there will your heart be also."

(Lk. 12:33-34)

We learn further that in Acts there was brief enthusiasm in the earliest Church for holding "all things in common"—a "consumer communism of love," as Ernst Troeltsch has termed it. But there was no general movement in the churches toward such a consumer communism. Certainly there was no common Christian economic program to organize all production socialistically. As we will see, we must not interpret this naively as a condemnation of these possible forms of social organization. The point here is that unlike people of our day, Christians of the first centuries did not move to alter social and economic structures.

All the themes to which we have just pointed are rooted in Jesus' summary of the Old Testament law. In response to the lawyer's question: "Which is the great commandment in the law?" Jesus replied:

"You shall love the Lord your God with all your heart, and with all your soul, and with all your mind. This is the great and first commandment. And a second is like it, You shall love your neighbor as yourself. On these two commandments depend all the law and the prophets."

(Mt. 22:37-40)

Here Jesus ties together two major religious-ethical teachings from the Old Testament in Deuteronomy 6:15 and Leviticus 19:18. Only God can be loved consummately and unreservedly without falling into idolatry, while a healthy love for neighbor and self can become inclusive and reciprocal. Certainly these commandments, when identified with economic issues, require Christians to seek the neighbor's economic well-being, even as they seek their own.

Forgoers and Stewards: Two Lifestyles for an Economic Ethic

As we look more closely at the economic ethic embodied in the New Testament we find it actualized in two contrasting economic lifestyles. While these two ways of thinking and acting are different, they are not contradictory or ultimately conflicting. In order to understand them it is helpful to consider two New Testament individuals as role models. They depict, in "letters writ large," two types of persons who strive to love God totally and their neighbors mutually. The first of these two role-symbols is Paul (although others of the first apostles could be employed here). The second is Zacchaeus, the rich Jewish tax-collector.

As we have seen, Paul, like his Lord Jesus Christ, rejected the wealth, status, and prestige he might have possessed as a Pharisee. His courageous discipleship often brought him suffering, privations, attacks, imprisonment, and threats to life itself. He summarized his experience:

> . . . danger from rivers, danger from robbers, danger from my own people, danger from Gentiles, danger in the city, danger in the wilderness, danger at sea, danger from false brethren.
>
> (2 Cor. 11:26)

Throughout the remainder of this book the role that Paul embodied will be termed that of the economic "forgoer"—one who renounces nearly all economic possessions and resources.

Jesus, in calling persons into the mission of his kingdom, certainly called many to become forgoers.[2] He himself chose this stance. When sending forth his first followers, both the twelve and the seventy-two, he expressly commanded them to take no money or possessions while on their mission.

Jesus did not, however, summon all of his disciples to become forgoers. He recognized another, broader, less austere economic ethic for those disciples not called to become forgoers. This other public economic ethic was more readily universalizable and was required of all disciples: All others are summoned to become stewards.

Zacchaeus is the New Testament person who most fully represents the second role. He is described in Luke 19 as a rich, chief tax-collector. Many of his Jewish compatriots despised him for being a henchman, a traitor who served the Roman oppressor. Yet we learn from Zacchaeus that a steward is one who shares a proportionally generous part of his or her economic goods out of a genuine concern for the well-being of others.

Recall the dramatic meeting between Jesus and Zacchaeus, as recorded by Luke (19:1-10). Jesus invites himself to the tax-collector's home. As soon as they arrive Zacchaeus exclaims: "Behold, Lord, the half of my goods I give to the poor, and if I have defrauded anyone of anything, I restore it fourfold." Giving away half of his goods means that he went beyond the requirements of Old Testament tithing; compensating four-fold for defrauding means that he strove to avoid all cheating. Jesus replies cryptically: "Today salvation has come to this house, since he is also a son of Abraham. For the Son of Man came to seek and save the lost." Jesus makes no explicit reference to the economic practice that Zacchaeus had just outlined. What does all this mean?

It is commonly recognized that Luke is the Gospel writer who most severely criticizes the wealthy and the economically advantaged. Yet he is the only one of the three Synoptics who includes any reference to Zacchaeus. For whatever reason, Luke affirms that this rich tax-collector had an encounter with Jesus that deserved inclusion in the written record of the Gospel. Luke implies that Jesus gave silent approval to Zacchaeus' policy for procuring his income non-exploitatively within a corrupt tax-collection system, and for sharing that income in significant proportions.

Zacchaeus and his steward ethic become, then, crucially important as a parallel to the forgoer ethic to which some believers are called. We conclude that Jesus accepted Zacchaeus as a prosperous but just and caring tax-collector, and as a person moving into Christian discipleship. We conclude from all this that there is a non-ascetic dimension to economic stewardship that needs to be recognized and accepted.

The reader might ask whether too much is being read into this dialogue, since Luke does not report Jesus making explicit reference to the economic commitments so important to Zacchaeus. However, this is a silence that speaks loudly. Jesus was apparently satisfied with Zacchaeus' pattern of stewardship. He must have perceived beneath Zacchaeus' economic policies the faith and intentions of one ready for deeper commitment to the kingdom.

This interpretation of the Zacchaeus story correlates well with the overall direction of Luke's Gospel. In Luke's account Jesus does speak approvingly of this despised tax-collector. Certainly Jesus felt no need to cross-examine Zacchaeus in the manner in which he had queried and challenged the rich young man in Luke 18. Recall that this young man, too, had professed genuine concern for eternal life. Soon, however, Jesus exposed how this young man's prior commitment was to his wealth and to the status and pleasures it assured.

In addition, Jesus' implicit approval of Zacchaeus' economic ethic takes on added significance for us today in the face of the fact that much of the New Testament was written in a setting of eschatological expectation, an expectation of the imminent coming of the kingdom. Scripture scholars tell us that Luke was trying to downplay this belief and to stress those teachings and events in Jesus' life that would prepare the disciples for a full life-time on earth. Thus this example of a responsible economic life is important. Here is a development that points toward Luther's later affirmation of secular vocation as crucial to discipleship. As we will see, part of the challenge in discerning a responsible economic ethic for Christians in later historical eras is the fact that such matters were not very well developed in New Testament times because of this very assumption that the end of time was so near.

Thus, this incident is important because it sets forth a universally applicable, public economic ethic of radically proportional, but not total, sharing. The heart of this proportionally inclusive ethic is what it demands of all stewards: They must be, in proportion to their possessions, accountable for the well-being of others. To repeat a text very basic to the steward economic ethic: "Every one to whom much is given, of him much will be required" (Lk. 12:48).

Richard J. Cassidy has described the significance of Jesus' meeting with Zacchaeus.

It is, however, in Jesus' encounter with Zacchaeus that we find the best example of his attitude toward those who have embraced his teachings regarding surplus possessions. . . . He is thus no longer among those to whom Jesus said, "Woe to you who are rich." . . . Instead, Zacchaeus has joined the ranks of Jesus' faithful disciples, those who have heard Jesus' words and put them into practice.[3]

Here Jesus commends one who has taken "a substantial step toward putting Jesus' teachings into practice."[4] An advantaged steward is, in other words, one who possesses surplus wealth beyond that needed for survival, minimal comfort, and certain positive values in cultural enrichment.

It needs to be emphasized that the steward ethic carries many of the same disciplines as that of the forgoer. Neither of them is to become anxious about even necessary food, drink, or clothing; neither is to become attached to material possessions. Both ought to beware of covetousness. The clear, obvious difference between them is that a steward shares an accountable portion, but not all possessions. A steward is a faithful disciple who is strongly approved by the Jesus of Luke's Gospel if this interpretation proves to be sound. Neither Jesus nor Luke calls upon all believers to become forgoers. However, in the biblical economic ethic every disciple must become either a forgoer or a steward. There is no other alternative.

This interpretation of the dialogue between Jesus and Zacchaeus means that the authentic steward may retain a degree of material welfare beyond that of the forgoer—a degree that stewards must determine. Still, this lifestyle, which deliberately entails keeping more than is needed for survival and simple comforts, must be lived with full awareness of the dangers to Christian commitment. Christians learn from their Lord that the possession of some money lures them to desire more money. Powerful acquisitiveness can proceed to consume them with anxious, egoistic self-assertiveness. Then the love of money degenerates into a demonic worship of mammon. As Martin Hengel reports the attitude in early Christianity, "Mammon is worshipped wherever men long for riches, are tied to riches, keep on increasing their possessions and want to dominate as a result of them."[5] As soon as stewards rise to the income level where they attain a surplus, they are confronted with a subtle, private temptation: a temptation to expropriate some or all of this surplus for themselves. How easily they can devise new wants, cloaked as needs! Put another way, the well-off steward must shun the allurements to self-indulgence that a surplus makes so inviting.

All stewards must divide their income and property into two basic funds: a use fund and a surplus fund. The use fund is the portion of their money that provides necessities, reasonable comforts, cultural enrichment values, and savings for future contingencies. The surplus fund, on the other hand, is that portion of an authentic steward's possessions that is not needed for use functions and should not be expended for personal or family enrichment or savings.

The surplus may be shared with others in need or disbursed to religious movements, community agencies, and justice causes. It is to be channeled into policies and actions that structure greater justice and efficiency into the economy. Stewards are morally forbidden to shift surplus funds into satisfying personal and family wants and felt needs. The surplus of stewards will be either committed to new policies and programs to strengthen justice and efficiency, or will be corrupted into self-centered advantage.

It is important to provide a further word concerning forgoers and stewards. All that has thus far been written here concerning them has sought to delineate their supportive relationships on behalf of the impoverished. Now we must emphasize that in the biblical economic ethic, poor persons also become forgoers or stewards.

Recall Jesus' parable in which the master of the household entrusted his property to three servants while he went on a journey. The first received a five-talent portion, the second two, and the third one. The point of the story was Jesus' condemnation of the one-talent recipient for not putting his small portion to work (Mt. 25:4-30). This person failed to be a responsible steward, even when he had so little. Recall also the incident where the destitute widow contributed "out of her poverty" her last penny to the temple treasury. Jesus highly commended her, even though she had so little to give. Her contribution was appraised as "larger" than those of the wealthy. She became a selfless forgoer (Mk. 12:41-44). Committed forgoers or stewards, even when impoverished, are not lazy or obsequious; they do not ask for charity but for justice and dignity. Indeed, as we will see in subsequent chapters, the traditional interpretations of giving and receiving, of charity and justice, must be widened and transformed by a modern awareness of what human initiative can accomplish and what human dignity requires.

The remainder of this book is an effort to investigate the role of authentic stewards. We will ascertain how they individually, and in Christian communities, can integrate the biblical economic ethic into their neighbor-centered lifestyle. This lifestyle becomes for advantaged stewards a twofold mission: in management of personal surplus and in shaping the structures of economic interaction in society.

The approach to economic life proposed in the scriptures is full of implications for us today. Still, before moving to our own situation, it will be helpful to consider how Christians in an earlier era tried to live out this biblical economic ethic. For this reason we next examine the teachings of the early and medieval church concerning the responsibilities of the Christian in economic affairs.

Patristic and Scholastic Teaching on Economic Matters

When the early church fathers began to articulate what Christian faith would mean for the economic affairs of the people of their day, they were careful to base their analysis on the wisdom of biblical sources. Thus it is no surprise that we find many of the same themes running through their teaching as were dominant in the economic ethic of the New and Old Testaments.

Like the Israelites of old, the early Christians felt a strong sense of community. Like Paul, they understood themselves to be a part of Christ's body and were thus integrally related to one another. The suffering of one affects all others. In addition, the early church carried forward Jesus' warning that they must not become attached to things. Wealth and the attachment to things are impediments to life in Christ because they deaden the sensibilities of the person. The *Didache* and other early writings denounce greed and the neglect of the poor that accompanies it.

The earliest Christians were generally poor, but it was not long before the question of private property required the church's attention. Some followed the forgoer model. We have seen the testimony of the Acts of the Apostles concerning the sharing of goods in the Jerusalem church. Still most did not give up all their possessions. Eventually there were even wealthy persons counted among the believers. When the church leaders formulated a doctrine of private property they began with the Old Testament insight that God as creator is the only absolute owner of material goods. All human "owners" were in fact only stewards, and they could hold that right of stewardship only if they used those goods in the service of all God's people. As Gregory of Nyssa taught:

> If one should seek to be absolute possessor of all, refusing even a third or a fifth [of his possessions] to his brothers, then he is a cruel tyrant, a savage with whom there can be no dealing, an insatiate beast gloatingly shutting its jaws over the meal it will not share. [6]

Similarly, Ambrose of Milan and John Chrysostom taught that Christians must consider themselves no more than caretakers of the earthly goods they possess. Gregory the Great, pope from 590 to 604, admonished: "When we minister the necessities of life to those who are in want, we are returning to them their own, not being bountiful with what is ours; we pay a debt of justice rather than fulfill works of mercy." [7]

When we look upon this stance not from the point of view of the responsibilities of ownership but from the perspective of the impoverished, it might be termed the just entitlement of the poor. This doctrine of just entitlement was developed during the era of the church fathers. These leaders envisioned how God in his original creation established a perfect order for human life. They held that, prior to human disobedience in the Garden of Eden, humankind needed no imperfect institutions, such as slavery, civil government, and private property. After sin and the "fall," however, God ordained such institutions as private property and other social systems as "remedies for sin." In a fallen world of sinners, God's natural and civic laws established property rights and duties, which, if justly administered, could deter ruthless aggressors from stealing others' properties.

These church leaders went on to develop clear rules designed to legalize personal property ownership rights, to protect property holders from robbery, and yet to prohibit the wealthy from exploiting the poor. Their overall aim was to assure that the biblical system of private property would maintain economic justice for everyone, rich and poor.

There was a clear, common realization among these ethicists that the power of the rich posed a persistent threat to the economic needs and rights of the poor. How could this natural, inevitable imbalance favoring the advantaged be offset by a higher level of distributive justice? Their Christian answer was to recognize that the wealthy had a compensatory obligation in justice to bestow from their surplus the goods needed to sustain the deprived. This countervailing justice could become a momentous, radical basis for reducing the economic discrepancy between the over-possessed and the under-possessed.

This economic ethic was more fully developed in medieval Christian theology by Thomas Aquinas. Most Christians think of Thomas as the defender of the traditionalism and stability of the feudal system. However, in economic matters he insisted that under the stress of need, the poor person could be justified in the revolutionary act of stealing from the rich.

To see how this was, we must keep in mind that Thomas described three systems of laws that Christians would have to consider in answering questions about their economic life. There was human or civil law promulgated by the king or ruler. This system of laws was to be the working out of the particulars for the higher system of natural law that was a part of all created things by the very fact that God had created them. Everything was created by God with a purpose, and it is the natural "law" of that thing to fulfill that purpose. This whole system of natural law was subordinate to the eternal law which, as Thomas explains, God himself embodies in the divine reason's conception of a thing.

Thomas points out that there are very good reasons behind the private possession of property and thus very good reasons for establishing human laws to support private ownership. Everyone is more careful to procure and care for one's own goods than for goods held in common, and this process also has the advantage of ensuring peace, since there is no dispute over who makes the decisions about articles of property. However, when it comes to the *use* of those goods, the person who possesses them does not have the right to use them in any way he or she wishes. Here is where the natural law takes precedence over the human law about property rights. Since material goods were created by God for the very purpose of meeting human needs, the possessor of goods has the obligation to use them in accordance with their nature—to meet needs. Thus, if a rich man has more than he needs and a poor man is in urgent need of goods like those the rich man possesses, the rich man has an obligation to share them. In fact, says Thomas, the poor man is justified in taking those goods if the rich man will not give them to him.[8]

Thus we see that during the whole of the history of Christianity up through the Middle Ages the wealthy have always been recognized as having a major obligation to the poor. The poor have always been seen as having a just entitlement claim upon the rich. A. J. Carlyle has summarized the theory of property in medieval theology. He follows the general theme introduced above: Some legal organization of ownership became necessary. The state and its laws provided, legally, for the rights of private property—but only as a concession to sin. Yet, in Carlyle's words, it was always assumed that the legal institution of private property

> cannot override the natural right of a person to fulfill basic needs from the abundance of that which the earth brings forth. This is what the fathers mean when they call the maintenance of the needy an act of justice, not of mercy: for it is justice to give to

people what is rightfully theirs, and the needy have a moral right to what they require.

When, therefore, the fathers say that almsgiving is an act of justice, there is little doubt that they mean that the man who is in need has legitimate right to claim for his need that which is to another man a superfluity.[9]

Thus, ownership of private property means that the rich are accountable for meeting the essential needs of the poor from their own surplus wealth. The seriously impoverished have a clear and prior entitlement or just lien upon the surplus property of the wealthy.

Six Background Assumptions and Two Ethical Principles

We can now summarize the elements that form the foundation of the economic ethic of the biblical, patristic, and medieval eras by enumerating six "background assumptions" and restating two concrete ethical principles. Although some of the background assumptions are not explicitly listed quite this way anywhere in scripture or in early Christian writings, they are part of the unspoken and presumed world view of the Judeo-Christian tradition. Let it be clear that this does not make them less important but more important. The captains of two baseball teams may discuss the ground rules at a particular playing field but seem to ignore the most basic rules of the game. That the batter is out after three strikes is an unspoken rule. Similarly in describing the stream of thought of a writer or a whole civilization, those insights into the most basic facts about life sometimes go unstated. But to think clearly on economic matters we must state these very assumptions clearly.

1. The world is gift to all humanity; private ownership is never absolute.
The world—everything that exists—was created by God, and God "saw that it was good." This denies any dualism, where the

material realm would be considered evil and the spiritual realm good. The doctrine of creation considered the economic realm and all others to be arenas where religiously important events occur. In addition, God as creator alone possesses the world and all that is in it (see, e.g., Deut. 10:14-15 and Eccles. 3:12-13). Through the covenant, Israel was reminded time after time that the control or "ownership" that humans have over the good of the world is limited. We who use or even "possess" material things do so only because they are God's gifts and only as stewards of what really belongs to him.

As a result, the doctrine of private property throughout the tradition has always allowed only a qualified, not an absolute, ownership. Within Old Testament theology this qualified right of property was, like all else, rooted in the covenant. The many warnings in New Testament and patristic writings against excessive attachment to material things are well known. Parallel with these are instructions concerning the nature of property itself. The *Didache* exhorts the sharing of possessions as a limit on ownership: "Share your possessions with your brother, and do not claim that anything is your own. If you and he are joint participators in things immortal, how much more so in things mortal?"[10]

Similarly, Gregory of Nyssa, Ambrose of Milan, and most church fathers put strong restrictions on ownership—restrictions based on the creaturely nature of all material things.[11]

In medieval Christianity we find Thomas Aquinas, as a prime example, treating the question of property as intimately related to the doctrine of creation. In Thomas' view, humanity's dominion over material things consists only in the use of them, and even then their use must be for the common good; God alone has complete dominion over their natures.

Whether in the language of covenant or metaphysics, the tradition has recognized God's creation of the world as circumscribing the rights of ownership. As we will see in Chapter 4, most modern visions of property rely on the philosophy of John Locke and stress an initial effort of labor as the justification for private possession. This is seen as granting the owner complete control over a thing. The Judeo-Christian tradition *cannot* support such a claim.

2. The human person is both individual and communal.

Crucial to the Old Testament vision of economic life was the fact that Israel was seen as the people of God, a community. Hebraic religion was not primarily a one-to-one relation with God. Rather, God's action created a people of his own, and each Israelite related to the Lord as a member of that people. The argument from New Testament and patristic sources runs parallel. In Thomistic terms, following Aristotle, the very rationality that characterizes the human person renders every human person a social and political being. Throughout the tradition, both love and justice are held up as literally essential dimensions of human life.

As we will see in Chapter 6, the modern economic conception of the human person is one of a self-defined and complete individual who relates to others to achieve his or her ends. In contrast, the Christian vision stresses the community and "the common good" (in addition to the goals of individuals) as robust categories of analysis for an economic ethic.

3. Human life is historical.

This third background assumption refers to the way the Judeo-Christian tradition has looked at the sequence of events from day to day and year to year. Things did not just happen; there was a purposeful unfolding of events.

According to the Old Testament scholar Gerhard von Rad, this historicizing of experience in ancient Israel began with a common celebration by the whole people of Israel of festal events that had been celebrated singly in different places. "The idea of history which Israel worked out was constructed exclusively on the basis of a sequence of acts which God laid down for her salvation."[12] With the later rise of the prophets, Israel came to see even *new* events as sharing in the same character as the older founding acts of Yahweh in the nation's past.[13] What remained clear throughout was that the everyday life of the individual believer and of the community had a religious significance. Neither the economic realm nor the political nor any other area of human life was an amoral or nonreligious affair.[14] We will see in Chapter 7 how this relation of faith and history led to the development of Christian social ethics and the obligation to transform social structures.

4. Sin is a part of human life.

This background assumption is well known to Christians, but its significance for an economic ethic is often overlooked. Good and evil are pivotal categories in economic life. Not every preference of mine is good, and the fact that I can afford something does not mean it is all right to buy it. Some economic goods are more basic than others. When I obtain a luxury item—one I do not need—I use up resources that might have been used to provide the necessities of life to someone else. As we will see in Chapter 6, relying on "the market" as the sole or even the primary economic structure often entails overlooking the power of sin in the world. At the same time, the reality of sin appears in the fact that all of us tend to look to our own comfort and would probably not work as hard as we do if effort, individual initiative, and perseverance did not bring monetary reward or the esteem of others. One of the strengths of "the market" is that it is built on this insight into human sin and self-interest. The Christian economic ethic discredits any naive assumptions about ending social sin by merely doing away with capitalism.

5. All earthly power is subject to divine rule.

With the development of monotheism in Israel came the conviction that all gods and all earthly rulers were ultimately subject to Yahweh's rule. Not only were the rulers in Israel subject to the Lord but, as the prophets warned, even the Assyrians and Babylonians fulfilled God's will.

In the New Testament, Jesus reminds Pilate that he would have no power at all over him were it not given him from above. The very word used in Greek for "power" *(exousia)* denoted a force—whether possessed by Jesus or by the anti-Christ—that came ultimately from God. Similarly, all earthly power and even what we today would call "social forces" and "social reality" come under the sway of God's domain. As Stephen Mott argues, "social reality" is the basic meaning of "cosmos" in the New Testament.

"The world" is not primarily a place but rather a system of relationships and values which have come under God's judgment.[15]

A similar theme is found in Thomas Aquinas, where all earthly powers, like everyone else, are to operate in accord with the natural law. The religious importance of the political and economic life of medieval Christianity cannot be doubted in the face of the detail with which Thomas considers such issues. Of course Thomas, like the scriptural and patristic sources before him, did not appeal to the possibility of democratic social change to improve or abolish evil social structures. Although we will not examine this possibility until Chapter 7, we should note here that the inclusion of efforts to change social structures—in addition to moral appeals to those actually in position of authority—is not really a radical extension. In Thomas' words, "Whatever can be rectified by reason is the matter of moral virtue."[16]

Most people in the modern world agree, at least in principle, that citizens have the right to shape social institutions by design. The Christian vision of earthly power implies that the shaping of such institutions should occur according to moral standards. While this view does not provide any detailed blueprint, it does undercut a number of positions that oppose this effort, such as all libertarian appeals to "freedom of the individual" based on the subjectivity and relativity of "personal preferences."

6. The sinfulness of earthly powers requires prophetic confrontation and critique.

Because all human effort and all human institutions will be tainted by sin, prophetic confrontation of sin is crucial. The Hebrew prophets condemned the leaders of Israel for deceiving themselves into thinking they were fulfilling God's law without providing justice to the widow, the orphan, the sojourner, and the poor. Christians striving to live out an economic ethic must not only attend to their own personal lifestyles but must also challenge economic structures, confront the powerful, and run counter to popular opinion when justice requires it. It is one of the background assumptions of the Judeo-Christian tradition to examine carefully the background assumptions of every era and civilization and to challenge those world views when they form an ideological barrier to full human life.

In addition to these six background assumptions we will now restate two clear ethical principles that must be included in every Christian economic ethic. The first is that each person is to be either a forgoer or a steward; there is no other choice. Some will give up all but the barest material essentials. Others will not forgo so completely but will live responsibly and share proportionally. The second moral principle is that the poor and oppressed are justly entitled to a share of the wealthy person's riches. These two principles, along with the general perspective represented by the six background assumptions, provide Christians with some basic tools for addressing economic life.

Yet in this very analysis we are now confronted with a difficult problem that we must face candidly. It surfaces most clearly in the just entitlement favoring the poor. It is also evident in the forgoer role and still present in the steward role. This vexing problem can be brought into focus by a key question arising out of Chapter 1: If the biblical economic ethic is enduring, why has it failed to implant more of its principles into the actual economic behavior of individuals and the actual economic policies of nations? The answer to this question can also pinpoint the serious difficulties encountered today by the forgoer/steward and just entitlement principles.

To many people the very language used in affirming the higher economic justice of these two principles sounds utopian, extremist, and impractical within our modern context. Where can we find significant numbers of forgoers giving away everything, or modern stewards developing proportional sharing far beyond the ten-percent tithe? Indeed, is there not a very insignificant number of regular tithers in most of the mainline churches? How many of today's church people advocate actual policies where extremely poor persons are authorized to impose claims upon the excess wealth of the rich? Are not most such programs today branded as wild-eyed fanaticism? In short, is the biblical economic ethic, as it is being interpreted in this study, essentially unworkable?

It is precisely in answer to such pertinent and tough questions as these that we need to return to a concern voiced in Chapter 1. There, recall, we raised the definitive question, How can the Christian economic ethic *exert reformative structural power over U.S. capitalism* (and over other forms of economic organization in other countries)? We found in that first chapter that a positive answer to this question requires an analysis of two kinds of action: *individual* and *structured.* We learned further that structured action can be at the voluntary level of inwardly created expectations, or at the compulsory level of externally enforced rules or laws.

We stressed the necessity for sound moral structures that would disentangle the enduring Christian economic ethic from dependence upon powerless abstract ideals and powerless individual (unstructured) action. We also learned that operative norms are neither abstract ideals nor disconnected individual actions. Rather, operative norms are considered worth following in actual behavior: One feels one ought to conform to them. The Montgomery bus boycott was introduced as a significant case example, wherein Mrs. Parks, Martin Luther King, Jr., and others developed a sound moral structure for effecting large-scale, nonviolent power.

Later in this book we will elaborate the ways Christians can today actively employ this knowledge of operative norms to help shape individual behavior and social structures. But before we end our short study of the medieval period, we will look more closely at how the Christian economic ethic was embodied at that time. Operative norms were crucially important then as now. Unlike today, people then did not view those operative norms as open to alteration by conscious decisions about democratic social change. Nevertheless it is highly instructive to understand how those norms worked at that time.

The Important Connective Function of Operative Norms

The biblical economic ethic was always an ethic directed to specific historical-economic situations: to Moses and his leadership in the Exodus, to Amos and his prophetic mission to the Northern Kingdom. The same is true of Thomas and his shaping of so much in medieval Christendon, and of all Christians in any other particular time and place.

Recalling our short treatment of operative norms in Chapter 1, we can say that in every historical period sound operative norms are rooted in the empirical situation, in conscientious intentions, and in a set of values articulating a vision of what society and the individual can be. At the same time operative norms always thrust into a particular set of policies and actions. The remainder of this chapter will examine at least some of the significant factors surrounding the actual operative norm that patterned life and history within the medieval economic situation. Later we will face the task of relating the Christian economic ethic to the mindset and world view of us moderns.

Prior to the reinvigorated research by medieval scholars within recent decades, one might have thought that medieval Europe was tradition-bound and controlled by rigid customs. We propose, as a more accurate assessment, the phrase "primarily traditional." Evidence for cumulative change within early, middle, and late feudalism is now widely recognized within historical, literary, and religious perspectives. Certainly the seeds of the Renaissance were sown during the last centuries of medievalism. Still, during that era, the Christian economic ethic and the traditional economic situation developed side by side.

All predominantly traditional economies prior to modern capitalism were quite limited in their capacities to produce a rising output of goods and services. Several major restrictions were structured into their performance. First, these economies had fairly stable technologies. The rapid development of machinery and skills to which we have become so accustomed was unknown. Systematic research—both pure and applied—was not undertaken. Traditional European society produced such geniuses as Leonardo da Vinci and Michelangelo, to be sure, but universities, business, and government had not learned to "invent how to invent," as Alfred North Whitehead has put it. Second, these societies had no large surplus production. That is, most of what was produced by the farmers, artisans, and others was necessary just to keep the system going: food for people; clothing, implements, and buildings just to replace worn-out items. Compared to our economy today, the medieval economy produced only a small surplus over the production necessary for the life of the system. Since economic growth can come only from reinvesting this surplus, a small surplus limits the possibility for growth. Third, these traditional societies did not have the economic institutions necessary for structured saving and investing. In the modern era, capitalist economies depend on banks, stocks, bonds, and other investment devices, while socialist economies depend on systematic government decisions about expansion. The medieval economy had none of these.

Another important element was the Church's uneasiness over moneymaking. Most significant was the fact that during those centuries the medieval church singled out one of the seven deadly or capital sins as requiring special condemnation. This was the sin of covetousness or avarice—an "inordinate desire for riches." Thomas specifically stressed what the author of First Timothy had taught: "The love of money is the root of all evils." According to Thomas, "Covetousness, as denoting a special sin, is called the root of all sins, in likeness to the root of a tree, in furnishing sustenance to the whole tree. For we see that by riches a man acquires the means of committing any sin whatever."[17]

Within the context of this religious and moral warning, economic activities could not but be carried on within an ethos and world view resistant to moneymaking. The economist Robert Heilbronner points out, "Men of affairs in the twelfth and thirteenth centuries occasionally inserted codicils in their wills urging their sons not to follow their footsteps into the snares of trade."[18] Indeed, a devout merchant might well close up shop for the day if by early afternoon he had acquired the income he depended on for his livelihood. This could assure that he was not falling into the deadly sin of covetousness!

There were other highly visible marks of the impact of Christendom upon economic life. Most forms of usury—lending money for interest—were condemned as sinful. Church leaders sought to determine and maintain just prices and wages, in cooperation with secular officials. Heilbronner describes the relatively static medieval economy.

> The idea of an *expanding* economy, *growing* scale of production, and *increasing* productivity was as foreign to the guild-master or fair-merchant as to the serf and lord. Medieval economic organization was conceived as a means of reproducing, but not enhancing, the material well-being of the past. Its motto was perpetuation, not progress.[19]

Both of the two biblical economic role-types, forgoers and stewards, were very respected persons. The traditional medieval way of life wielded sufficient influence to prevent moneymaking from becoming a prevailing norm for "success." Certainly the culture of Christendom did not exalt the self-sufficient and self-made individual. From the forgoing of St. Francis to the stewardship of wealthy individuals, it was an age when acquisitive economics was subordinate, not dominant.

Recall that our second ethical principle espoused a moral justice that upheld the right of the impoverished to be provided necessities by those possessing surplus wealth. This was to be done not as an act of charity but as a minimal requirement of the just entitlement. Too often, however, the implementation of this altruistic ideal was left to the vagaries of almsgiving and mendicancy, the practice of begging.

We have illustrated above how the biblical economic ethic activated its forgoer/steward and just entitlement principles within Christendom. Now we need to delineate the specific nature and functioning of the operative economic norms in this total process of building a sound moral structure. Here we submit our formulation of the central operative norm that moved millions of the medieval faithful to feeling and believing that they ought to conform to a pattern of disinterested economic behavior, as decreed by the church:

Faithful, obedient worshippers ought to expect one another to fulfill the duties of their God-given stations in life and should curb all temptations to greed.

Recall our treatment of sound moral structures at the end of Chapter 1. There we saw that *operative norms* constituted a kind of intermediate force in any moral structure. Good operative norms perform a connective function. They keep individual behavior tied in to the just values of an overall vision and, by leading to concrete policies, prevent that vision from being just a pie-in-the-sky dream to which only lip service is paid.

The operative norm just cited for this medieval period fits very well into such a structure. It was well integrated into an overarching vision of all creation and stressed the way in which humanity was to exist according to God's laws. We need only be aware of the vast yet detailed metaphysical vision of scholars like Aquinas to understand the scope of that vision. At the same time this operative norm was effective in structuring the economic activity of thousands of persons in medieval society as those people went about their daily tasks to assure sustenance for themselves and others.

Two cautionary comments are in order here. The first is that in spite of our applying this analysis of operative norms to the medieval period, we must not be so naive as to think that every person or even every Christian person of that era faithfully followed this ethical norm completely. In addition, we must not be blind to vicious negative elements in the ethos of that period. Ignorance, superstition, dogmatism, vulgarity, brutality, and conditions near slavery all too often permeated that world of Christendom.

Our claim, however, stands: This operative norm *did* structure economic life. Unlike later eras, where people saw themselves as *choosing* a vocation, people of the middle ages felt it their duty to live out the station in life that God had given them. And unlike later eras where many Christians saw the gaining of personal fortunes as thoroughly consistent with their faith, medieval Christians generally held such activities in disdain. These two parts of the norm were really operative in that era because, as we saw in Chapter 1, people considered them not as external legal obligations but as ways of living that are worthy of being followed, as lines of conduct for which any good believer would naturally strive.

Our second note of caution also deals with a possible objection to applying this operative norm analysis to the middle ages. We do not claim that either the average person or even leading scholars such as Thomas Aquinas employed concepts like "operative norm" in their understanding of themselves. Such terms were developed in modern sociological theory—an analysis that can help twentieth-century Christians be better aware of how social morality works and thus be able to make it work better. Chapter 7 will examine this in detail. Still, it should be said that, for example, many of the moral norms Thomas cites as part of the natural law are also among the operative norms of the era. People really did live by them.

But if our analysis were used only to analyze the past, it would not be of much help in a book like this. As we will see later, one of the most significant changes to occur in the transition to the modern era was that people came to view social structures—forms of government, the rules for economic activity, and so on—as capable of being changed. Once these structures are seen not as eternal but as open to human alteration, there is the possibility of reshaping social structures and individual activity by a conscious transformation of operative norms in accordance with a genuinely humane overarching vision of life. In our day, when the self-sufficient moneymaker is exalted as the epitome of success, this shift is sorely needed. But we are getting ahead of ourselves here; we have other work to do before arriving at the question of the Christian economic ethic in the twentieth century.

The next two chapters introduce the new age of change effected by the Protestant Reformation and the Commercial Revolution (Chapter 3), and by Lockean Liberalism, with the Commercial Revolution continuing to be a force for new dynamics

(Chapter 4). These developments cover continental Europe from the beginning of the sixteenth through the seventeenth centuries. This means, in other words, that we will examine the impact, or lack of it, of the Christian economic ethic in those two crucial centuries, as that ethic was reinterpreted by Luther and Calvin. Their religious endeavor must also be seen in its interchange with the secular historical situation, especially the Commercial Revolution and the many forces of the Renaissance.

It remained for John Locke to submit the traditional ethos of England to a shattering new image of human beings and of the society, economy, and government they were to provide for themselves. Lockean or Classical Liberalism ushered onto the historical stage the possessive individual who drives to brush aside the biblical operative norm against covetousness. The consequences were to become momentous.

3

Luther and Calvin: Ethical Dilemmas of the Commercial Revolution

The sixteenth century provided the prelude for a dramatic era of modernization in Europe and the West. The medieval world was in steady decline. The Renaissance was moving toward its zenith in its transition from classical civilization into neoclassical art, modern philosophy, and modern science. Indeed, a new humanistic spirit discovered the "humanity of the classics," as John Hermann Randall aptly puts it.

On the more material side of history was the explorers' swift discovery of the rest of the world. Within roughly one brief century beginning in 1486, hardy European explorers ventured into virtually every part of the world that was accessible by water. One crucial invention had made possible the spread of literacy and learning during this era: the development of printing from movable type. This first occurred at Mainz in 1447, with Gutenberg developing his press by 1450.

Jean Bodin of France developed the concept of political sovereignty—the theory that helped create the modern nation-state. In his *Republic,* published in 1576, he defined sovereignty as "supreme power over citizens and subjects, unrestrained by law." Throughout earlier traditional biblical societies, political thought had held that beyond all human laws were the higher laws of God, nature, and custom. These ultimate laws circumscribed, in theory, the power of the ruler to make *new* laws; the ruler could only promulgate or activate laws that were consistent with those laws already existing in the mind of God and in the structures of nature and tradition.

Bodin, in other words, addressed himself realistically to the emerging historical situation where centralized governments were steadily gaining greater power and authority. To implement their new power these states needed to make new laws. Bodin, along with Machiavelli and Thomas Hobbes, provided the philosophical basis for the first modern national states.

It was within this historic era that the Protestant Reformation began transforming Christendom. Indeed, the coming of Martin Luther and John Calvin instigated wide-ranging Christian movements bent on fashioning a new "fit" between the biblical economic ethic and the emerging historical economic situation. We must also recall that there were other important religious forces affecting change, especially new free church and sect associations and the Catholic Counter-Reformation.

Our treatment of this period will be limited to Martin Luther and John Calvin. It was clearly their leadership that initiated and shaped the Protestant Reformation. Would the versions of the biblical economic ethic developed by these two men empower them to constrain the expanding commercial revolution, unabashedly bent on moneymaking? Or would this new pursuit of wealth subvert the ethico-economic mission of the Reformers?

To restate them in the language of this study, these questions ask: Would Luther and Calvin build into their societies a firm and adequate moral structure that intermeshes conscientious intentions, just ultimate values, and an accurate assessment of the factual situation to develop publicly operative norms that marshal the power to guide policies into responsible and just economic behavior?

Martin Luther: A Transitional Economic Ethic

In his famous study *The Social Teaching of the Christian Churches*, Ernst Troeltsch describes well both the traditional and the modern aspects of Luther's life. On the one hand Troeltsch summarizes those aspects of the Reformer's economic ethic that make Luther appear as a traditional medievalist:

> It is against all law, both Natural and Divine, to wish to rise in the world, to break through existing institutions on one's free initiative . . . to improve one's manner of life, or to improve one's social position. . . . (T)he continuation of the patristic and medieval prohibition of usury is taken for granted. . . . (A)ll labour organizations and all titles of possession are regarded as means of preserving a social order which is free from competition.[1]

It is here clear that Luther is not bent on replacing the traditional economy with radical new structures of business and economics.

Troeltsch also finds contrasting evidence of a "new" Luther that depicts his initiative as he pioneers into different economic values and policies. Here is evidence of Luther's new thrust, erected upon his understanding of biblical economic ethics.

> Industry was urged upon all as a duty, property held in perpetual tenure (mortmain) was secularized . . . ; above all the control of the Church in the sphere of economics was removed. . . . The discharge of one's duty by honest work is the best service a man can render to God, and the love of one's neighbor which is exercised in the duties of one's calling is better than charity, which exalts beggars. . . . (T)he whole idea (of medieval begging and almsgiving) is corrupted by the ideal of a holiness consisting in "good works."[2]

Luther failed to develop a consistent interpretation of new forgoer and steward roles that could enable disciples to assume leadership in the sixteenth century. Certainly there was no emphasis upon the entitlement of the poor to the surplus wealth of the rich. We will now seek to penetrate to the roots of his failure to apply effectively his interpretation of the biblical economic ethic within the emerging economic situation in Germany.

Luther strikes a fatal blow against the traditional forgoer role, which previously tended to dominate the biblical economic ethic, especially in earlier Catholic medievalism. His urging of industry for everyone as a duty, his unconcealed preference for agriculture as the most beneficial lifestyle, his secularization of property (which meant the abolition of monasteries and convents), his severing of the church's control over economics, and his elevating of secular work to a major Christian vocation in service to God and neighbor—all of these were significant new gropings toward a new vision, new operative norms, and new policies. They point to a Luther who was subjecting medieval Catholicism to a sharp economic challenge. In the emerging Lutheran interpretation of the biblical economic ethic, the role of the forgoer was no longer a dominant force.

The farthest-reaching shock for Catholicism came, however, from the drastically altered role Luther conceived for the steward. This responsible new steward could serve the poor more beneficially *not* by giving them alms (which merely "exalted beggary"), but by doing honest work as the "best service one can render to God" and by loving one's neighbor within the duties of one's calling.

Immediately we should stress that Luther here moves to the very threshold of a creative and powerful new version of the steward role in the biblical economic ethic. Then he fails to pass through that door!

Luther's traditional rural stance bars him from utilizing the just entitlement in the vital new way his analysis of secular work and vocation makes possible. In other words, Luther misses the crucial summary of the church fathers' stance that we noted in Chapter 2: that the person in need has a moral right to lay a claim upon the superfluous wealth of the rich.

Luther does not recognize the ultimate moral and economic rights of the poor as interlocked with the ultimate moral and economic obligations of the rich. In the volatile new pressures of the commercial revolution, especially in such disruptive events as the peasant's rebellion in Germany, Luther emphasizes the duty of the poor not to instigate violent revolutionary change.

The result was that the potentially creative thrust of Luther's doctrine of vocation, to be fulfilled in all legitimate secular institutions, was short-circuited. He envisioned the Christian as offering love and enacting justice for the neighbor by means of "honest

work" in the "duties of one's calling." But without the just entitlement on behalf of the poor neighbor, this secular work and duty
was to be performed within the norms of one's job *largely as it had
been done for centuries in traditional, rural Germany!* In the final
outcome, therefore, Luther buttresses the economic status quo.
He failed to take the lead in building a sound new moral structure
within which a new breed of stewards could reconstruct more just
and efficient operative norms appropriate to the commercial
revolution.

Why does Luther develop this ethical weakness? After all, as
Karl Holl has demonstrated conclusively, Luther was seriously
searching for a new economic ethic. He undermined the Catholic
system of almsgiving and beggary. He struggled unsuccessfully
for effective ways to oppose an emerging capitalism. He even
supported the dying guilds as one step in such opposition. He
initiated the first "community chest" that struggled to provide
charity for those willing to work.[3] In the end, however, his
economic policies were too little, too late. Again, we ask why.

Luther's politico-economic efforts to rebuild a sound moral
structure failed because his ethic was essentially interior and
individualistic; it never moved firmly to a plane beyond the conscience, with its subjective moral point of view; never to a level
where publicly operative norms constrained responsible role-
behavior. Holl sympathetically and responsibly interprets this
privatistic foundation for Luther's ethics:

> From the unconstrained sense of unity with God, Luther now
> derives, in addition, the right and obligation of the believer to act
> even without the compulsion of law, i.e., out of his individual sense
> of the divine will to produce by his own creative act the proper
> form of morality in a specific instance.[4]

Holl, unfortunately, does nothing to stress Luther's need to
complete his existential love ethic as it was activated by an
inward, divinely willed conscience. Christians must move on to
the problem of an adequate moral structure, with its operative
norms in economies, politics, and church—norms that can structure new policies.

Luther unintentionally shifts the radical demands of the just entitlement, as developed by Jesus and many of the church fathers, to the conventional job-performance of all workers of the realm. His theology and his economic ethic led him to give too much approval to the historical situation of the commercial revolution.

John Calvin and Economic Life Within the Holy Community

John Calvin came to his Geneva mission endowed with many of the qualities required for his particular task. Indeed, he was in many ways a giant in this arena of social morality. Even his untimely death (at age fifty-five) could not bar him from exerting major influence throughout Western Christianity. One needs only to recognize the caliber of Calvinist leaders in Switzerland, France, the Low Countries, England, Scotland, and North America to be moved to acclaim him as a strong mentor for all of those in his strand of Protestantism.

Luther was trained to be a monk; Calvin to be a lawyer. Luther died in 1546, age sixty-three; Calvin in 1564, age fifty-five. These facts point to factors that may help explain the two men's different roles in the Protestant Reformation.

Calvin's legal training equipped him to lead in the political reorganization of both the secular and the church communities in Geneva. The fact that Calvin's life span extended almost a score of years further into the Renaissance and the commercial revolution was significant. The dominance of tradition was waning. Calvin perceived the necessity for a new economic ethic and new policies in both business and government. The mercantilism at the heart of the commercial revolution signaled a shift from a traditional economy to a stronger market economy, but not yet the full-fledged, modern capitalistic market. Governments initiated regulations and control over business in order to gain favorable balances from trade.

Calvin had a far more positive social goal for the Christian community than did Luther. Indeed, Calvin envisioned the church becoming a "Holy Community," with members helping one another to become more faithful and supportive disciples. In this community their supportiveness entailed both an inner moral point of view and a public structuring of operative norms. Thus, Calvin intuitively moved toward a *fuller moral structure* in his interpretation of the biblical economic ethic.

Involved in these contrasting assessments of the Church and its mission was a more important difference between Luther's and Calvin's understanding of what it meant to be called by God into one's earthly vocation or "calling." As we did with Luther, we will examine Calvin's approach to God's mission for believers.

We have seen that Luther believed that God was summoning Christians to live out their vocations in the traditional ways of earning livings. Calvin, on the other hand, stressed that God often called people into *new* vocations that should initiate new economic policies in both the congregation and society for upbuilding the Holy Community.[5] Here a brief statement from Troeltsch provides another of his relevant summaries of Calvin. As "the organ of salvation," the church "ought to prove itself effective in the Christianizing of the community, by placing the whole range of life under the control of Christian regulations and Christian purposes."[6]

This is a helpful point at which to cite some of the data concerning Calvin, as gathered by Troeltsch. This short overview discloses how Calvin went beyond Luther in formulating a new version of the enduring biblical economic ethic, within a new politico-economic setting.

Calvin's important doctrines of one's calling affirmed the freedom to move into new vocations; there was no effort to maintain the agrarian way of life, as in Luther. Frequently Calvinist clergy became socialists; Lutheran clergy did not. "Productive credit" was encouraged under certain conditions, but not "usury credit," and not living off interest. Hard work, abstention from luxury consumption, and freedom to participate in new commerce and

production resulted in savings and capital accumulation for investment—all of this Calvin viewed as good for society, if Christians
were given the grace not to develop covetousness. Earning
profit, under certain conditions, was regarded as a sign of God's
approval of one's enterprise.

> The greatest possible emphasis was laid upon the idea that true
> Christian dignity regards questions of rank and position as mat-
> ters of entire indifference, while on the other hand, every position
> of privilege is regarded as an obligation to the whole community.[7]

This latter statement makes clear that Calvin was struggling
to tune the biblical steward into the emerging commercial revolution, even while he was departing farther than Luther from the
biblical forgoer role. Calvin's use of the tradition of relative natural
law (what God ordained for sinners after the human "fall")
became a dynamic force for change. He went far beyond Luther's
more negative role of repressing sin and of caring for one's
neighbor within the patterns of traditional agrarian duties.

Calvin, in sum, went beyond Luther as he incorporated the
enduring biblical economic ethic into his economic program for
the unique economy of Geneva. Like Luther, he de-emphasized
the traditional forgoer role. But unlike Luther, he went on to
create important elements for a new steward role. This was
clearly illustrated when Calvin arranged a state loan to finance the
manufacturing of cloth and velvet in Geneva "in order to give
work to the poor and unemployed." Thus, his entrepreneurship
enabled the impoverished to become industrious producers, not
idle beggars. When this had to be given up because of competition from Lyons, the "manufacture of watches was introduced
with the same aim."[8] In all these developments Calvin differed
from Luther by organizing new structures with which to implement what the advantaged owed to the disadvantaged in various
forms of just entitlement action.

The following is another way of summarizing the contributions
of Luther and Calvin. Luther failed to disentangle the principled
biblical economic ethic from its deep roots in medievalism. Still,
his emphasis upon the performance of duties entailed in secular

vocations, as a positive way in which to serve the economic needs of one's neighbors, constituted an historic step toward more modern forms of steward action.

Calvin, on the other hand, pressed more consistently toward such disentanglement from the more static life of the Middle Ages. His primary problem was that he unwittingly entangled his version of the biblical economic ethic too extensively with, and, at times, too subserviently to the commercial revolution and then, eventually, to the later industrial revolution. It was not given to Calvin to foresee how the acquisitive spirit of capitalism that emerged in the late eighteenth and nineteenth centuries would corrupt the more disciplined capitalism that he strove to build in Geneva.

Max Weber reminds us that by the late eighteenth century Calvin's this-worldly asceticism in economics had deteriorated too often into Benjamin Franklin's ethic of shrewdly calculating self-interest.[9] The religious basis for the economic asceticism of Calvin "had died away" by the time of Franklin's discipline of penny-pinching. Indeed, Calvin's doctrine of the biblical steward and the steward's obligation to the poor increasingly eroded as the seventeenth and eighteenth centuries witnessed the disintegration of traditional Christendom.

John Wesley was a contemporary of Benjamin Franklin. Wesley, the founder of Methodism, perceived a crucial moral difficulty structured into capitalism. Calvin probably would also have perceived this crisis if he, like Wesley, had lived after John Locke and Adam Smith had launched their respective theories of modern capitalism. As we will see in the next two chapters, Locke tried to remove the medieval condemnation of private wealth-seeking, and Smith went beyond such justification of self-interest to glorify it as the road to prosperity for the nation. Wesley's reaction was far different:

> I fear, wherever riches have increased, the essence of religion has decreased in the same proportion. Therefore I do not see how it is possible, in the nature of things, for any revival of true religion to continue long. For religion must necessarily produce both industry and frugality, and these cannot but produce riches. But as

riches increase, so will pride, anger, and love of the world in all its branches.[10]

The Commercial Revolution: An Economic Force for Change

We move now from the sixteenth into the seventeenth century. Alfred North Whitehead has termed this the "Century of Genius." He wrote concerning its remarkable eruption of thought and invention:

> Three main factors arrested attention—the rise of mathematics, the instinctive belief in a detailed order of nature, and the unbridled rationalism of the thought of the later Middle Ages. By this rationalism I mean the belief that the avenue to truth was predominantly through a metaphysical analysis of the nature of things. . . . The historical revolt was the definite abandonment of this method. . . . In religion, it meant the appeal to the origins of Christianity; and in science it meant the appeal to experiment and the inductive method of reasoning.[11]

This study's focus on economics makes it appropriate to concentrate briefly on the commercial revolution, which reached its zenith during the seventeenth century. It became one of the early modern movements with which the biblical economic ethic needed to come to grips. Three major economic factors were central to this era: (1) an expansion in world trade, with new marketing centers cropping up across Europe, (2) a marked increase in the money supply, especially gold and silver bullion taken from the Old World, and (3) procedures that improved bookkeeping and accounting.

The heart of this commercial expansion was the doctrine and policies of mercantilism. Feudalism, with its many small manors and principalities, steadily disintegrated in the face of the rising size and power of the new commercial class and the centralized nation-states. These new governments, especially Spain, Britain, France, and the Netherlands, began to develop rigorous regulations of both trade and manufacture. These nationalistic regulations replaced early guild and customary controls. The prime objective was to secure favorable balances of trade.

Some forms of mercantilism, led on by the apparent effects of the precious metals imported from the New World, assumed that the sheer accumulation of gold and silver bullion assured national wealth. Britain and France, on the other hand, tended to the theory that trade that earned a favorable balance was the key to national prosperity. Thomas Mun, a leading mercantilist in England, published his *England's Treasure by Forraign Trade* in 1664. The following passage constituted his ode to economic nationalism, greatly encouraged by mercantilism:

> Forraign trade . . . is the great Revenue of the King, The honor of the Kingdom, the Noble profession of the Merchant, The School of our Arts, The supply of our wants, The employment of our poor, The improvement of our Lands, The nurcery of our Mariners, The walls of the kingdoms, The means of our Treasure, The Sinnews of our wars, The terror of our Enemies.[12]

More than a century later Adam Smith, in his *Wealth of Nations,* initiated a critical assessment of mercantilism, in both its bullionist and its balance-of-trade versions. Then by the end of the eighteenth century, the economic trend, especially in England, was shifting from the commercial into the industrial revolution. In the latter, the central theme was no longer government regulation, but laissez-faire competition in the marketplace, within a context of John Locke's "possessive individualism," as C. B. Macpherson terms it. In Chapter 4 we will examine this political-economic phase of modernization emerging in the industrial revolution.

Recapitulation and the Task Ahead

The United States is currently enabling some 180 million of its people to achieve high levels of economic success—self-sufficient or mutually inclusive achievers. This well-off majority has been conditioned to expect employment as well as annual wage increases proportional to their present incomes. Career vocations also frequently entail a number of fringe benefits and supplemental incomes.

Serious structural strains, however, are built into this U.S. "successism." The economy is also structuring about forty-six million persons into economic "unsuccess"—into the lot of the locked-out and seriously disadvantaged poor. They seldom or never enjoy long-range career vocations.

How is it possible that so many economically successful church members are helping to legitimize the procuring of ever larger annual incomes as a key to success, when so many impoverished are barred from such success? Professing Christians need to winnow out a realistic, enduring biblical economic ethic that can strengthen a more just and efficient economy in our time.

In a brief but broad-ranging historical study we are developing an overview of what happened when the biblical economic ethic sought to inculcate its values and economic lifestyle into several historical epochs. We have completed our inquiry into the biblical age, the patristic period of the early church, and the medieval centuries. We have also viewed the Protestant Reformation and the commercial revolution during the sixteenth and well into the seventeenth centuries. We will next examine the period of Lockean Liberalism, with its original notions of property, the state, and economic individualism. This can be dated from roughly 1670 well into the eighteenth century, say 1760. Finally, we will explore the modern epoch, from the laissez-faire economy of the initial industrial revolution beginning about 1760, up through social welfare capitalism, and even more recent trends whose beginnings we are only now able to sense.

The basic Christian economic ethic is drawn from the Hebrew scriptures, from the New Testament traditions of Jesus, Paul, and Zacchaeus, and from the patristic and medieval church fathers. These activated the roles of forgoer and steward, both of which inculcate inclusive, not exclusive, economics. The forgoer tilts the center of concern to the well-being of others at the price of self-deprivation; the steward sustains a mutual concern for the well-being of others and self, so far as economic factors are involved.

The second guiding principle in the biblical economic ethic was developed by church fathers, especially after the Council of Nicea in 325. They affirmed the just-entitlement principle, according to which economically advantaged disciples owed, from their surplus wealth, a debt of justice to the seriously impoverished. During the medieval centuries the economic setting was one of traditional scarcity. In such a situation the church upheld operative norms that condemned economic hoarding and wasting. Modern types of capitalist and Marxist economies had not yet developed. By the sixteenth century, however, the Renaissance and, more specifically, the commercial revolution and Protestant Reformation began to confront this traditional biblical economic ethic with radically different economic accountabilities. Soon new patterns of economic life were making their appearance.

Luther and Calvin were the Christian leaders in the endeavor to relate the biblical economic ethic to this emerging commercial revolution. Luther largely discarded the forgoer ethic and only partially originated a new steward role. His creative thrust was to elevate secular work and its duties as providing more beneficial help for the poor than does the giving of funds to charity. In this, however, he did not emphasize the just entitlement of the poor. Hence his interpretation of the biblical economic ethic was reduced too much to doing one's job within the status quo of sixteenth-century Germany.

Calvin, like Luther, de-emphasized the forgoer role in economics and worked to create a new steward role. His policy for the steward went beyond Luther's in the creation of jobs for the poor. Calvin's total social ethic became a cornerstone upon which he erected some of the guidelines for an adequate moral structure in economic life during the commercial revolution. He was not, however, granted the acumen to discern dangerous future entanglements with an emerging capitalism, an awareness that came later to John Wesley and Max Weber. It was not given to Calvin to foresee how the acquisitive spirit of capitalism that emerged in the late eighteenth and nineteenth centuries would corrupt the more disciplined capitalism that he strove to build in Geneva.

In this book we are developing a careful methodology to guide us in disentangling the principled biblical economic ethic during those various historical epochs. It is the absence of clearly structured operative norms in the church's economic ethic that becomes the missing link between inner moral expectations and structured policies. An operative norm triggers structured action because the norm is "considered *worthy* of following in actual behavior: thus, one feels that one *ought* to conform to it."[13] Here the inner "ought" motivates people to do their public duty not because they must, but because their own sense of responsible behavior leads them to it.

This means, in other words, that developing a sense of inner "ought" concerning public issues means building sound moral structures. We have learned from the Montgomery bus boycott that people have the interactive power to produce a viable economic ethic only when individual moral action is structured into norms that are operative (whether through expectation or requirement).

We move further into our historical investigations as we turn to Chapter 4. There we examine the next modernizing era, the decisive impact of classical liberalism, by focusing on the work of John Locke and on the possessive individualism he described and promoted.

4
Lockean Liberalism:
A Radical Shift
from the Biblical Economic Ethic

A second period of modernization, following the commercial revolution, accelerated the tempo and scope of political and economic change. This was particularly true in England and her North American colonies. Such terms as "classical liberalism" or the "enlightenment" denoted new philosophical, ethical, and cultural forces. Constitutional or parliamentary democracy characterized the Anglo-American political scene, capitalism the economic in its early stages.

Since our primary concern is economic, it is pertinent to note that no vocational economists made their appearance until late in the eighteenth century. There was as yet no such academic discipline as economics. Two philosophers, however, became significant "bridge" thinkers as political economists, joining politics and the rudiments of economics. These two were Thomas Hobbes (died in 1679) and John Locke (died in 1704). For our purposes, we will concentrate on John Locke and the Liberalism to which he contributed much.[1]

Locke developed original insights into the nature of the moral self, into how such selves relate in political experience, and into how they can legitimately acquire and use the material goods of nature and society. He was a leader in shifting Western political economy from its roots in the biblical tradition of economic obligation into the new soil of sensate pleasure and possessive individualism.

Locke's Theory of God's Natural Order and How Private Property and Government Came into Being

In his *Second Treatise on Government,* John Locke conceptualized his fanciful picture of what economic experience was like in the original state of nature. His doctrine of God's creation presupposed neither the biblical perfect order prior to sin nor the "fall." Indeed, Locke largely ignored traditional orthodox theology. Instead, he improvised his novel doctrine of a deistic God, of a flawed but not totally depraved sinful human nature, and of an idealistic natural law within which privileged, middle, and upper classes were to govern.

We can quickly summarize his vision of the state of "freedom" and "equality" in which rational human beings are created.[2] The problem is that as industrious, rational individuals acquire their own property, they must protect it against encroachments by covetous, irrational rivals. In that natural state each responsible, rational citizen has to become police officer and judge, in order to protect his or her own property. Locke devises a "remedy for the inconveniences of the state of Nature." In order to offset this "inconvenience," upright citizens have the good sense to contract together to establish civil government. Hence individuals, "however free" in their natural, pre-contractual state, "unite for the mutual preservation of their lives, liberties, and estates, which I call by the general name—property."[3]

When critics of American politics today charge that the government is primarily established to protect the rights of property, many Americans respond with indignation. Yet it is clear that Locke himself repeatedly asserts that the chief end of government is to safeguard citizens' properties. Citizens unite for peaceable living in a political state "in secure enjoyment of their properties." People come under the laws of government and "therein seek the preservation of their property." They would not tie themselves up under government "were it not to preserve their lives, liberties, and fortunes, . . . the preservation of property being the end of government and that for which men enter into society. . . ."[4]

Locke's famous Chapter 5 on property, and how individuals can rightfully possess it, is crucial. He begins with what seems to be a remarkably communal vision.

> God, who hath given the world to men in common, hath also given them reason to make use of it to the best advantage of life and

convenience. . . . Nobody has originally a private dominion exclusive of the rest of mankind.[5]

Yet alongside this natural property belonging to all people in common, there is one form of property that is from the beginning *exclusively* each person's private possession.

> Though the earth and all inferior creatures be common to all men, yet every man has a "property" in his own "person." This nobody has any right to but himself. The "labour" of his body and the "work" of his hands, we may say, are properly his. Whatsoever, then, he removes out of the state that Nature hath provided . . . , he hath mixed his labour with it, and joined to it something that is his own, and thereby makes it his property.[6]

Thus persons have a basic property in themselves, in their body and hands. It is this foundational property that empowers and authorizes them to appropriate from nature their private property in things, in land, fruits, animals, and other goods.

Locke starts off, in other words, with a radical communalism where each person has individual access to the common bounties of nature. Thence each individual can convert the private property of one's own self into the appropriating power that issues from the "labour" of one's body and the "work" of one's hands. From this absolutely private self-possession, Locke proceeds to explain and justify the right to preempt the bounties of nature exclusively for oneself. At one moment he presupposes equality and mutuality in appropriating everyone's property from the common riches of nature, and then he shifts to a property belonging only to individuals. In one fell swoop Locke challenges the very foundations of the biblical economic ethic and its inclusive structure of property obligations to those lacking property. No longer do we read anything about the duties of stewards; no longer do the poor have any significant claim on the superfluous wealth of the rich. Here is an entirely self-centered theme that legitimizes individualism within its context of a dawning capitalism.

Immediately a troublesome question arises. What if an inventive and energetic individual acquires more from nature's storehouse than he or she really needs? This, Locke concedes forthrightly, could become exploitive. Indeed, he is ready with a moral principle. Each procurer can acquire ethically only as much from nature as one "can make use of to any advantage of life *before it spoils.* Whatever is beyond this is more than his share, and belongs to others. Nothing is made by God for man to spoil or destroy."[7] Natural spoilage, then, seems to place a definite limit upon at least some of the items gathered from nature. There is a limit upon the quantity that acquisitive individuals can retain for themselves.

Again, however, no sooner does Locke seem to affirm an obligation in justice for property holders than he promptly discards it. He repudiates his own vision of persons peacefully laboring according to the natural law, wherein one can acquire only enough to fulfill one's needs, before his possessions spoil. He perceives that humans invent a new mechanism—one that makes it not only legitimate but entirely beneficial and just for some individuals to accumulate wealth. Let Locke introduce this potent new mechanism:

> . . . I dare boldly affirm . . . that the same rule of property—viz. that every man should have as much as he could make use of, would hold still in the world, . . . had not the invention of money, and the tacit agreement of men to put a value on it, introduced (by consent) larger possessions and a right to them. . . .[8]

Locke then concludes that while allowing a harvest of nuts to spoil is immoral if others are hungry, if a person would give that harvest

> for a piece of metal . . . he invades not the right of others; he might heap up as much of these durable things as he pleased; the exceeding of the bounds of his just property not lying in the largeness of his possessions, but the perishing of anything uselessly in it.[9]

Locke has here legitimated the unlimited seeking after wealth required for capitalism (and which was the major barrier to the acceptance of capitalism by the Christian churches). Locke (along with Hobbes and other thinkers of his day) provided a new kind of Genesis story of creation, and its implications have been earth-shaking. No longer will the biblical economic ethic—with its forgoance, stewardship, and just entitlement—furnish moral foundations for the emerging secular ethos. Instead, Hobbes, Locke particularly, and the first major proponents of a laissez-faire economy appear during the waning years of the commercial revolution. Modernization in the West was to leap forward at a dramatic new pace.

Locke's Ethic of Possessive Individualism

In order to pinpoint the dynamic change that Locke's brand of individualism wrought, we turn to the insight of C. B. Macpherson, in his now-classic book, *The Political Theory of Possessive Individualism*. Macpherson's assessment of Locke begins with Locke's understanding of the individual:

> The individual in a possessive market society is human in his capacity as a proprietor of his person. . . . his humanity does depend on his freedom from any but self-interested contractual relations with others; his society, i.e. his one area of relatedness to others, does consist of a series of market relations.[10]

This particular form of individualism espoused by Locke, Macpherson calls "possessive individualism." He finds the roots of this acquisitive individualism in Hobbes and in the Levellers, particularly in John Lilburne and Richard Overton.

Macpherson traces in more detail other consequences of an individualism based on possession or ownership as a root metaphor. The "possessive quality" in liberal-democratic theory

> is found in its conception of the individual as essentially the proprietor of his own person or capacities, owing nothing to society for them. The individual was seen neither as a moral whole, nor as part of a larger social whole, but as an owner of himself. . . . Society becomes a lot of free equal individuals related to each other as proprietors of their own capacities and of what they have acquired by their exercise. Society consists of relations

of exchange between proprietors. Political society becomes a calculated device for the protection of this property and for the maintenance of an orderly relation of exchange.[11]

Thus, for the purposes of our inquiry into the Christian economic ethic, the following three developments constitute major negative consequences flowing from Locke's Classical Liberalism.

1. Locke almost totally reversed the long biblical tradition that warned against evils in covetousness and the love of money.
Money becomes for Locke the positive factor that obliterated the original equalitarian society he had fantasized. Money was the mechanism that released and encouraged people to acquire as much wealth as possible. It did this by eliminating almost all ethical constraints arising from the spoilage factor. Durable money solves this messy problem. Locke's only social accountability, as individuals appropriate wealth, centers in the minimal taxes required to finance small, laissez-faire governments. Certainly taxes could remain insignificant so long as the "best government is the one that governs least." (Recall that the U.S. government could impose no federal income taxes until a constitutional amendment permitting them was adopted in February 1913.)

2. Locke undermined the steward's obligations and the just entitlement of the poor.
Locke recognized no role for forgoers and stewards and never paid heed to the just entitlement of the poor. As William T. Bluhm puts it, "He mentions no limit on the right of individual acquisition nor any obligation in the use of property. . . . The great purpose of the political order designed to fulfill the natural law is, therefore, to protect life and property, not to secure its just distribution and use."[12]

Locke was confident that his historical basis for the approval of wealth-seeking eliminated personal and institutional obligations to the poor. After all, Locke assumed that humankind as a whole had at least tacitly "consented" to the exchange of perishable commodities for money, with its assurance of hoarding without spoilage. He conjectures that all wealth, at least originally, had been earned by the labor of people's bodies or the work of their hands, as he phrases it. Did not this clearly imply that the impoverished (or their direct ancestors) were definitely responsible for their precarious station? They had failed in the race to appropriate money. Here we can clearly discern the fateful seeds that were to develop into modern vocational "success" or "unsuccess."

We need to ask at this point, however: Is not this indifference to the plight of the poor dangerous? Might not they, in times of economic privation, use their ballot to elect a government more responsive to their needs? Locke had good reason, however, not to worry about this threat, as we will see.

3. Locke designed a "democracy" that denied the right to vote to both the idle and the working poor.

The simple fact was that Locke had nothing to fear from the vote of the indigent and all laborers because they were virtually disfranchised. He developed an "inherent differential in rationality," as Macpherson termed it, which excluded the laboring classes (along with beggars, alms-takers, and vagrants) from the ballot. Indeed, this exclusion of laborers meant a so-called democracy that needed their work but that denied their political rights. "Not merely the idle poor, who had been treated as outcasts from Tudor times, but the labouring poor as well, were now treated [as] almost a race apart, though within the state."[13]

All of this meant a shift from feudal status society to modern contract society. Land, resources, and labor would be owned by individuals and would be alienable or salable. Salability meant that landowners, merchants, and workers could offer their land, goods, or labor for sale in a competitive market. Countless new contracts would have to become ratified day in and day out between landowners, manufacturers, merchants, entrepreneurs, and laborers.

It is within the context of this emerging contractual market economy that we can perceive the far-reaching, injurious import of Locke's emphasis on the workers' natural property right to their own bodies. What seems to be a profound right to the labor of one's body and the work of one's hands becomes a useless possession—*if one cannot find an employer who will contract for this labor at a living wage.* Macpherson probes into the subtle hoax that Locke introduced:

> Once the land is taken up . . . those without property are . . . dependent for their very livelihood on those with property and are unable to alter their own circumstances. The initial equality of natural rights which consisted in no man having jurisdiction over another cannot last after the differentiation of property. To put it another way, the man without property in things loses that full proprietorship of his own person which was the basis of his equal natural rights. . . . civil society is established to protect unequal possessions (after the invention of money), which have already in the state of nature given rise to unequal rights.[14]

Only the possession of property "things" could secure for people their right to become full-fledged citizens.

Within a century Adam Smith and other new-breed economists were to build this possessive individualism into the emerging injustice (and remarkable productivity) of the industrial revolution.

Limitations in Locke's Social Ethic of Freedom and Equality

We are now in position to appreciate the extent of the economic revolution that Locke's acquisitive ethic initiated in England and then elsewhere. This second revolution meant a zest for possessive, not traditional, markets. Everything seemed to be open to contractual bargaining. Everything and every person seemed to be up for sale or hire. Let the buyer beware!

It is precisely in the face of the lasting impact of Locke's possessive individualism and its possessive market society that we do well to probe the basic socio-ethical values upon which Locke rested his liberalism. As we read the *Second Treatise,* two value-terms frequently meet our eyes: "freedom" and "equality."

Both are central to Locke's state of nature and the law of nature that governs this state. Thus he starts from the state in which all persons would naturally be: " . . . that is, a state of perfect freedom to order their actions and dispose of their possessions and persons as they think fit . . . without asking leave or depending upon the will of any other man."[15] Immediately he adds that this natural and original state is also one of " . . . equality, wherein all the power and jurisdiction is reciprocal, no one having more than another. . . ." Locke finds freedom and equality most fundamental to his hypothetical state of nature.

We have earlier seen, however, that when we attempted to follow his train of reasoning that moved from a mythic state of nature to the hard realities of English politico-economic history, we had to be on guard against the subtle enticements in both his logic and his interpretation of facts.

Freedom, or liberty, became the password for all who entered the ranks of liberalism. Locke's particular version of freedom became, however, tightly linked with persons' concern for property and the liberty to share in profitable exchanges in the new contractual marketplace. This meant that the possessive aspect of his individualism surfaced in both economics and the monadic, isolated nature of each independent self. This further "freed" all potential employees to contract for a job in Locke's new possessive market only when the employer freely decided it would be profitable to offer such a contract. This contractualism of the early industrial revolution became "free" to enact laws that refused labor the right to meet and organize unions. In sum, workers were now free to be proprietors of their bodies and hands, but it was the employers who had the really decisive freedom—the freedom to make such bodies and hands marketable or unmarketable within possessive individualism.

Lockean freedom, on the more positive side, upheld key civil liberties—personal, political, religious—and assured greater toleration for minorities. Locke should be honored for his role in these advances in individual and social freedom, as far as they went. But these commitments could not go far enough, given Locke's espousal of an economic freedom that could not assure increasing numbers of persons the primal power to translate their labor into a decent livelihood.

When we move to Locke's second ethico-political value, *equality*, we encounter even more serious tension in his liberalism. Here his possessive individualism seemed to make everyone equal in the original state of nature, by dint of designating everyone's body and hands to constitute their innate and inalienable property. Yet what did this really mean? Actually, it meant nothing more than an elemental biological equality that empowered everyone to supply all basic physical needs in a bountiful but purely imaginary nature.

We note, next, that in Locke's mythical natural order there existed another type of equality—the never-ceasing equal "inconvenience" where all proprietors had to protect their two kinds of property: their (1) body/hands property and their (2) object/ "thing" property, acquired by means of the labor and work of their body/hands property. Throughout our remaining consideration of Locke, we need to keep clearly in mind these two properties and what happens because of them.

Finally, persons freely chose to shift from the "inconvenience" of their natural, individualistic arrangement to a new political order that protected everyone's property. They did this, presumably, to provide a new dimension of equal property protection.

Precisely at this point, however, we have already seen that the equal-protection aspect of the new politico-property system backfired in the faces of those who found themselves possessing a body/hands property *and nothing more!* If no one offered them employment in this contractual, employer-employee economy, there was no other way by which they could utilize their so-called innate and inalienable body/hands property to procure the "thing" property they had to have to live decently. To assure that there was absolutely no other way, recall that Lockeans and others left the idle and the working poor without the right to vote. Thus, ironically, the ballot became the supreme symbol of inequality.

To cap all this inequity, Locke now reasoned that the invention of durable money legitimized successful employers in piling up ever-greater wealth. The earlier natural spoilage limits no longer applied to durable money. Wealth could be acquired with no worries about becoming covetous.

At this point we can sum up three serious shortcomings in the Classical Liberalism to which Locke contributed so much. *First,* his theoretical freedom became too integrally dependent upon the possession of object/ "thing" property. *Second,* his theoretical equality was utterly dependent upon everyone's being equally endowed with innate and inalienable body/hands property. But this farfetched property notion could become operative only when employers conferred upon employees the power to translate their body/hands property into just wages and actual object/ "thing" property required for self-fulfilling living. *Third,* emerging capitalism freed successful entrepreneurs from all medieval restraints upon piling up ever-greater wealth. The biblical warning against covetousness was obliterated.

The Practical Problem of Democratizing Governments

We have now assessed Locke's politico-economic revolution based upon possessive individualism and his inadequate theories of freedom and equality. Next we will inquire into manifest and latent flaws that have periodically undermined democratizing endeavors in these United States. These weaknesses have not been expunged during more than two hundred years of nationhood. Our democratizing "blood count" is ominously low when compared with that of most other political democracies.

We note at the outset that fifty-five delegates (many of them Lockeans), participated in the constitutional convention in May 1787. We sense the high vision they affirmed in their Preamble to the Constitution. Still these highly conscientious and competent founding fathers were guilty of structuring three irreparable flaws into their new-born democracy.

First was their acceptance and indirect approval of one of the cruelest systems of slavery ever concocted by humans. Some 460,000 blacks were slaves (20 percent of the nation's population as of 1770), who were denied utterly the "blessings of liberty" that the founders had fought so heroically to secure for themselves and their posterity.

From the very inception of this nation, the "half-free, half-slave" impasse was to haunt and tear asunder the "grand experiment." By the 1980s we have learned through recurring tragedies that the fallout from the democracy/slavery contrariety was to bear its evil fruit right down to today's white racism.

The *second* of these three weaknesses is termed the Lockean syndrome, or what Macpherson calls Locke's possessive individualism. One result of this syndrome is the contradiction Macpherson finds between economic liberalism and political democracy. In this strained situation democracy is requiring direct and full equality ever more relentlessly.

Direct equality means that indirect factors, such as money, social status, race, or other extraneous elements, cannot deprive the poor of their share of political and economic resources. Decent incomes, adequate educational facilities, and competent health care are three assets, in other words, without which persons cannot confirm their dignity as human beings in modern democracies. Full equality means that the poor and disadvantaged must be able to join with the advantaged in generating new forms of socio-political power. Until both direct and full equality are achieved, the United States is flawed by fractional democracy; only a fraction of the potential power for justice and equality is being marshaled. And obviously, the very phrase "fractional democracy" is a contradiction in terms.

Along with its agonies resulting from the failures of a half-free, half-slave impasse and the Lockean syndrome, we find also embedded in the patriotic mood of this nation a *third* basic weakness: political extremism. Put most succinctly, extremism is patriotism run amuck! It is a superpatriotism that splinters a society in the process of exalting its "good Americans" and castigating its "un-Americans." This patriotism of extremists is contrived by persons who cannot comprehend the "state of mind" that undergirds authentic democracy. This democratic "state of mind" is obviously a staunch commitment to pluralism[16] that "remains commonly accepted as the fixed spiritual center of the democratic political process. . . ."[17]

Eduard Lindeman makes clear that people must do one thing if they are to enact authentic democratizing: They must discipline themselves to a unity that can be achieved only through the "creative use of diversity."[18] Extremism undermines the safety and order required to maintain a creative diversity.

The Deepening Conflict Between Economic Liberalism and Political Democracy

Our next task is to let Macpherson, Alan Wolfe, and others who have contributed to the theme thrust us into an awareness of the clash between liberalism and democracy. Unfortunately, the nature of economic liberalism and of political democracy, and deeply rooted encounters between them, have not been clearly interpreted. We must seek clarity.

Recall first that Locke's economic liberalism has little to do with full democratizing, with supportiveness toward the liberties of the propertyless, or with full equality. Indeed, Alan Wolfe insists that the very words "liberal democracy" are a contradiction in terms. He finds classical or economic liberalism, as formulated by Locke, Jeremy Bentham, and John Stuart Mill during the seventeenth into the nineteenth centuries, always tilted toward the economic rights and freedoms of property-holders. It was free men, writes Wolfe, who "would buy and sell land, commodities, and each other's ability to work in an atmosphere unencumbered by . . . obstructive regulations. Liberalism was the ideal political philosophy for an emerging powerful capitalist revolution."[19]

Alongside economic liberalism, another set of revolutionary forces were to emerge during the nineteenth century. They were cited by Macpherson and Wolfe as democracy and full equality. Political democracy, in contrast to an economically oriented liberalism, arose in opposition to the "very conditions that liberalism tried to create." It was not until the nineteenth century that the rising working class demanded universal suffrage, rights of women and minorities, and control over the market in labor. Democracy emphasized two themes that liberalism did not: direct equality (in opposition to the indirect equality of the market) and participation of all "in the affairs of the human community."[20]

Wolfe points out that in spite of the differences between (economic) liberalism and (political) democracy, these two could live in relative harmony so long as Western societies engaged in a continuous process of economic growth! Liberal nations could acquire their property and profits alongside democratic provision for more equality and more participation of workers in the industrial process.

Then in the twentieth century, particularly in the 1970s, came a collapse in continuous economic growth or, as Wolfe puts it, the end of "expanding expansion." Liberal capitalisms were now barely holding their own economically. Thence Wolfe concludes that liberal democracy's crisis is very real. "Its roots lie in the fact that in western societies the economic system is liberal and capitalistic while the political system is formally democratic and therefore potentially socialist."[21] If people have the right politically to redefine the rules of the game, they may well opt for a very different set of rules.

In the light of this background from Locke, Macpherson, and Wolfe, we can summarize what our word "democratizing" signifies. Lockean possessive individualism improvised an economic liberalism that aimed at securing a complex of politico-economic rights for the propertied, while seeking to lock out the poor politically. Then, during the eighteenth and especially the nineteenth centuries, laborers and the poor pressed for a political democracy based upon direct equality and participation by everyone in the community. Now, with "expanding expansion" slowed or halted, the strains between economic liberalism and political democracy are becoming sharper.

By the 1980s, signals from this strain were becoming louder and clearer in this nation—a surge of political-economic pressures from the right and left; a weakening of the center; more

extremism, less consensus. Our task of democratizing governments is confronted by many aggressive challenges.

At this point it is helpful to draw upon Amitai Etzioni and
Warren Breed to help us assess this deepening struggle between
right, left, and center. For the condensed model of *democratizing*
that we are developing, we must reckon with three negative
forces operative in all politico-economic activity—forces that
become ever more powerful in the pressures activated by the
mass media: *alienation, inauthenticity,* and *"the appearance of
responsiveness."*

Breed uses "alienation," largely in the Marxian sense, to refer
to the situation of persons who experience both a "feeling of
resentment" and an "expression of objective conditions which
expose a person to forces beyond his understanding and control."[22] Breed next brings in Etzioni's crucial bond between
alienation and inauthenticity: "A relationship, institution, or society is inauthentic if it provides the appearance of responsiveness
while the underlying condition is alienating."[23] Breed then intro-
duces us to the decisive factor: the insidious manner in which
inauthentic structures "devote a higher ratio of their efforts than
do alienating ones to concealing their contours and to building the
appearance of responsiveness."[24] Here is a sharpening of Marx's
classic work on alienation. Here inauthenticity, by building an
appearance of responsiveness, becomes more deceptive than
does alienation.

We are now confronted with a complex of factors, rooted in the
Lockean vision and exacerbated in more recent centuries and
decades. The current struggle between those who own and
control economic wealth and those government bodies and citizens attempting to place limits on the negative effects of economic factors must be seen in its full historical context. Such
strife over justice issues is not being newly imposed by rabble-
rousing leftists but is the predictable outcome of the enfranchise-
ment of the poor and outcast. As the political and economic
battles heat up, justice seekers will have to attend carefully to the
tactics of political extremism, inauthenticity, and the appearance

of responsiveness to which those with vested interests in the
unjust economic system resort.

Summary and a Look Ahead

We have completed our inquiry into Lockean economic liberalism
and its stance with respect to the self, nature, society, government, property, and economics. We have seen how Locke largely
ignored Luther, Calvin, and the Reformation's attempt to shift the
biblical economic ethic of stewards into the economic ethos of the
commercial revolution.

Within the larger context of ethics and economics, we must
stress that Locke's liberalism failed to develop a sound and
adequate moral structure. His economic liberalism failed to develop freedom for the propertyless, only freedom for the propertied. It remained for a new dimension of democracy to emerge in
the nineteenth century: political democracy that emphasized
direct equality and the participation of everyone "in the affairs of
the human community."

The inherent conflict between economic liberalism and political
democracy was significantly submerged through the process of
economic growth. Then, in the mid-1970s and on into the 1980s
"expanding expansion" in most of the capitalist nations has been
slowly weakening. This slowdown has sharpened the conflict
between the surging right (which has endeavored to resuscitate
Lockean liberalism under today's banner of supply-side economics and conservative politics) and the wavering left (which is
groping for new ways to coordinate more planned, demand-side
economics and more egalitarian politics). In such a time, it
becomes ever-more urgent for those committed to full democratizing to probe the dynamics of alienation, inauthenticity, and the
appearance of responsiveness. But we are getting a bit ahead of
ourselves here. Many other crucial developments have occurred
between Locke's day and ours, and we now turn to at least some
of them.

5

New Challenges
to the Christian Economic Ethic:
Revolutions Within Revolutions

The disruptive and at times even shattering events in culture,
economics, and politics that have occurred throughout history
have become noticeably more frequent since the sixteenth century. It was, however, with the beginning of the industrial revolution (roughly about the year 1760) that the scope, intensity, and
frequency of those upheavals became so great that the shape of
people's lives was altered in a matter of decades rather than
centuries. The pace of change has been accelerating. Since World
War II we have been experiencing what might be called the
revolutions of high technology. The last half century has seen
change so fast that five to ten years is enough to bring about
major shifts in the contours of human life itself. The lives and
cultures of persons throughout the earth are being increasingly
disoriented. Walter Lippmann well summed it up in a phrase from
Aristophanes: Whirl is King, having driven out Zeus.

In this chapter we will attempt to summarize a few of the major
trends and problems affecting us in the modern world, and the
economic thinking that has accompanied them. Much will of
necessity be left out, but we hope to outline enough of our
current situation to allow us a point of departure for the constructive analysis to be presented in Part Two. We begin with perhaps
the single most important watershed in modern economic history: the industrial revolution.

An Overview of Economic Events and Ideas

Periodically in history, the invention of new means for producing goods brings about massive economic and social change in a fairly short time span. In the eighteenth century a new source of industrial energy, steam power, was the key that unlocked the energy of coal and transformed the structure of the whole production process. With steam power human beings could break out of their dependence on the comparatively weak forms of human, animal, and water power.

The eighteenth century became the period, especially in England, when many practical mechanics and inventors moved rapidly toward the new factory system powered by steam. In 1733 John Kay invented the fly shuttle, an improvement in the process of weaving. During the same year John Wyatt developed a spinning machine to speed up the other phases of textile production. Richard Arkwright created the water frame in 1768, thus enabling water power to improve and increase the output of spinning. Then came a more specific focus upon steam power. As early as 1698 Thomas Savery invented a steam engine, though it was not efficient. Thomas Newcomen followed with an improved version in 1705.

It remained, however, for James Watt to conceive, in 1765, the first condensing steam engine, which eliminated defects in the Savery-Newcomen models. Watt obtained his first patent in 1769. Then followed the chaotic yet productive years when workers and engineers had to be trained to operate safely these powerful new steam engines; when capital had to be raised to finance larger, more costly factories; when laborers had to be "domesticated" for long hours of oppressive factory toil.

We can aptly designate the industrial revolution as the union of steam with the factory system. Financing large and costly manufacturing plants, railroads, and mines resulted in a speedup of methods for raising capital, especially early in the nineteenth century: selling common stock, then preferred stock, and finally bonds. Great Britain and the United States took the lead in advancing the new world of economics and business, with Britain the forerunner from 1760 into the late nineteenth century.

At the same time as these historic developments were taking place, a whole new branch of human knowledge came into being: economics. It is true, of course, that many pre-modern thinkers addressed economic topics. Medieval scholars did. The great Greek philosophers Plato and Aristotle did. Yet before the eighteenth century all treatments of economic matters were rather minor references within works dealing primarily with other concerns, usually ethics. In view of the vast changes in economic life that were taking place in the move from traditional medieval economy to modern industrial production, a simultaneous increase in the amount of thinking about economic life comes as no surprise. Many pamphlets and shorter treatises had been written by others before him, but the undisputed "father" of modern economics was a Scottish moral philosopher named Adam Smith.

In 1776 Smith published his well-known *The Wealth of Nations*. In it he attempted to make sense of the economic structures that had been developing over the preceding century or two. He did so with the explicit purpose of making "an inquiry into the nature and causes of the wealth of nations." (In fact, this is the full title of the book.) In doing this Smith combined an analysis of economic life with roughly the same general presumptions about possessive individualism as we saw in Locke in the preceding chapter. The end result was a book which so forcefully articulated the spirit of capitalism that his arguments are the primary ones used by defenders of the capitalist system even today.

So much has happened between Smith's time and ours that it is important to become aware of the major shifts in economic life since then. As we will see, there are two insurmountable problems in employing the economic philosophy of Smith to chart a course for our economy at the end of the twentieth century. The first is the weakness of the individualist position based on the political tradition from Locke. The second is the fact that our economic system today is so different from the system which

Smith knew that his views alone no longer accurately describe the forces that shape economic life today.

We will return to an analysis of the individualist position in Chapter 7, but we can now outline some of the shifts in the structure of the economy over the last two centuries. To do so, it will be helpful to refer to the analysis of economic life provided by Joe Holland and Peter Henriot, S.J., in their *Social Analysis: Linking Faith and Justice*. There Holland and Henriot break that two-hundred-year period of industrial capitalism into three stages. The first two stages are widely known and employed by many commentators: laissez-faire capitalism and social welfare capitalism. They articulate the third from more recent work of theirs and others: the stage of national security capitalism. We will take each in its turn and examine both the state of the economy and the content of economic theory that predominated during that time.

1. The Era of Laissez-Faire Capitalism

The industrial revolution brought a tremendous surge of economic activity, first in England and then in country after country elsewhere. The raw physical productivity of the new industrial processes was great enough to reward economic innovators (often referred to as "entrepreneurs") with sizeable profits even though the vast majority of workers were to wait decades before much of that "trickled down" to them. Some of the already wealthy invested part of their fortunes and received large returns on their investments. Others who were definitely not wealthy were able to combine inventive genius with entrepreneurial ability and formed very successful businesses. And some, of course, invested large sums in efforts that fizzled for any of a variety of reasons. The lure of great profit drew many onward and incited feverish activity in new economic enterprises.

While there was great variety in the form and size of each business or factory, the basic outline can be generalized. Each business was self-contained, usually owned and managed by the same individual or family. The larger businesses, such as the textile factories, hired workers for a weekly or monthly wage.

The workers, for their part, were often rural people who had left their traditional homes because of poverty there and the promise of a better life in the cities. Improvements in transportation such as canals, faster oceangoing ships, and eventually railroads, led to an extension of markets so that a centrally located factory could economically use raw materials shipped from great distances and could sell its products to even more-distant consumers.

Adam Smith lived amidst this newly developing economic structure and presented an analysis of its workings. His was not the best summary of technical innovation (several major inventions used widely in Great Britain by the time *The Wealth of Nations* was published did not even get a mention there), but his analysis of the economic forces at work was by far the most perceptive of his day.

If he were pressed for the most basic cause of human prosperity (and therefore the key to ending poverty), Smith would give us a three-part answer, beginning with the division of labor, moving to exchange, and then on to self-interest. He begins the first chapter of *The Wealth of Nations* with part of his answer: "The greatest improvement in the productive powers of labour, and the greater part of the skill, dexterity, and judgment with which it is any where directed, or applied, seem to have been the effects of the division of labour."[1]

By the division of labor he means the breaking up of fairly complex procedures into several simpler tasks and the specialization of human labor so that different individuals work exclusively on one or another of those simpler tasks. This leads to significantly greater productivity than if each worker were to do all of the steps individually. (If each worker in a modern auto factory had to produce a complete car alone, not many cars would be built.) Smith gives three reasons for this. The individual develops greater dexterity in doing the one specialized task than if required to do many tasks; no time is lost shifting from one operation to another; and a labor-saving invention that increases productivity is more likely to be discovered by an individual whose whole attention is focused on a single task.[2]

Smith uses a now-classic example of the manufacture of pins to demonstrate the increased productivity brought about by dividing the process into eighteen distinct operations. This method, he asserts, is two hundred times—perhaps, he says, even four thousand times—more productive than when each worker makes the whole pin from start to finish. Even if he exaggerates a bit out of enthusiasm for the idea, Smith's point is well taken. Looking at all the things necessary for simple survival, it is quite clear that each of us would be less well off if we had to produce for ourselves every article we use.

Yet as important as the division of labor in society is, Smith knew that exchange (the second part of his answer) was equally important. For the division of labor

> is not originally the effect of any human wisdom, which foresees and intends that general opulence to which it gives occasion. It is the necessary, though very slow and gradual, consequence of a certain propensity in human nature which has in view so such extensive utility; the propensity to truck, barter, and exchange one thing for another.[3]

Only humans exhibit this propensity, he argues, and only they are so dependent on other members of the species for survival. Yet in spite of our dependence on others, we do not have to resort to servile and fawning attention to the other to get what we need. In fact, he says, depending on the good will or charity of the other probably will not work very well. There is a better way, since in trade, *each* party to the transaction is able to trade away something considered to be of lesser value for something considered to be of greater. Since the other will gain (at least by the *other's* standards of greater and lesser value), an exchange can be proposed to appeal not to sentiments of charity but to the other's self-interest.

Self-interest is the third and final part of Smith's answer to the question about prosperity and poverty. He puts it in his own inimitable fashion:

> It is not from the benevolence of the butcher, the brewer, or the baker, that we expect our dinner, but from their regard to their

own interest. We address ourselves, not to their humanity but to their self-love, and never talk to them of our own necessities but of their advantages.[4]

Self-interest, leading to exchange and to the division of labor, is the key to understanding how and why economic interaction comes about. "Nobody but a beggar chooses to depend chiefly upon the benevolence of his fellow-citizens," and even the beggar depends on the self-interest of others when he or she *spends* the coins received from mendicancy. Self-interest is what makes the economic world go round. And as it does, the advances in productivity, which we have seen are in part caused by the division of labor, occur in all sectors, including the transportation industry. As transportation becomes cheaper, those who are the most efficient at producing a certain item can serve an even larger geographic area. This allows for greater division of labor and subsequently, greater wealth in society.

Self-interest can certainly have a darker side, but Smith contends that competition will hold abuse in check. If there are several bakeries for me to do business with, no one baker can mistreat me or charge me too much without my trading instead with one of the competitors. Competition among economic actors is the best guarantee that self-interest will work to the advantage of all, in spite of the *intention* of each individual to work only for self-advantage. The baker will treat me well because of his or her own self-interest. While some would look to government regulation for protection from self-interested exploitation by firms, Smith reminds us that since the owners of firms would willingly collude and get government help to legitimate their cartels, governments are not as a rule to be trusted with the authority to authorize some monopolies and ban others.

Idealists (especially Christian idealists) who would simplistically depend only on love to move economic actors or who would naively expect only altruistic behavior from civil servants and governments have much to learn from Smith. Self-interest has undeniable power in our lives and, within limits, is a strong force for good. Take an example from daily life. When we push a

cart through the grocery, do we pick up torn or damaged packages of food, or do we choose those that look the best to us?
Choosing the poorest would certainly leave a better choice for
the next shoppers. *Should* a responsible Christian or other citizen
be altruistic here and purchase the worst foodstuffs? While we
intend good for the other members of our family who will eat the
food, are we simply acting *selfishly* in choosing the best for *our*
family and leaving the rest for others?

Smith does not treat these moral questions in *The Wealth of
Nations,*[5] but his point is that looking out for our own self-interest
has generally *good* effects—and for more than just me and my
family. Later in this chapter and in Chapter 7 we will address the
shortsightedness of this belief in the virtues of self-interest, but
for now let us consider the wisdom in Smith's perspective.

If shoppers acted perfectly altruistically, they would
unnecessarily be buying food that might be spoiled, and this could
result either in the disposal of the food just before it is to be
prepared or in an unhealthy meal if the food is used. Moreover,
the grocery store will have little economic reason to change its
behavior, since it can go on selling these damaged packages. But
if the store is left with unsold packages of spoiled food because
shoppers refuse to buy them, it has an economic incentive to be
more careful in its purchasing and handling of food. The manager
will be more likely to reprimand those employees who are care-
less; or, if the food is being damaged before it gets to the store,
the manager will complain to the supplier or change to a different
supplier. The supplier then has an economic incentive to find out
whether employees of the supplier are at fault or whether poor-
quality packages are being bought from food processors. The
chain of events goes on.

The initial self-interested refusal of grocery shoppers to buy
damaged or spoiled food may, in the end, lead a vegetable-
canning company to improve its procedures to cause less damage
to food containers. This step represents a more responsible and
efficient use of the world's food supply and a more careful stewardship of God's gifts.

Thus self-interested behavior on our part can bring about both better meals for us and more responsible behavior on the part of people a thousand miles away whom we do not know and will never meet. In terminology that has become more popular after Smith, the "market mechanism" (whereby consumers express their preferences through what they buy) leads to "economic efficiency" (so that the cannery either improves its handling of cans or goes bankrupt because other canneries do a better job). Adam Smith was clearly enamored of this process of self-interested behavior, and like most of the intellectuals during the period of laissez-faire capitalism he focused on its positive results.

Yet while the idealist is wrong to stress only the purity of altruistic intention as the key to healthy social life, Smith, too, is wrong to think that a good economic system can be simply structured around self-interest. After all, the period of laissez-faire capitalism was one of tremendous hardships for workers and the unemployed.

Many factory owners found it in their self-interest to pay low wages in return for long hours, to employ children as young as six years old for as many as twelve or fourteen hours a day, to neglect the purchase of even the most basic safety devices. The records of British parliamentary inquiries into such abuses recount the often-brutal conditions. Thus the self-interest of consumers to choose the lower-priced of two identical items made at two different factories meant that even if some factory owners wanted to be more responsible to their employees, that extra responsibility would cost them more money, and their higher-priced goods could not compete with the lower-priced goods of their less scrupulous competitors. When some are allowed to be irresponsible, the market mechanism forces the rest down to the same level—or forces them out of business. At the very time when industrial productivity was rising faster than ever, working conditions were far harsher than those prior to the industrial revolution.

Working people, of course, did not bear all this silently. Many workers found great appeal in the analysis of capitalism provided by Karl Marx—an analysis which saw the owners of capital expropriating for themselves the wealth that workers were producing. Marx himself thought that a new, socialistic form of economy would arise because of a workers' revolution (perhaps through political means, perhaps through violence) in the face of worsening living conditions. In fact, it was the Russian revolution at the end of World War I that provided ground for the first national transformation of economic structures in reaction to the evils of laissez-faire capitalism. (In its place arose a system of totalitarian communism, with its own series of evils under which the people of the Soviet Union live today.) In the United States and Western Europe, a different series of events transpired.

Slowly through the nineteenth century, the material life of the workers came to share in at least some of the greater wealth produced in the economy. For years the economic historians have debated the causes for this increase in the material well-being of workers. Defenders of capitalism see it as an inevitable development of the system. Critics of capitalism point to the struggles of working people. In any case it is clear that by the end of the nineteenth century and the first part of the twentieth century a shift was beginning to take place. The brutal harshness of earlier laissez-faire capitalism was giving way to a capitalism where the welfare of the middle and lower classes was improving.

2. Social Welfare Capitalism

All attempts to break history up into neat periods come up short, but it is clear that the capitalism of most of our current century has had a different character from that of a hundred years earlier. While the working poor and unemployed continued to live lives of severe scarcity, large parts of the working class came to enjoy some measure of economic security. As we look back on this change, two major influences stand out.

The first is the struggle of workers to form labor unions and to use that organized power to force concessions from those who owned the factories where they worked. Union organizing was resisted from the start by management and owners. Its opponents argued that forcing a firm to offer a certain wage is a violation of freedom and that firms should be free to hire whomever they wish. Workers countered that the power of a large employer negates the freedom an individual worker should have.

By the end of the nineteenth century, the predominant family-owned business of Adam Smith's day was giving way to a new model for firms—the national corporation. Major firms could then depend not just on their own company guards to put down worker protests and actions but also upon the force of municipal police and at times even national troops to protect their interests. In many places workers responded to such physical threats in kind. Too many people today have forgotten the battles, bloodshed, and loss of lives that accompanied the birth of unions.

The second major influence in the transition to a new phase of capitalism was the growing political influence of working people. We saw in Chapter 4 how the Lockean world of economics and politics allowed for only wealthy males to vote in a so-called democracy. Slowly this changed.

In England, urban males who did not own property were allowed to vote beginning in 1867, those in rural areas only in 1882. In the United States, white males had the right to vote since the founding of the republic, but black men could not until after the Civil War (and even then, prejudice and discriminatory laws kept most of them from doing so until a century later). Women were finally granted the right to vote only in 1920 in the U.S. and in 1928 in England. Thus, while progress was slow, the disenfranchised were beginning to be allowed access to the democratic process. Clearly, even after the "right" to vote was granted, the inexperience of previously excluded voters, and the prejudice of those who had held the vote exclusively, postponed much of the effectiveness these new voters were destined to have eventually. Since blacks and women had been excluded from the political process for so long, it took many years for strong norms concerning active political involvement to become operative in those groups. Still, the growing movement to democratize the limited democracies of the United States and other Western nations had an influence on the political climate within which capitalism was developing.

At the same time, the greater productivity of industrial capitalism allowed for more resources to be invested in schools and other social welfare functions of government. Greater education led more citizens to be better informed about, and more involved in, politics. The strife in the movement toward unions also radicalized many workers who became much more active in the local and national political process.

During this period, economic science continued to develop in its efforts to analyze the economic activity of society.[6] The orthodox branch of the discipline became far more technical, incorporating calculus, statistics, and other areas of advanced mathematics into its formulation of economic theory. Dissident economist objected to this and to the general abstractness and bias toward capitalism in the majority view. Marxian economists continued the critique begun by Karl Marx during the laissez-faire period.[7] Under the leadership of Thorstein Veblen, a new group of American economists, known generally as Institutionalists, developed a scathing critique of the economic and cultural scene.[8] Even within the generally orthodox school of economics which was known for its adversion to government involvement in the economy, there were economists in the later stages of laissez-faire capitalism who were strong adherents to Utilitarianism and who were thus willing to propose many government programs in an effort to achieve the "greatest good for the greatest number."

The economist most thoroughly identified with the spirit of social welfare capitalism is John Maynard Keynes. His influence within economics, and most importantly within politics, did not come about until the 1930s, long after many of the reforms of this phase of capitalism began. It was because of the disastrous effects of the Great Depression that Keynes' proposals for government oversight of the economy were largely adopted. Prior to that time, most economists took the economy to be self-correcting, but as Keynes put it in 1935, "The outstanding faults of the economic society in which we live are its failure to provide full employment and its arbitrary and inequitable distribution of wealth and income."[9]

With unheard-of millions of workers unable to find a job, the government took on the responsibility of using its fiscal and monetary policy to keep the economy running as smoothly as possible. This general sense that the government had to step in existed before Keynes' *General Theory* was published, but his work solidly lined up the economics profession with the general thrust of the new form of capitalism in which the welfare of the general population became an explicit political concern.

This reciprocal influence between the economic realm and the political had led earlier to the repeal of laws that made labor unions illegal and resulted later in several political victories for organized labor. Unions spread throughout much of the industrialized sector of the economy. Unions then became the primary force for legislation directed at the social welfare of the nation and at their own well-being as organizations. Nearly all the laws and programs generally referred to under the title "the welfare state" resulted from the efforts of unions: child-labor laws, the forty-hour work week, social security, minimum wage, and in later decades, Medicare and Medicaid, job training for low-income teenagers, and a number of other "anti-poverty" programs.

Thus while the basic economic unit in the economy, the corporation, was growing from a local to a national and even international operation, the economy was taking on a more humane face. The profit motive was, of course, still the driving force of corporate activity, but economic life was losing some of the brutality of the earlier period of laissez-faire capitalism. Even large firms began to speak of "corporate social responsibility," which in the terminology we have been using is an example of a strengthening of the public norms about how corporations should operate.

One of the central issues facing capitalism today can be put as a question: Is this phase of "social welfare industrial capitalism" (to use Holland and Henriot's phrase) proof that capitalism is becoming more and more humane and is providing greater justice to more and more people, or is this phase simply a temporary respite in a movement driven by economic forces ultimately unrelated to justice concerns?

The strength of capitalism, especially in its social welfare phase, has always been that it encourages solid effort, individual initiative, and innovation, that it produces a wealth of goods and services for the populace, and that it has supported a fairly strong democratic sense among the people of the nation. Unfortunately, there are ominous signs that a harsher form of capitalism is developing.

3. National Security Capitalism

Many critics today see a new phase of capitalism emerging. Such changes, if and when they occur, are always subtle and cannot be clearly viewed until many years have passed. Still, several changes in the character of capitalism are visible and seem to be pointing to an era when many of the positive elements of social welfare capitalism may be lost.

As always, developments in technology are crucial. With almost unbelievable speed in transportation and electronic communications at their disposal, very large transnational corporations can act as easily all around the globe today as national firms could within the U.S. just fifty years ago. While larger operations have generally brought economies of larger scale, the difficulty of keeping track of widely spread plants and offices used to be a barrier to growth. Now supersonic air travel and satellite communication systems and computer networks allow firms to coordinate efforts in Singapore and Brussels just about as easily as in Los Angeles and New York. This makes it economically possible for transnational corporations to choose the country where goods will be produced almost without regard to where they will be sold eventually.

Beginning in the 1960s but accelerating in the 1970s and early 1980s, more and more transnationals have closed older manufacturing facilities in the United States and have built new factories in countries where wages and taxes are lower. This same phenomenon has been occurring since even an earlier date within the U.S., as older plants in the unionized industrial areas of the North are closed and new ones built in "Sunbelt" states where union organizing has been less successful, due in some cases to anti-union state legislation.

Such reinvestment of capital in new areas has a devastating effect on the people and communities where the firm has been operating for many decades before pulling out. In many cases, especially where the firm has been the major employer in a small town, the result is catastrophic. The only recourse for finding employment is to move, and hundreds of families are forced to pull up roots and find another place to settle. While the corporation moving out looks only at its own balance sheet, it imposes huge social costs on other firms (in related "service industries") whose businesses have depended on the plant's workers as customers, and on the city or town as a whole, as families and neighborhoods are split when people must choose between living there unemployed or moving to another area.

There is likely no evil intent whatever on the part of the corporation closing the plant. In most cases the firm believes it has been forced to do so by its competitors who are already located in low-wage, low-tax areas of the country or, more frequently now, the globe. The situation is very much like that in the laissez-faire phase. Recall how at that time well-intentioned entrepreneurs who did not want to treat their workers so severely either had to do so anyway or were often forced out of business by the low-priced goods that less scrupulous businesses could offer. Now, too, firms are pointing to competitive pressures as the reason why good intentions about not causing those social costs must give way to profit-making realism. In fact, the competition *has* gotten stiffer.

One of the factors in the world economic situation that is different now from what it was during most of the phase of social welfare capitalism is the strength of the nations competing with the U.S. Throughout most of the twentieth century the United States has not had to compete with such strong rivals as we do today. Japan and West Germany spent much of that time rebuilding from the devastation of war. Today their standards of productivity set the pace for the world. During that earlier period it was far easier for the U.S. Congress to pass, for example, positive health and safety legislation, since firms that then faced higher costs simply charged U.S. consumers higher prices, and the ultimate consumer paid the full and true cost of producing those goods in a more humane production process.

Now, however, when competing plants in Japan, Indonesia, or Taiwan provide those same goods at lower prices (because of lower wages, fewer safety standards for workers, and/or lower taxes made possible by fewer social services), firms with plants in the U.S. are forced by competition to keep their prices lower. This puts a squeeze on profits and leads them to want to move those operations to the low-cost areas of the world.

Morally, the effects are ominous. When a nation does not have to worry much about firms moving out to other countries, the level of justice can be significantly raised by political action. However, when the threat of the flight of capital investment to other nations is present, then higher costs required by more responsible behavior may well lead firms to cut back activities at home and move much of their manufacturing abroad. And where do those new plants get built? In nations with low levels of social services for their citizens, strong anti-union laws, a low level of civil rights and civil liberties, and cheap labor. In short, in nations with undemocratic, authoritarian, often military, governments that are aligned with the local wealthy class and that recognize little responsibility to lower-income people.

Because any sort of international or world government seems impossible in the foreseeable future, this basic reality of international competition seems destined to predominate. The legislated restrictions on all competitors that brought about the shift from laissez-faire capitalism to the more humane social welfare form will not be available now that markets have grown to be larger than national governments.

Political debates in Northern "Snowbelt" states in this country now often contain attacks on the "business climate" of the state as being too negative and pushing businesses out to other, usually Southern, states with "better business conditions." While some laws are simply badly drafted and needlessly inefficient, in effect these claims urge that the standards of economic justice of the state be lowered. We are now hearing such talk openly and regularly at the state level, and it is appearing with increasing frequency in discussions of national policy in relation to the business conditions of other nations. The moral tragedy is that we in this country have only begun the process of providing elementary justice to women, blacks, Hispanics, and American Indians, and yet these meager gains are now in danger within the international economic system.

We can see, then, that freedom from military governments, death squads, and poverty in the Third World is not simply a justice issue for those nations alone. As partial as are the justice standards of the United States economy, even these will be in danger if the forces of transnational competition are allowed to prevail without regard to their effects on social justice. We can also see how certain economic interests within the U.S. have much to gain by a foreign policy that supports right-wing dictators throughout the world. The naive illusion that popular revolutionary uprisings are Russian creations covers over the reality that even a popular revolution completely unrelated to the Soviet Union would represent a setback for firms seeking an "ideal" business climate and could well signal the fall of numerous other military dictatorships that provide safe and secure labor forces for transnational firms.

In this book we are focusing on economic life in the United States, not on that in the Third World, where even more severe problems exist. Still it is not difficult to see the commonality of interest among working people of all nations. Many workers who are threatened by (or unemployed because of) the transfer of jobs to other nations react instinctively against both the firms who are moving and the workers in those other nations who take the new jobs. However, given the realities of international competition among transnational firms, workers and the unemployed poor in the United States need to cooperate with the working people of other nations. It is in the interest of these U.S. citizens to push Congress and the President to shift U.S. foreign policy to support democratic reforms and truly free labor unions in Third World nations. The preservation of structures for economic justice at home requires the establishment of similar structures elsewhere. The force of competition in the international economic and political system will otherwise be too strong.

We must be clear about the intentions of the various participants in our economic system. This threat to justice can come about without either U.S. firms or the U.S. government consciously trying to pervert the interests of citizens or workers here or abroad. The issue is the workings of the international economic system. Even well-intentioned individuals take actions that have what they see to be unfortunate side effects. A responsible economic ethic requires a transformation of the system itself and not simply a change from bad intentions to good.

The analysis of the current phase of capitalism provided by economic science shows anything but a consensus. Some mainstream economists assert that although the situation has changed in some ways since the days of Adam Smith, the basic outlines of competition among firms remain and the governments of the world should push for free trade and generally stay out of economic affairs. Milton Friedman is perhaps the best-known advocate of minimal government role in the economy; if a firm, large or small, goes bankrupt or just decides to move its plant to another area of the globe, governments should not interfere. Some economists such as Lester Thurow advocate new economic institutions such as a national investment bank to give U.S. firms the same advantages that others enjoy.

> It [the national investment bank] certainly represents more government in the mixed economy, but the time has come to recognize that if we are going to compete with some of our more successful industrial neighbors, we are going to have to change the way we have been doing things in the past.[10]

Still others like David M. Gordon stress the need to develop solid, long-term jobs through support of "community-based" enterprises rather than depending solely on the profit motive to induce firms to change their behavior in ways required for the society's good.[11]

In short, there is a wide variety in the analyses of and recommendations for our current economic situation. But this is not really new. While there is some agreement about what has happened in the past, only hindsight made that possible. In every era, current events are not nearly so well understood as those of the past, where time has allowed a fuller perspective.

Two Major Disintegrative Problems

We have seen in brief overview the development of our economic system from its earlier form at the time of the industrial revolution up to the present. Before moving on to the task of developing tools for establishing a stronger economic justice, we will first take time here to examine two particularly important problems facing the United States in our current phase of industrial development: the limits to physical and social growth, and a syndrome of structured economic weaknesses. Both call for new thinking and new values. Both require a fresh approach to policies and priorities in business.

1. Limits to Physical and Social Growth

There is too little awareness of the real significance of growing "shortages" of physical commodities and almost no awareness of the encroaching problems of social scarcity. The decade of the 1970s marked an awakening of public consciousness to the fact that the physical economic growth of a growing population on a planet of fixed size leads inevitably to problems.

> Suddenly—virtually overnight when measured on a historical scale—mankind finds itself confronted by a multitude of unprecedented crises: the population crisis, the environmental crisis, the world food crisis, the energy crisis, the raw material crisis, to name just a few.[12]

The strain on raw materials illustrates the problem dramatically. As one reputable source estimated it, industry will extract more minerals from the earth during the last third of the twentieth century than have been drawn from the earth throughout all of previous history.

An awareness of such limits has alarmed many people, but economists as a group have been generally unimpressed. The reason for this is an important one, and most citizens have not understood the wisdom of the economist's position, but it is equally important to note what the economic analysis leaves out.

Economists have objected to much of the uproar about vanishing resources because some of the earliest studies on the limits to growth neglected any reference to the role played by prices in their projections. Thus, for example, the first Club of Rome report, *The Limits to Growth,* extrapolated current petroleum consumption to estimate how long the world's known oil reserves would last. The study used three projected rates of growth per year, ranging from a "low" estimate of 2.9% to a "high" estimate of 4.9% growth in consumption per year.[13] In fact, the rapid rise of oil prices due to OPEC has caused such significant conservation of energy and substitution of other energy sources for oil that in recent years there has been at times little and at times no growth in yearly consumption of petroleum in the United States.

As economists stress rightly, when a particular resource comes to be in short supply, its price rises, and not only do consumers use less of it, but producers will search the world harder to find more of it than had been previously discovered. The price mechanism works in such a way that literally running out of a resource will happen very slowly. Since the oil in wells that are easiest to drill is used first, the last oil to be produced will be much harder to pump out and much more costly—so much so that the last barrel of oil on earth will almost certainly never be used. So in one sense the physical limits to growth are not as severe as some assert.

At the same time the physical limits to growth are quite real, even if they are not as alarming as some may think. In particular, as goods become more costly, the limits that our whole economy is approaching cause the most hardship for low-income people, who are least able to cope with the higher prices caused by growing scarcity. This is a topic we will return to in Chapter 7. On the world scale, the physical limits to growth mean that it is literally impossible for all the world's people to possess as many material goods as we, the relatively wealthy of the world, own. To compare the United States with China alone, the approximately 150 million automobiles that Americans own would mean that about 900 million cars would have to be made for the Chinese people to have as many per capita. Not only would the amounts of steel, aluminum, rubber, etc., be staggering, but the drain on world oil reserves would make it impossible. In effect, the reason why we are never going to actually run out of oil is the same reason why the people of China will never have as many automobiles as we do. The price will rise, and the poor will not be able to afford to drive. The physical limits to growth have tremendous implications for efforts to achieve economic justice at home and abroad.

It remains for us to alert ourselves to another dimension of the limits to growth: social limits. Fred Hirsch builds an analysis of these social limits by differentiating what he terms "material" from "positional" economies. A *material* economy is one that invents technological means to increase production per unit of labor input. The *positional* economy, on the other hand, must deal with a very different kind of scarcity—one that has to do with

> all aspects of goods and services, work positions, and other social relationships (particularly all non-material aspects of privilege) that are either (i) scarce in some absolute or socially imposed sense, or (ii) subject to congestion or crowding through more extensive use.[14]

This can be put another way: In the positional economy the "non-material aspects of privilege" cannot be democratically and equitably spread to everyone. If they are, congestion results and the privileges evaporate.

Hirsch then warns of strains that are inevitable here and now because of social, non-material scarcity. The following instances of frustration and conflict confirm that there are just not enough of non-material privileges to go around:

• As housing conditions become more congested in cities, more persons aspire and struggle to acquire more attractive scarce scenic land farther out on the edge of the city. But this movement produces more "auctioning" wherein the costs of scarce lands are bid up. Only limited numbers can afford the affluent exurbanite role.

• As the economy strains to increase its physical output, the necessary managerial and technological leadership cannot be provided without ever more sophisticated "screening." Such screening calls for rigorous selectivity, training, and evaluation; all of this develops into tougher requirements, "obstacle cours- es," and testing. In this rugged competition and crowding in the quest for executive positions, there are many disappointed "losers," who feel themselves in a high-pressure rat race.

• Finally, all of this confronts winners with "unrelieved conges- tion" in their extended eight o'clock and five o'clock traffic. Also, the more advantaged who can afford to travel widely find themselves overwhelmed by the congested airports and mass movements of tourists.

These instances are sufficient to warn that many of the advan- tages advertised in material economies as expanding satisfactions actually deteriorate into increasing headaches. *This is especially true as more persons attain affluence that enables them to compete.* Note that it is precisely the successful growth of the material economy that produces deepening strains of social scarcity in the positional economy. Affluence does not produce a satisfied society.

Roger Shinn draws upon Hirsch's study to indicate strains that are deepening in the positional and affluent society. Shinn shows that humans have developed societies where everyone could have enough to eat. "But if you have the basic necessities of life, you then want things that will always be scarce and always available only to a minority."[15] Secluded vacation facilities and Old Master paintings are not compatible with mass consumption. Thus, everyone may aspire to be in the upper half or upper quarter of society, but this is not possible, just as not all or not even 51 percent of college football teams can win on any given Saturday. Shinn aptly summarizes Hirsch:

> . . . every increase in general prosperity makes it harder to secure
> some amenities of life. To raise the ladder may be no help to the

people on the bottom of it . . . because some things everybody
wants are available only to those near the top of the ladder.[16]

Shinn then echose Hirsch's conclusion: that we must structure
into today's social organizations a new supporting "social morality." Indeed, we too are convinced that a new social morality is
needed, one we proposed, centered on the values of the steward's proportional inclusiveness. We will now probe this possibility, first, by returning to Hirsch's argument.

Hirsch concludes his study of the social limits to growth by
calling on William S. Vickrey, an economist. Vickrey points to a
boundary that differentiates (1) where the individual "can give
free rein to his personal predilections," and (2) where the person
acts (we hope) "in accordance with ultimate ethical values."[17] Too
often, concludes Vickrey, the glorification of economic freedom
tends to "confuse individuals as to where the boundary between
the two cases lies."

Then Hirsch comes in loud and clear to state his basic conviction: that social scarcity "shifts the boundary" between the two
areas, annexing a portion of what had been legitimate self-
interest to the sphere of social obligation. In addition, social
scarcity

> increases the danger that neglect of this social sphere will corrode
> the basis necessary for pursuit of private objectives in a market
> economy. The glorification of economic freedom thereby threat-
> ens to destroy it, much as breast-beating patriotism all but
> destroyed the nation state.[18]

This lesson was painfully learned in the 1950s, during the "Red-
baiting" by such leaders as Senator Joe McCarthy. The simplistic
individualism preached by so many today is similarly misplaced.

It is within this situation of social scarcity (which Vickrey and
Hirsch examine) that we submit our social justice stance, built
upon the role of operative norms and the steward's ethic of
proportional inclusiveness. We believe that these ethical "tools"
can sharpen our grasp of a new *social morality* and demonstrate
that the biblical economic ethic can serve us more effectively in
our time than during any era in the past. It is our conviction that

disciples, especially stewards, have an opportunity to create a new society and a new structure of ultimate values and specific policies.

2. A Syndrome of Structured Unemployment and Low Productivity

A second undeniable dimension of our current economy is the dogged persistence of problems in employment and productivity. The difficulty here is not that no one has any idea about why these problems endure—a multitude of answers are given. The difficulty is that so many of the answers conflict, many proposed solutions have been tried and found wanting, and in nearly every case, those citizens who have had to pay the price of the original problems and the failed remedies have been those already at the low end of the income scale.

Unemployment has for decades been steadily growing as the most significant weakness of our economic system. We will review the situation shortly. But before doing so, we should remind ourselves of the jobs the economy has provided for millions of Americans.

One of the major difficulties faced in the employment arena over the past several decades has been the increasing numbers of Americans who have been looking for jobs. Of course, the population has risen, and this means more citizens of working age have sought work. Even more importantly, however, has been the rise in the *percentage* of Americans looking for jobs. In 1950, for example, 55.2% of the population held (civilian) jobs and another 2.9% were unemployed. Thirty years later, 58.5% held jobs and 4.2% of the population were classified as unemployed.[19] Thus, between 1950 and 1980, an extra 4.5% of the population was either working or looking for work.

Many different factors have led to this rise in the portion of Americans active in the labor market. To take just one subgroup of the population, white women have experienced a significant change in their participation in the market. Most single women had all along been holding down jobs, but the change affected many women who had traditionally worked at home as mother and wife. Basically, today there are many more so-called "working mothers." (The term itself indicates an unjust and disparaging attitude to work done at home, but that is not the point here.) During that same thirty-year period, the number of white women with jobs in the market rose from about seventeen million to over forty-one million. In 1950, about a third of white women held paying jobs; in 1980, over one half did. [20]

Thus the U.S. economy has provided a large number of jobs to Americans. But unemployment is still a crucially vexing problem. Put in its simplest terms, since an unemployed worker could be assisting in the production of the nation's wealth (making products, installing plumbing, or whatever he or she might do), it is a tragic and immoral waste to leave that person idle. We as a nation keep that person from contributing economically and thereby harm both that person's sense of self-worth and the material well-being of the society. Economically speaking, if there had been employment for the over ten million people unemployed for long periods during the recession at the end of the 1970s and the beginning of the 1980s, we would have had not only more products and services produced, but the wage incomes received by those ten million could have spurred the economy. In addition, the drop in costs of unemployment benefits and other welfare payments to needlessly unemployed persons would have helped reduce the federal budget deficit. Still, in spite of all the good that comes from lower rates of unemployment, the problem has not only persisted but worsened.

One of the ways to understand the growing problem of employment in the nation is to view the *patterned increase in unemployment in our economy.* This change has become evident through three decades—the 1950s, '60s, and '70s—and clearly seems to be operating during the '80s. This pattern is the "upward creep" of unemployment rates. Data on unemployment rates for each decade since World War II reveal a persistent increase in the rate of unemployment, the percent of the workforce that is unemployed but not so discouraged that they have given up the search for work. We can summarize this in Figure 2. [21]

FIGURE 2
The Lowest Unemployment Rate in Each of Three Decades

Decade	Lowest Unemployment Rate of the Decade	Year
1950s	2.9%	1953
1960s	3.5%	1969
1970s	4.9%	1973

As with every use of statistics, we must be careful to understand the limitations of the numbers. The percentages are lower than the actual number of "unemployed" in the country would indicate. The official government definition of an unemployed worker does not include many people whom most Americans would consider unemployed: for example, someone who was able to find a two-hour-per-week part-time "job," or someone who after looking for work for a year gave up the search out of discouragement. Still, even though the statistics in Figure 2 understate the extent of unemployment at any one time, it is quite clear that the unemployed portion of the U.S. work force has been rising over this past thirty years. This trend has been countered significantly only in the midst of the wartime economies of the early 1950s and in the 1960s.

At the same time as problems of employment have become more troubling, the technological change that has been propelling the modern industrial economy since the industrial revolution has brought about more sophisticated machinery, communications, and control equipment and other forms of what economists call "capital goods." Processes that used to take mostly labor power and a bit of equipment (termed "labor-intensive" production) are giving way to others that depend more on a smaller amount of highly skilled labor and a large amount of complicated and expensive equipment ("capital-intensive" production).

This development has had two contrasting effects in the lives of workers. The first is the very positive one of a higher standard of living. Not only do more productive machines create more wealth for society at large, but the individual worker working with the equipment is now able to produce more output per hour of labor. Thus, the worker's wage is higher because of both the greater skill he or she probably has in order to operate the machine and the higher productivity the machine makes possible. The real income of the vast majority of people has risen because of the technological advances of the modern era. (Of course, those who own the equipment enjoy a higher standard of living as well, even if not because of their receiving a higher wage.)

At the same time, however, when more productive equipment is used it will take fewer labor hours to produce the same number of products as were produced previously. Obviously, if the same number of products were produced, fewer workers will be employed. This is the worry of many working people. On the other hand, since the greater income for workers and owners stimulates the economy, there will be some increase in the demand for those products, and this will create a need for more workers than would be necessary just to reach the old level of production. Whether total employment rises or falls depends on the relative sizes of these two effects.

In any case, even when the growth in the economy leads to a greater number of jobs, there will certainly be dislocations in employment. That is, as one trade (say, typesetting for newspapers, magazines, and books) becomes more capital-intensive through the introduction of computerized processes, the demand for the labor of typesetters will fall. So even though new jobs may be available in the production of silicon chips for computers, an unemployed typesetter possesses the "wrong" skills (and probably lives in the "wrong" part of the country) to take advantage of the openings in computer manufacturing. One of the reasons why labor unions and working people more generally have been so concerned about any moves to capital-intensive methods is that the corporations involved have historically taken so little responsibility for the "adjustment process" that imposes steep costs on the working class.

Ethically, we face a dilemma. Greater productivity will benefit the people of the nation, and new methods will help improve productivity. (Factory owners are right in saying that the nation would still be riding around in horse-drawn wagons if the automobile industry had been prevented from developing new products and methods.) Yet the dislocations that inevitably occur in the midst of technological change have harsh effects on some people (the workers left without work) and beneficial effects on others. Clearly, standards of justice must be brought to bear in this process.

The second dimension of the syndrome of problems structured into the U.S. economy has to do with productivity, the output per labor hour for the economy as a whole. That output is not rising as fast as it used to. A recent report to the President of the United States from the Business-Higher Education Forum laments our lackluster response to "America's competitive challenge."[22] Many other analyses have reached similar conclusions.

We have seen the increasing sharpness of the competition between nations in recent years. Those nations that traditionally have been second to the United States in economic leadership in the world, West Germany and Japan, have experienced significant increases in productivity over recent decades. Yet there has been a clearly identifiable reduction in the productivity increases of the American economy. During the twenty years after World War II, yearly productivity increases were over 3%; from 1965 to 1975 they were slightly over 2%; throughout most of the decade of the 1970s they were barely over 1%. Predictably, the recession that followed caused even poorer results. What has been happening?

The well-known economist Lester Thurow analyzes this phenomenon in his *The Zero Sum Society*.[23] Many have pointed to lower expenditures on research and development as a fundamental cause, but productivity began to fall in the mid-sixties, considerably before the fall in research and development budgets.

Others point to inadequate investment in plant and equipment, but investment as a portion of overall production in the nation rose rather than fell at the very time when productivity was falling. Still others assert that an interfering government manipulated by strong "distributional coalitions" (to use Mancur Olson's phrase[24]) reduces productivity. But the United States is remarkably unencumbered by regulation and government involvement in the economy when compared to Japan, the nation with the *highest* rates of productivity increase in the world.

Rather, Thurow traces the problems in productivity to three major sources. The first is a set of problems experienced by three particular industries: mining, construction, and utilities. The second is a shift in consumer choices to spending more money for goods and services that happen to be produced in industries that have lower-than-average levels of productivity (e.g., services, retail trade, and construction). This is no "mistake" for consumers, since they obviously want, for example, more services today than fifty years ago. Nor is it a criticism of the importance of these sectors of the economy; they provide crucial elements for people's lives. It simply means that, technologically speaking, less can be done to improve the output per hour in these areas than in the rest of the economy on average.

Thurow identifies the third source of the slower rates of growth in productivity as "idle capacity," the economist's term for factories and other capital goods that are operating at lower production levels than those for which they were designed and built. Statistics collected by the Federal Reserve Board, the Commerce Department, and independent research institutes tell the story. While even in times of prosperity our economic system does not use its industrial system to capacity, the governmental decisions of the past two decades in particular have used an economic slowdown (leaving even more capacity idle) as a policy tool to combat inflation. This strategy has, as we have seen, the terrible effects of severe unemployment. In addition, should those in political power choose to employ this approach (with or without adequate social welfare provisions for the unemployed), one additional predictable effect will be a fall in productivity, since, historically, output per hour falls in a recession. Thurow blames a full thirty percent of our productivity slowdown on such deliberate decisions to counteract inflation by restraining demand.

While there are a large number of issues associated with the slowdown in productivity, the one thing that seems agreed upon is that the problem is not simple. As Thurow puts it,

> If you remember that productivity has been growing at about 3 percent per year for as long as we have been measuring productivity growth (well back into the nineteenth century), and that our neighbors have achieved growth rates double or triple this in the last few decades, it is very unlikely that there will be a simple cure. Current productivity growth rates are deeply embedded in the structure of our economy, and major changes will be necessary before we see major improvements.[25]

Summary and a Preview of Part Two

In this chapter we have seen just some of the outlines of our economy's history and current situation. We have viewed the shift from the laissez-faire capitalism to the steps toward greater institutionalized concern for workers and the poor in social welfare capitalism. We also saw the beginnings of the reappearance of some of the harsher elements of that earlier phase as competition between regions and nations makes it as difficult for the economically responsible state or nation today as it was for the benevolent entrepreneur a century and a half ago. The rewards of lowest-cost production are great and form a swift current that pushes along even those who would rather not go. Only a basic restructuring of the riverbed itself can allow for a rechanneling of that power to serve human needs better.

We looked as well at two current underlying problems of our economy and its people: physical and social limits to growth, and a syndrome of structured problems surrounding employment and productivity. None of these problems will be easily resolved in the near future. These and other predicaments call for a careful consideration from several critical perspectives. Badly needed here is a dialogue between economics and ethics. All too often economists dismiss proposals for more ethically responsible policies as naive and inefficient. All too often ethically attuned citizens either feel impotent in their lack of economic knowledge or, what is just as bad, simply ignore it.

Part Two of this book is designed to assist the reader in the process of interrelating economic and ethical perspectives. Chapter 6 looks to several crucial ideas in economic analysis both to appreciate the wisdom implicit in them and to critique the limitations they represent. Chapter 7 examines social justice and its relation to that central concern of economists, efficiency. Chapter 8 investigates several concrete economic issues today and suggests operative norms that Christians might decide to work on in the larger society. Chapter 9 returns to the analysis of operative norms begun in Chapter 1 and examines the life of the small disciplined community that will have to be at the heart of any true effort to empower the Christian economic ethic in today's world.

PART TWO

Toward an Effective Christian Economic Ethic Today

6

Beginning an Ethical Assessment
of Economic Analysis

It is probably safe to say that the greatest difference between the modern world and all previous eras of human history is the immense capacity for altering and controlling our surroundings that we have developed over the past two or three centuries. We move mountains to mine copper in Montana, then ship it to Japan to be formed (along with iron ore brought from ten thousand miles away) into finished products that are packed and shipped back across the ocean to be sold to consumers in the U.S. and elsewhere. The reach and force of our technological grasp is awesome.

An equally important development has been the growing conviction that we as human beings can alter and control our social institutions. To illustrate: For centuries, most people—both peasants and nobility—had taken it for granted that the traditional political systems of Europe were permanent. The wealthy and powerful had, of course, a much greater capacity to put their wishes into effect, but they, too, long assumed that the political structures were not open for change. Slowly, however, the rising merchant class came to insist on limitations to the power of the king and nobility. Eventually this idea grew to the point that people saw themselves as citizens who together could alter the form and policies of government and who, in fact, should take responsibility for the nation's political structures. Thus, for example, at the time of the American Revolution, many colonists were convinced that King George was abusing his authority and violating their basic human freedoms. As a result they felt not simply that they were justified in rebelling but also that they *should* rebel and design a new and more just governmental structure. There was, of course, a strong dose of self-interest in their rebellion, and in spite of the Declaration of Independence, the Constitution did not recognize the full rights of slaves and women. Still, the general principle was that people have the right to choose their own social structures.

A similar attitude developed with regard to the economic realm. The traditional economic structures were no longer considered good simply because they were traditional. Rather, the people—or in practice, their political representatives—not only could but should alter and improve economic structures. For example, in the early nineteenth century the British Parliament debated and eventually repealed the "corn laws," restrictions on the import of grain from the Continent that were supported by the older, landed gentry and opposed by the rising merchant and manufacturing class. Although many such debates through the years have occurred over what the economic rules of the game should be, it was and remains a fundamental principle of democracy that the rules of the game should be *decided upon* and that the people of the nation should make that decision.

Even our laws about what "property" is and what rights property-owners have are the outcome of decisions. When new structures such as the business corporation evolved in the seventeenth and eighteenth centuries, laws had to be decided upon to specify their status, rights, and duties. Thus, for example, business corporations are "limited liability" organizations because of a political decision to lessen the liability of their owners. If a corporation goes bankrupt, the stockholders of that firm cannot be personally sued by people to whom the corporation owes money. This differs from the definition of a business partnership, where, upon bankruptcy, the partners might lose not just their business investment but their homes and personal property as well.

In the modern world, then, economic structures are supposed to be subject to public decision. But there are serious limitations on this principle. Existing economic structures largely determine which groups get what in our society; and this, in turn, largely determines which groups have power to influence those public decisions about economic life. As we saw in Chapter 1, large numbers of Americans live in dire poverty and have very little real influence on Congressional decisions about economic matters. At the same time some persons have very large incomes and wield disproportionate power not just in the economic realm but also in politics. In addition, the size of economic units—especially of the multinational business corporation—has grown so large that two new problems have arisen.

The first is that the firms themselves have become some of the most influential actors in political decision making through lobbying and campaign contributions. The second problem is that the firms' significance in the economy places limitations on what legislators might be *able* to do—as when a town changes its policies for fear a large firm may move out or when Congress votes large subsidies in the form of loan guarantees to prevent the bankruptcy of major employers such as Chrysler or Lockheed.

Still, in spite of all defects in our systems of representative government, the fundamental democratic principle relating to economic life stands: The people through their government have the right to alter economic structures. In the modern world people have come to realize that the political and economic rules of the game are not eternal. Nation after nation has chosen democracy over monarchy and a more or less "free" market system over feudal economic arrangements. Even those individuals referred to as conservative "free-marketeers" believe it is the right and duty of democratic governments to decide on economic structures; they just argue that the government should see the wisdom of choosing to stay out of daily economic activity.

But let us stop a moment and reflect on where we are in our discussion of the modern world. So far in this chapter we have recognized two facts. The first is that most citizens of the modern world see that at least at some times it is important for people to alter the basic political or economic rules of the game. The second is that most feel that the people of a nation have the right and duty to reject bad rules of the game and set up good ones—even though the nation does not go around changing basic structures very often.

We now are left with a question: What difference do these two facts make for a Christian economic ethic? Just because something can be done does not mean that Christians *ought* to do it. And just because most people think something should be done does not mean that *Christians* should think so. How should Christians be involved in altering social institutions?

Rethinking Social Institutions: The Example of Slavery

In our earlier discussion we have seen several examples of how the faith community held up certain ethical principles to guide human action in everyday situations. We have looked primarily at the Judeo-Christian approach to economic life, but the same process is involved in ethical reflection on every realm of human life. Believers strive to live out a life of faith. True Christian faith has always required that all realms of the believer's life be transformed by that faith. The Christian, as a sinner, will always fall short of the demands of the gospel, but Christian ethical principles have nonetheless been developed to address the question: What does faith require of me in this situation?

To see how religious principles can help transform social institutions, it is instructive to recall a particular moral issue that has caused well-meaning Christians great difficulties down through the ages: slavery. Such an example illustrates well the process whereby Christian ethical insight is refined over the years and is made real by operative norms that transform relationships both of individuals and institutions.

In both ancient Israel and the early church community, slavery was taken for granted as a natural part of social life. This is not surprising, since slavery was a part of nearly every society in the Mediterranean basin for thousands of years. Still, having faith in God led Israel to put restrictions on slavery. The book of Leviticus, for example, directs that no Israelite could be held permanently as a slave the way a slave from a foreign nation would be. In New Testament times, St. Paul did not preach that Christians should abolish slavery, but he did call for a more humane master/slave relationship for Christians than was usual for others.

In the modern period, just as people came to an awareness that the old political institution of the monarchy was not an eternally given part of life, so Christians and others came to realize that the social institution of slavery did not have to be a part of life. That is, not only did modern Christians, like Paul before them, see that their faith required a more loving personal relationship between master and slave; they also came to realize that their faith called for a better institutional framework where children of God did not treat one another as master and slave in the first place.

The question as to how ethically sensitized people actually are able to transform society and eliminate sinful institutions such as slavery will be addressed in a subsequent chapter. There we will further develop the process touched on earlier whereby communities can build sound moral structures by empowering operative norms. Our concern here with the question of slavery, however, is first to see how Christians came to recognize the importance of eliminating this particular social institution, once they as citizens of the modern world realized that such social institutions can be transformed.

The first element to keep in mind is that Christians do not live in a vacuum. As believers, Christians do hold to certain values and orientations that are not shared by all in our society, but much of the debate about slavery took place around issues that were not primarily religious. There was the biological question whether "Negroes" were different from Caucasians. There was the political question of whether the Constitution could support a prohibition of slavery. There was the economic question of what emancipation would do to the economy. There was the psychosocial question of whether emancipated slaves would be able to "handle" their freedom. For each of these questions, the thoughtful Christian had to consider both what the debates within the secular disciplines of natural and social science had to say and what the values and principles of the Judeo-Christian tradition had to contribute.

As we look back on the dispute over abolition, it is difficult for us to appreciate the pro-slavery side of the issue. Slavery seems clearly inhumane and so definitely un-Christian. The arguments for slavery on biological, political, or theological grounds seem transparently biased and self-interested. What is important for us to realize is that ultimately most people came to see that the equality among people of different races was more basic than their differences. Within the Christian churches, after centuries of abuse, believers came to see that all men and women, as creatures of one Creator, as sons and daughters of one God, are more alike than different. Christians and others came to employ this background principle of equality—and other principles such as love of one's neighbor—to adjudicate between conflicting arguments. While one side argued that Negroes were more ignorant and less educable than whites, the other side argued that they were members of the same human species as whites and were just as fully human. The fundamental principle of the equality of all God's children ultimately led Christians to reject the first argument.

It is a fundamental premise of this book that we are now in a critical situation with regard to our whole economic system, a situation analogous to that surrounding the problem of slavery in the last century. We have seen the economic problems outlined in Chapters 1 and 5. We have outlined the basic biblical and patristic approaches to economic life in Chapter 2. We have in later chapters witnessed the difficulties that Christianity in the modern period has experienced in trying to analyze and shape economic life according to the vision of what a fulfilled and fulfilling life would be. What we now need to do is to enter into the current debate on economics and to weigh the competing arguments about economic life against the fundamental insights of the Christian message.

An Ethical Assessment of Economic Ideas

It is quite natural that in dealing with economic problems Christians should depend heavily on the discipline of economics for a description of the situation. Thoughtful believers have long ago ceased ignoring the social or natural sciences simply because they are "secular."

At the same time, however, for Christian ethics to use the insights of economics is not so simple and straightforward as most economists believe. Within the discipline of economics it is usually assumed that while economists as ordinary citizens have their own values and convictions, when they act as scientists they are supposed only to describe what is going on in the economy. They are supposed to leave it to others to use that description in judging whether what is happening ought to go on. Most economists see themselves as providing description, not prescription; as social scientists, they want to leave to others the choice about what to value.

If things really were this simple, life would be a lot easier. But the economist's usual understanding of the relation of economic science and human values runs into difficulties on two levels.

At the most obvious level, a problem is posed by the fact that on a large number of important issues economists as scientists debate among themselves as to what is going on in the economic realm. Are the major oil companies exacerbating the energy problem for higher profits, or is just OPEC to blame? Does less unemployment cause more inflation, or must one of these problems be solved before the other will get better? Are multinational firms the best hope for development in the Third World, or do they actually cause underdevelopment? As we listen to economists from the right, left, and center we can hear different answers to these questions about what is going on in the economy.

At a deeper level, however, we find that in the very process of trying to describe what is (and trying to avoid the question of what ought to be) the economist starts with some basic assumptions that are value-laden and not value-free. In addition, since these assumptions are starting points, they are unproved and, at least within the science of economics, are unprovable. In fact, many of the disputes among different "schools" of economists—conservative, liberal, radical—can be traced to different starting assumptions. Different schools of economic thought look at the same world, but see it differently. They consequently come to different recommendations for economic policy.

We saw in the debate about the abolition of slavery that there were many conflicting claims that needed to be weighed against one another. The Christian tradition proved valuable in recognizing that even though whites and blacks were not equal in every way, they were equal in the most important and fundamental sense. A similar situation exists in the realm of economics. Many descriptions of economic life are provided. Each has some degree of truth to it, and empirical investigation is a crucial test of any description. But the fact remains that different starting points and conflicting visions of the world need to be weighed against one another. We contend that the basic insights of the Christian tradition must be employed in assessing the adequacy of the assumptions that operate below the surface of economic description.

Most economists in the United States share a set of assumptions about the human person and economic activity. Technically speaking, these assumptions are a part of the "neoclassical" school of economics. We will simply refer to this as "mainstream" or "orthodox" economic theory. Employing this approach, economists have made highly valuable contributions to the well-being of people here and abroad. At the same time, however, orthodox economic science has had significant negative effects—effects that economists themselves often overlook. In the rest of this chapter we will examine five basic economic categories of mainstream economics. We will view the economist's understanding of each and will see how the Christian tradition requires a critique and expansion of each concept.

1. Scarcity
Mainstream economists today universally take "scarcity" as the fundamental problem with which economics is concerned. The

orthodox definition of economic science is "the study of the allocation of scarce resources to achieve alternative ends." For example, with limits on the amount of iron ore and labor available for making steel, we must choose between more tractors or more autos, between more military tanks or more steel girders for buildings. What people would like to have always exceeds what is available. This is what the economist means technically by scarcity.

But there is a serious problem in taking this definition of scarcity as a starting point for economic science. Nearly everyone sees that "scarcity" is the fundamental problem of economics, but the scarcity that most people see is different from the one economists speak of. Most people speak of scarcity in the sense of not having enough to live a fully human life. Their concern over scarcity is represented in fears about whether the food and housing bills can be paid, whether a Social Security pension will be sufficient, whether the unemployed worker can find a job, whether the malnourished child of the Third World will live past the age of twelve. The shortcoming of the economist's definition of scarcity is that all these concerns are grouped along with a desire for ever-larger stereo speakers and ever-longer boats for recreation.

The economist is right in pointing out that people's wants exceed what is available, but this conceals an even more important insight. For economists, the problem of scarcity applies to all commodities: The inability of a family to buy food is treated in the science in the same manner as the inability of a family to purchase a yacht. For nearly everyone else, it is untrue to say that a well-to-do family that wishes it could afford a yacht is experiencing the same kind of scarcity as the poor family that wishes it could afford a balanced diet. From the point of view of the Judeo-Christian tradition, scarcity as poverty, as the lack of what it takes to live a full life, is an evil that all in the community have the responsibility to eliminate. Scarcity as the gap between unlimited wants and what is available, however, is a sign of human greed, something that the Bible has always referred to as the sin of covetousness.

M. Douglas Meeks has argued that the economist's preoccupation with scarcity contradicts a truly Trinitarian conception of economics because it overlooks what the New Testament calls the "pleroma" or fullness of God's gifts in the Spirit.[1] To speak of that fullness is not to deny that multitudes live in destitution but rather to point out that there is enough to go around if justice prevails. Justice would imply not only a redistribution of wealth but a realignment of the production system so that, for example, the best agricultural land in the Third World would be used to produce basic food for domestic consumption and not the more profitable cash crops for export to the industrialized world.

Thus an ethical assessment of economic arguments will confirm the view that scarcity is a crucial economic problem, but not primarily in the way economists generally mean it. Scarcity as physical poverty is often underrated by economists. Scarcity as the excess of wants over available goods is important but not important enough to make it the starting point of our study of economic life. We do need to choose among alternative ends in the allocation of scarce resources, but we miss the most real sense of scarcity if we treat all wants as equally significant. Of course, economists do ultimately make a distinction between different kinds of "wants": Some wants are fulfilled by expenditures of money, while others are not. In order to understand this difference, we need to examine the economist's notion of the market.

2. The Market

Mainstream economists appreciate "the market." They mean, of course, not the corner store but that series of social patterns of interaction between people who have something that others want and those others who are willing to pay in order to get it. The original "owners" (say, manufacturers with goods, or laborers with their labor power) look for the best offer for their product or service, while the buyers (say, consumers or employers) look for the lowest-priced source of what they seek. Competition (with other sellers) keeps owners from charging too much, while competition (with other buyers) keeps each buyer from being able to force sellers to lower their prices unduly. In addition, the hope of profits entices producers to make new products that consumers would like to have. The "free market"—one unencumbered by government restrictions—is viewed as a marvelous mechanism for setting national economic priorities without the need for national debate. Consumers' value systems determine where the nation puts its time and resources.[2]

The assumptions implicit in such confidence in the market have been criticized from both secular and religious points of view. The first problem is that wealthy consumers can fulfill far more of their wants than the poor can. Thus, relying on the market to determine what goods the nation will produce allows the wealthy a far greater voice in setting national economic priorities. In Chapter 1 we saw the great disparity in income (the number of dollars earned each year) between the rich and poor, and the even more alarming difference in wealth (the dollar value of the property a person owns at the end of the year). Economists will admit that if the current distribution of income between the rich and the poor is judged to be bad from the moral point of view, then the national economic priorities set in the free market will also be wrong until a redistribution of wealth and income is achieved. It is quite clear that the Christian principle of the just entitlement of the poor does in fact require such a redistribution. The obvious conclusion from this moral assessment is that although the market mechanism may be employed to achieve certain goals, Christians cannot have a naive confidence in market outcomes.

We should note that a good number of economists—particularly "conservative" economists—are caught in a problem in regard to the distribution of income in society. In spite of the concessions just cited, many advocates of "the market" oppose programs of redistribution of income on the grounds that only poverty (euphemistically called "market forces") will provide enough incentive for the poor to exert themselves. This stance bespeaks some important and questionable assumptions about the human person and self-interest that we will examine later in this chapter.

A second problem raised by relying heavily on the market is the implicit assumption that the firms in the marketplace actually do compete with one another. We need not deal with the technical economic definition of "perfect competition" here, but we can note that most economists do recognize that in many industries, the few, very large firms that dominate the industry often do not fully compete with one another in spite of the ideal of competition of the free market. Explicit collusion and outright price-fixing by firms is, of course, illegal in the United States, but there are more subtle ways to "administer" prices.

A significant example of such behavior is "price leadership," a procedure described even in introductory economics textbooks as prevalent in the American steel industry. One firm announces a price increase to be effective at some future date, and the other firms then generally announce the same price rise effective on the same date. Now and then the first firm is out of line and later alters its price change to match what the other firms are doing. This adjustment process occurs about four times a year and effectively eliminates much competition (which the firms euphemistically call "cut-throat" competition) in which one firm might lower its prices to attract more customers. There are other ways that competition can be and is reduced, but the point is that to the extent that competition *is* reduced, economists themselves admit that the operation of the market will produce less than optimal results.

At another level it is important to question the wisdom of relying on the market mechanism to set national economic priorities even if we first solved the problems of the deprivation of the poor and the failures of competition among firms. Advocates of the market appreciate, first, its automatic operations (no bureaucracy has to act before market adjustments occur) and, second, its impersonal operation (no person or group gets to decide what adjustments are ultimately made). The first of these claims involves the notion of "efficiency," to which we will return presently. The second—the impersonality of the market—raises a very important question for Christian ethics: Is an occurrence better simply because no person or group decided it should happen?

To answer this question it is important to see why proponents of the market respond by saying yes. Many, though not all, of them would argue that any person's values or ethical positions are simply personal subjective preferences. If this were true, then a policy decision by Congress or a government agency or a neighborhood council would be just an expression of preferences of the people in that group (and of any others who might be able to have some influence over them). Thus, in case of a shortage of gasoline, for example, rather than allowing a government agency to ration gas "arbitrarily," proponents of the market would advocate allowing the price of gas to rise to whatever price would induce consumers to reduce the amount they demand so there would be enough gas to go around.

The tradition of Christian ethics has consistently rejected the first step of this argument. Christianity has always denied the assumption that values are mere personal preferences. While it may not always be easy to decide which is the morally best course of action, the careful decision of a deliberative body ought not be dismissed as merely the efforts of one more "interest group." Some values *are* better than others, and sincere discussion in a group can improve a decision.

Not only does Christian ethics have greater respect for group decisions about the common good than do proponents of the market; the Christian tradition has analogously put less confidence in the initial preferences of individuals than do those same market advocates. While the latter have no standard by which to judge consumers' wants, Christian ethics has always held that some values—such as food and shelter—are more basic and more important than others—such as luxury consumption. Thus the market choices of consumers with money to spend may not be the best basis on which to determine what the economy should produce. In fact, if a decision had to be made about basic economic questions, the discussion and debate about priorities might well change many people's original personal "preferences" (for the better, we hope).

The Christian tradition has never granted ultimate value to the immediate inclination of individuals. Proponents of the market often call this attitude "paternalistic" or "totalitarian," but for Christians and others it is a matter of public morality. Although the action of the free market might at times achieve the best outcome, it does not necessarily do so. This is by no means to say that Christian ethics endorses the excesses of bureaucracy that occur in totalitarian forms of socialism but rather to assert that major questions of economic priority should be carefully weighed, debated, and decided upon in the light of fundamental moral values.

3. Efficiency

Economists—and just about all other human beings—value efficiency. No one thinks inefficiency is a good idea. Thus it is particularly difficult for well-meaning people to respond when in answer to proposals for humanizing our economy they hear, "That sounds nice, but it's quite inefficient." What is efficiency, and how is it related to moral concern?

Economists define efficiency as getting the greatest possible production out of any given amount of resources available. Alternatively, it can be seen as achieving any particular goal at the least possible cost in effort and resources. At a sort of commonsense level this is quite straightforward, but problems appear as we dig deeper. Consider two alternate procedures for, say, making steel: an older process and a more recently developed one that is more "efficient." The term "efficient" here means that the newer process produces steel at a lower cost per ton than does the old one. Now, however, consider two alternatives for a steel plant where the only difference between them is that one has a series of complex devices costing 300 million dollars in its smokestacks to reduce pollution by 90% while the other simply releases untreated smoke into the air. Which is more "efficient"? Clearly the second plant will appear to produce a ton of steel at a lower "cost," since from the point of view of the firm the costs paid by citizens who must breathe polluted air are not part of the firm's calculation of the "cost" of a ton of steel.

This case is a good example of the economic problem of "externalities" that we will examine in the next section, but like many other examples, it demonstrates the flaw in the usual use of the word "efficiency." In practice, that word generally includes only those costs of production that are measured in dollars and cents in the market. Although the steel mill with pollution control devices must pay for them, the mill with no such device need not pay for the privilege of imposing costs on people living downwind. Thus it is that many have complained about government pollution regulations because they reduce the "efficiency" of American firms. The advantages of lower pollution levels get lost in this casual use of the term.

To be fair to economists, we must note that the discipline of economics does clearly recognize that the negative effects of polluted air are indeed costs of producing steel—even if the steel mill does not have to pay those costs. This particular misuse of the term "efficiency" is most frequent among people in business and financial circles. Still, most economists do periodically lapse from a careful use of the term, as the next example shows.

We can now see that the gas guzzlers of the 1950s and '60s were very inefficient in their use of gasoline although they were nonetheless "efficient" economically since gas was so cheap at that time. Even today after our energy prices have risen dramatically, we still pay much less for gasoline, heating oil, and other forms of energy than do people in Europe and most other places on the globe. The economist will define efficiency in energy consumption with respect to the free market price of energy even though from an ethical point of view other concerns such as the availability of resources to future generations may loom large in the assessment.

Fundamentally, then, the word "efficiency" is forced to do double duty and is often misused in the process. The economist wants to use it in a value-free way—to designate achieving any goal with the least effort and use of resources. But even though the idea *could* apply to any goal and *could* include all costs, in practice both the goals sought and the costs considered are usually limited to those items that have a price tag designated in the market. In short, the "efficient solution" to an economic problem is usually equivalent to "the market solution."

When Christians reflect on the possibilities for an economic ethic in the modern world, they must keep "efficiency" in perspective. Whenever human values are involved that are not adequately represented in the market place—human dignity, the rights of future generations, the interests of the poor, etc.—then an efficient attainment of those goals may look remarkably inefficient from the point of view of the market. Even orthodox economists concede that once such values are incorporated into the list of society's goals, only government intervention can improve on the deficiencies of the market.

4. Property

In an effort to describe the economic situation without making a moral judgment about whether it is good or bad, orthodox economists have generally taken the institutional framework of the U.S. economy as given and have proceeded to analyze its workings. As a result, economists operate with the same assumptions about property as do most people in modern industrial society. They generally work with the understanding of private property deriving from the work of John Locke—which we saw in Chapter 4.

We have already seen the conflict between the assertion of nearly absolute authority of the owner over the thing owned and the Judeo-Christian insight into possession as stewardship. This disparity requires a rethinking of some of the usual rights and claims of ownership. This, in turn, will affect behavior on both an individual and an institutional level.

One of the moral problems that arises most frequently within current American economic institutions is the clash between moral principles and the firm's charter to produce a profit. From the point of view of the individual manager facing a difficult decision, this is most often felt as a clash between his or her "own" values and a responsibility to the stockholders who have a right to a significant return on their investment. But once we realize that ownership entails not only rights but also the duty to use possessions responsibly, the manager could be allowed as great a discretion in fulfilling the moral responsibilities of the firm as he or she is allowed in creatively seeking a profit.

When we step back and look at the larger issues in the economy, we find that this notion of a more limited ownership has equally important implications. In the last section we saw the example of air pollution by a steel mill. The usual presumption in our competitive society is that one person's rights will act as a limit on the excesses of others. No one is allowed to dump refuse on a neighbor's property, and if someone tries to do this, the neighbor can sue. But the release of toxic gases into the air by the plant is not challenged in the courts on the grounds of violation of ownership rights, since no one person "owns" the atmosphere. When the system of competing rights breaks down in cases like this, only direct action by government can alleviate pollution.

We should note that from the point of view of the steel company—operating with Locke's notion of property—the government's action appears to be an external and arbitrary limit on its rights. We can even hear assertions that government has "imposed" hundreds of millions of dollars in costs on U.S. business.

Yet if we really do believe the Judeo-Christian vision of all things as created for the good of humanity, then the atmosphere (such as the rivers, lakes, and oceans) is not presumed to be a cost-free dumping ground. Pollution is then seen as piracy of the public good. If it costs three hundred million dollars to reduce a steel mill's pollution to "acceptable" levels, then this amount ought not be seen as a cost imposed on business. Rather, it is a measure, to put it kindly, of the subsidy the firm has been receiving from the public that has allowed the pollution to go on. More bluntly, it is a measure of legalized theft as real as if the firm had, through a loophole in the law, been allowed to dump solid waste on a neighbor's land.

To widen the context even further, we can consider our nation's role in the international discussions about mining the floor of the world's oceans. At a number of conferences on a "law of the seas" the vast majority of the nations of the world have been calling for a special status for the oceans so that while they may be mined they cannot be "owned" absolutely. A world fund for developing nations could be established by a tax on all such mining. Many in the United States, however, have objected to this notion and, following John Locke, want to assert an absolute right for the firms who do the mining.[3] The Christian vision of property points toward some sort of communal possession of these extranational resources.

The "law of the seas" raises questions about economic structures of ownership in a situation where they are to be designed for the first time. The Christian economic ethic should also have a transforming impact on existing institutions of property ownership. The Christian tradition on its own does not provide ahead of time any exact definition of how a particular institution such as the firm should be structured; the details can only be worked out in an actual historical situation. Still, it seems clear that the firm ought not be viewed solely or even primarily as an organization of investors or owners who hire employees to perform certain tasks. It would be better to view the firm as an organization of persons of many sorts who have come together to produce goods or services for the benefit of themselves and the rest of society. Seeing the firm in this way and understanding the limits to private property, there is no reason why the ultimate decisions about the firm should be made by stockholders only. It would seem reasonable, for example, for the board of directors of a firm to be elected not just by the stockholders but by blue-collar workers and lower-level managers as well as upper management. In addition, some representation of consumers and of society as a whole would be very important, since in spite of the best of intentions, there will always be a tendency for the common self-interest of employees and investors to overshadow the rights and needs of persons outside the firm. Various arrangements would have to be tried and tested; some such attempts (entitled "co-determination") are currently being made in West Germany and elsewhere.

Although a more limited sense of private property is not sufficient to spell out new institutional forms precisely, it does indicate the direction in which to move.

5. The Human Person and Self-Interest

The fifth (and last) element we will investigate in this chapter may not look like an economic category at all. Economists are not in the business of developing and proving theories about human nature; they would like to leave that to philosophers and theologians. Still, in order to think about how people act and react as consumers and producers, economists work with a model of the human person. Mainstream economists think of the person as a "rational maximizer." That is, every individual has a set of preferences or values and some amount of wealth and natural ability. Using these financial and personal resources, the individual tries to fulfill those preferences to the greatest extent possible.

"Self-interest" is an important part of this understanding of the human person, but it is not always defined or understood clearly by either economists or their critics. On the one hand, the economist's official conception of "self-interest" does not mean that the individual engages in only "selfish" behavior. Some individuals value charitable actions, the economist explains, and thus those individuals get a kind of psychological "return" for activity that helps others. In the language of economics, individuals gain "utility" from actions they choose to undertake, whether those actions include buying heroin for themselves or working as volunteers at a community service agency. We will return to this notion later in this chapter, but here we note that this position can be well described as "psychological egoism," the belief that while not all behavior is consciously "selfish" in the narrow sense, all behavior is ultimately "self-interested."[4]

On the other hand, most mainstream economists believe that the "self-interest" of individuals is so strong that capitalism (which is based on each individual's looking out for his or her own interests) is not only morally better but is more feasible than socialism (which they think requires that individuals act counter to their narrow self-interest because the government organizes economic activity).[5] This belief that selfish activity predominates leads many proponents of capitalism to oppose any significant redistribution of income to the poor on the grounds that it would tend to destroy the incentive to work.

As we have seen in Chapter 2, the Judeo-Christian vision of the human person is more communal than all this. The person is recognized to be constituted in a social setting. The idea of self-interest is treated more subtly. Mainstream economics can say that all actions have some end or goal and that this end is an interest of the self who takes that action. But this sense of "self-interest" is not very interesting. Christianity has, rather, carefully made the commonsense distinction between actions where the intended beneficiary is the self (self-interested in the sense of "selfish") and actions where the intended beneficiary is another person or group.

The Christian tradition has always recognized the excesses of sin. But where capitalism counts on competition from other self-interested persons to hold self-interest in check, Christianity has always held out two additional prescriptions: a personal change of heart, and institutionalized requirements and restrictions. The individual can be exhorted to a less selfish lifestyle, and the structures of the community can be molded so that the basic needs of all persons are met and the self-interest of individuals corresponds more closely with the common good.

In fact, Christianity has always denounced any attempt to base social organization on self-interest alone. Behind this stance is an appreciation for the power of human sinfulness. In its critique of every social and economic system, Christian ethics points out the way those persons with power (i.e., "wealth" under capitalism) can subvert the usual checks and balances, can gain their own ends, and can legitimate their behavior by showing how "just" it is since they are not breaking any laws. In a careful study entitled *Economic Foundations of Political Power,* Randall Bartlett has demonstrated how an economic system based on individuals asserting their self-interest will, in the modern uncertain world, subvert any democratic government and render it a servant of vested economic interests.

Government actions will preserve the economic *status quo* since they arise from patterns of influence generated by the operation of the economic system. In a system such as we have described, the actions of self-interested, rational agents operating in an uncertain world will—rightly or wrongly—cause the structure of political power to rise from a firm economic foundation. This structure and its foundation are inseparable.[6]

At the same time as it challenges the foundations of capitalism, the Christian tradition also chides the naivete of those Marxists who would hope to eliminate human sinfulness simply by restructuring the economy. While the human person may, over generations, be shaped into a less competitive, less anxious and less selfish being than has been the case under capitalism, the doctrine of original sin recognizes that the human condition will never be free of a tendency to sinful forms of self-assertion.

Summary and Conclusion

Our intention throughout this book is to help thoughtful Christians reflect on and respond to the major economic issues of our day. Of course, some economic issues are highly technical and complex, and years of study of economics are required even to understand the arguments. A good example of this sort of issue is the debate over monetarism as a policy for the Federal Reserve Board in its regulation of the money supply. This book does not address those sorts of highly technical problems, but there *are* many important economic issues today that the reader will be better prepared to address. We will see a number of these in the next two chapters.

In this chapter we have examined five of the most basic elements in the economist's tool box. They certainly would not be such basic tools if they were not helpful in analyzing economic life. Yet, as we have seen, the use of these basic concepts by economists and others results in some unconscious biases and some erroneous conclusions when measured against the standard of the Christian economic ethic.

The economist's use of the term "scarcity" represents an important insight into our world, for it reminds us that we do have to make hard choices among competing goals. However, it tends to relegate the problem of actual poverty to a secondary status in the overall vision of the economy. Economists have a strong and almost instinctive faith in the market. In view of the problems that economists themselves note (the amount of competition and the existing distribution of income), this is overconfidence. There are two other ethical difficulties in relying on the market mechanism. This reliance tends to assume, first, that consumers' initial preferences ought to be the sole basis for setting priorities in the economy and, second, that the "impersonal" market determination is superior to careful group deliberation on fundamental issues.

We also saw in this chapter that concern with efficiency is a very important one but that this frugality in the use of resources generally overlooks those costs and benefits that are not readily measured in dollars in the market. Economists generally take current legal definitions of the rights of property-owners as given elements in the economy they describe. But a more limited sense of property ownership required by the Christian economic ethic would call into question many of the assumptions economists tend to hold and would generate alternative possible policies and structures for economic life. Lastly, we noted that the economic vision of the human person is inaccurate and tends toward certain policies and institutional frameworks that a more adequate understanding of the person could not support.

The point of this sort of criticism is not to reject the concerns and contributions of economists. Far from it. Rather, being critical of economic analysis allows the thoughtful person to put it to even better use, since both its shortcomings and its strengths are more clearly understood.

Earlier in this chapter we cited the debate over the abolition of slavery as an example of the way thoughtful citizens—including Christians—have to understand scientific as well as ethical arguments in taking responsibility for social structures. The same is

true today in our efforts to develop more just economic structures in the United States. We need to become conversant with
the major economic debates, and we need to be able to point out
the strength and weaknesses of standard economic arguments.
This chapter has been an important starting point in this effort.

We also, of course, need to be articulate about the dimension
of social justice within the Christian economic ethic. We turn to
this task in Chapter 7. In Chapter 8 we will integrate the demands
of social justice with our assessment of economic analysis and
examine social justice and efficiency in both the production of
goods and services and in the distribution of income.

7

Social Justice and Economic Efficiency

Social justice and economic efficiency often appear to clash. Consider a vivid example.

Beginning in 1973 the Organization of Petroleum Exporting Countries—OPEC—raised the price of crude oil dramatically. As a result, Americans and people all over the world have had to pay much more for their gasoline, home heating oil, and other related products. While everyone must pay higher prices, the poor are clearly the hardest hit, for they spend a larger proportion of their weekly income on various forms of energy and thus feel the largest percentage drop in income when energy prices rise.

In order to reduce the impact of higher prices for energy, the federal government established price controls on certain forms of energy. By law the prices of gasoline, home heating oil, and natural gas were temporarily kept from rising. This is a blessing for consumers—and the poor in particular—in that they do not have to cut back so much on food or other purchases in order to pay for necessities such as heat for the home and gasoline for the car. For the eighty-five-year-old widow living without luxuries and on a meager diet already, controls on the price of home heating oil are immensely significant.

This one very important good effect of price controls, however, is accompanied by two bad effects. Because everyone pays less for, say, gasoline than they would have to if the price controls were removed, people do not have as much incentive to cut down on wasteful or unnecessary driving. At fifty cents a gallon we may drive to the shopping center four or five times a week. At $1.50 a gallon (or more than $2.50 a gallon, as is common in Europe) we will probably be more frugal in our driving habits and do all our shopping for the week in one or two trips. That sort of difference, multiplied by the millions upon millions of people in the nation, amounts to a sizable reduction in the U.S. consumption of gasoline. In an era when we need to conserve energy more and more, higher prices help us as a nation to be better stewards of world energy resources. But price controls, which keep the price of energy from rising, reduce this tendency to conserve and actually encourage more consumption.

The second negative effect of price controls has to do with the longer-term question of supply. At any one time there are some oil fields where oil is being pumped out because the cost of producing a barrel of oil is less than what buyers will pay for it (which allows a profit to the producer), and other oil fields where the oil lies undisturbed because (as a result of location or rock structure, for example) the cost of getting that oil out will not allow for a profit; in fact, the cost might even be more than what buyers are willing to pay for it even if producers were willing to operate without a profit. But when the price to consumers rises, more oil fields are tapped and more oil is available to heat homes and run cars.[1] While price controls allow consumers to buy more cheaply the fuels coming from oil wells that are currently pumped, they postpone the exploration and development of oil fields where the costs of production are higher. In the long run, only higher prices will allow production from those untapped fields.

So we have a problem. While justice to the poor seems to call for relief from higher prices for such necessities as home heating oil and natural gas, conservation and availability of supply seem to call for just the opposite.

But we cannot stop here. The issue is even more complicated.

In the debate over what, if anything, the government should do to assist the poor in this situation, some people who oppose government involvement have gone beyond the arguments about economic efficiency. They have asserted that the rights of the oil companies and, ultimately, of their stockholders offset any alleged rights of the poor. These people argue that the stock-holder's right to be free from government interference is more basic than any so-called right by which an individual demands a handout from the government. They claim that since the oil companies have done nothing to harm that individual, it cannot be just to penalize the oil companies out of "justice" to the poor. This argument, in one or another version, was often heard from critics of the windfall profits tax proposed in the late 1970s.

When faced with these sorts of arguments, many thoughtful Christians have had trouble deciding how to think about all of this. The confusion arises out of a misunderstanding of the nature of justice, an error traceable to the individualism that has so often characterized American life. We will need to look first at the errors of this individualistic perspective before we return to the relation of justice and efficiency.

Individualism and Justice

A shrewd man once said, "Allow me to define the words and I'll never lose an argument." The first problem we encounter in the discussion of social justice is the frequent use of the term "jus-tice" to refer to only half of what real justice entails.

Everyone agrees that if you borrow money from the bank to buy a house, justice requires that you pay it back according to the mortgage agreement. Similarly, everyone agrees that it is unjust for a co-worker to take money from your wallet without your consent. Your duty to pay back the loan and your right to your property are both clear. This is the sense of justice that nearly all Americans recognize instinctively. And, of course, they are right. These are matters of justice. There is no doubt about that. The problem is that this sort of justice—justice in one-to-one rela-tionships—is only a *part* of justice. This kind is properly called individual justice.

The other half of justice, however, deals with situations where there is no explicit contractual agreement between or among people. This other half is social justice. It deals with rights and duties involving the character both of individuals and of the human community that creates and nourishes the individuals who are a part of it. That is, social justice deals with the relation between individuals and "the common good."

It is not that the common good is opposed to the good of individuals, since each individual can live in dignity and flourish only if the social, economic, political, and cultural context is healthy and humane. And it is not that individual justice is opposed to social justice and the common good, since the common good is severely damaged if individuals flout their voluntary agreements or violate one another's individual rights. Then not only do the individual victims suffer, but the character of the community deteriorates. Social justice and individual justice are by no means contradictory. In most cases, these two demand the same things from us.

However, while social justice and individual justice are not contradictory, they do at times conflict. Indeed, those issues where the two kinds of justice conflict are the most difficult ones of all. These are the issues where one individual's recognized rights cannot be fully respected without doing damage to another's rights or to the common good. Here are two examples.

The first is one we have already noted. Those people who own stock in, say, Exxon have certain generally recognized property rights, such as the right to the extra value of their stock when its price rises. At the same time, the poor of the nation have a right (less widely acknowledged) to enough fuel and other necessities to live a fully human life, even if the price of fuels rises dramatically because of OPEC. As we will see further in the next chapter, allowing the price to rise to free market levels will entail a major shift of income away from the poor (and also from the middle class). This will impose horrendous burdens on the already locked-out poor. When, on the other hand, we enact legislation (such as a windfall profits tax) that prevents the oil companies from receiving all the benefits of the higher price of oil, those who own those companies think that their property rights have been violated. We cannot have it both ways. Social justice for the poor conflicts with individual justice for the stockholders.

A second example falls under the topic of affirmative action to overcome discrimination in employment and education against blacks, Hispanics, women, and other groups. The economist Lester Thurow has compared the problem of discrimination to a foot race with two groups of runners. Each individual is competing against everyone else, but as we witness the race already underway, we note that everyone in one of the groups is wearing heavy ankle weights. Some of the faster runners with weights are ahead of some of those without, but on the average, the group with weights is behind. How would we make this a fair race?[2]

The individualist answer is to remove the weights from everyone's ankles; then no one has an unfair advantage anymore. But will this work? Will it then be a fair race if the one group is still, on average, behind the other? To make it fair you must either help those who used to have the weights or hinder those who did not until the two groups are more equally distributed along the track. While it is difficult to say how long this reverse discrimination should go on, it is the only way to make the race more just at this time.

Since blacks (to take just one of these groups) have been discriminated against in the past, the only way to do justice to them as a group is to compensate them now for past wrongs. One way to do this is to structure hiring decisions and graduate-school admission procedures so that, for any group of applicants with generally the same qualifications, black applicants would be given some preference over white ones. It would take decades for this procedure to bring about a significant change, but it would begin to make up for the injustice of the past. However, in any one decision to admit, say, a black student to law school because of race, there is an equally qualified white student who, expecting to be treated justly, is angry that the admissions decision was not made "fairly" since it was made on the basis of color rather than by random chance among applicants of roughly equal competence. The white student who is denied admission is discriminated against because of race—just what had earlier been happening to blacks! That student asks, "How can two wrongs make a right?" Once again, there is a clash between social and individual justice.

In each of these cases, a decision has to be made either in favor of the demands of individual justice and against the demands of social justice or vice versa. While the two kinds of justice are not at all times opposed (and in fact are not at most times opposed), still there are situations where they are. It is important for us to recognize that whether we as a society choose to assist the poor with energy costs and admit the black student to graduate school or whether we do nothing, we are in any case making a judgment about the relative importance of social and individual justice in those situations. This is important because many Americans tend to presume that only the advocates of social justice have the obligation to put forward good arguments for their position. They take for granted that the demands of individual justice are paramount, because they share one of the most widely held fallacies in America: individualism.

We have already seen in Chapter 4 how the individualism of John Locke presented such a challenge to the Christian economic ethic. The human person came to be defined as an owner of his or her person. C. B. Macpherson has called this "possessive individualism," since it is a form of individualism based on the idea that we are most fully human as possessors of our own qualities and capacities, owing nothing (or almost nothing) to society. As we have already seen, the outcome of this is that

> society becomes a lot of free equal individuals related to each other as proprietors of their own capacities and of what they have acquired by their exercise. Society consists of relations of exchange between proprietors. Political society becomes a calculated device for the protection of this property and for the maintenance of an orderly relation of exchange.[3]

Of course, very few people you meet on the street believe all of this literally, but this view of things has seeped quite deeply into the pores of most Americans and even, remarkably, of all too many Christians in this country.

The problem with this perspective is that it oversimplifies the complex interactions of human life. It presumes that only individual justice counts and that the only rights that exist are rights of individuals based on the individual's achievements and gifts. Justice means giving people what they deserve; and, in this view, what they deserve is in accord with what they have accomplished (or in accord with what someone else has given to them). However, this understanding of what makes people deserving is a chair with only two legs.

In his book *A New American Justice,* Daniel C. Maguire points out that the traditional rule of justice, "to each his own," must be translated as "To each according to his merits and earned entitlements" *and* "To each according to his needs."[4] Whether or not that second sentence is a part of justice is the crux of the divergence between individualists and advocates of social justice.

Maguire's approach is very helpful. Justice is the first assault upon egoism. Where selfishness says, "To me, my own," justice demands that other selves be recognized and respected. Why? Because the other person is worthy, is worthwhile. The other is also a self, like me, and is deserving of respect. Even though I tend to overrate my own worth, justice demands that I recognize the worth of others, not because of their usefulness to me but because of their being persons in the first place.

Individualists often overlook this. They assert that justice means that everyone should receive according to his or her merits, but they often do not stop to ask *why* everyone should be treated this way. And when they do, the answer is usually that all citizens agreed to this in the "social contract," that fictitious agreement to end the fictitious state of nature that we examined in Chapter 4. This response begs the question. Even if there had been a literal social contract eons ago, each of us today would still have to decide whether to respect the rights of others. The ethical question remains: Why should I?

The answer is as we have just seen: Others are persons. I owe something to the other because of the intrinsic worth of that person. *That* is why, when I make an agreement with that person, I should live up to it. *That* is why, when I steal something from another, I owe appropriate restitution. The rights of that person derive from the worth of that person, a worth that is characteristic of *all* persons, including me.

Now it is clear how the "second half" of justice is necessary. Since human worth is the factor behind the rights of individuals, we can see that defining justice as "to each according to his merits and earned entitlements" is not enough to ensure full respect for the worth of the person. The unemployed nineteen-year-old black youth may not have had anyone cheat him or steal from him or violate justice in one-to-one dealings with him, but he lives in a dehumanizing situation and his worth is ignored. The woman who works in a dead-end job as a bank teller while male tellers are promoted to more responsible positions may have explicitly agreed to her job and her wage and may not have experienced injustice in one-to-one dealings. But she is less fully human than she would be if challenge and advancement were as available to her as they are to her male co-workers. Individual justice is not sufficient to guarantee respect for the worth of persons.

Thus needs are as fundamental a part of justice as are accomplishments. As Maguire puts it, "needs give entitlements because of the worth of the needing person."[5] As we saw in Chapter 1, this view of justice can be seen reflected as far back as the Old Testament, where Yahweh demanded that widows and orphans be cared for in Israel. We have documented again and again in the Christian tradition how the just entitlement of the poor is a major theme in the Christian economic ethic.

It is worth noting that even in spite of rampant individualism, the criterion of need is at times recognized as a part of justice in the secular vision of justice held in the United States today. What about the situation of a mentally handicapped and terminally ill child? In his book *The New American Justice,* Maguire pointed to his own six-year-old son with an incurable degenerative disease of the central nervous system. Danny received free transportation to school while healthy children walked; he received far more attention from teachers and specialists than most of his peers. There was no prospect that this boy would ever become a "productive" citizen; thus, there was no social utility to granting him these extraordinary services. Yet most Americans would approve of his receiving these or at least some benefits beyond those available to other six-year-olds. Why? He deserved them. Why? Not because of his accomplishments, but only because of his needs. Because he needed more than the average six-year-old, he had the right to more.

An obvious objection arises. Are there not problems with using need as a criterion for the distribution of goods and services? Surely many people would say they *need* all sorts of things in order to get the political community to provide them without charge. True enough, but we are speaking here of fundamental needs, needs crucial to living a human life. Maguire calls these "essential needs" and defines them as "those without which self-respect and hope could not endure."[6] While there will always be disagreement over some items, there clearly *are* such needs. An adequate diet, basic medical care, education, and old age insurance are almost everywhere in this country recognized as essential needs. People therefore have the right to them.

We should make clear here, of course, that this right does presume appropriate effort by the needy person. Able-bodied men and women have no right to reject decent jobs and live off the community out of sloth. As members of the community they too have obligations to the common good. It is in the situations where personal effort cannot provide the conditions for self-respect and hope that the community has the obligation to intervene.

The more extreme forms of individualism would deny even this. They would say that while the wealthy in a society may choose to share some of their wealth with the poor, it is their choice, not their obligation. However, those who hold such extreme individualist positions are rarely able to bring themselves to say that greed and narrowness are as good as are care and concern for others. The writer Ayn Rand is a good example of such a person. The heroes in her novels do not admit that they owe anything to the common good, but they just happen to be willing to make unselfish use of their wealth to assist others from time to time. The fact of the matter is that without this convenient inconsistency they would in the reader's eyes lose all semblance of human beings worthy of admiration. Rand's individualism asserts that these heroes owe nothing to the common good, but she senses that her readers would label them despicable for acting accordingly. It is far more accurate to say that because we each *know* we have such justice obligations, we each instinctively expect and require appropriately just behavior from one another.

Justice and the Social Construction of Reality

We have seen how individualism misunderstands the moral obligations of individuals. It is important to go farther and recognize how individualism misreads the daily workings of human life. The former is a "normative" error, a mistaken conception of what *ought* to occur. The latter is a "descriptive" error, a mistaken conception of what *is* going on in the world. While an accurate description of human life does not guarantee good moral judgment, inaccurate descriptions usually lead to faulty moral decisions. We cannot appreciate the importance of justice if we misunderstand the communal dimension of human life.

Most people, especially Americans, are quite aware of how human life is lived as the life experience of individuals. Each of us is, after all, an individual. Our daily life is filled with the perceptions we experience and with the decisions we make as individuals, from the taste of the milk at breakfast to the decision whether we will read a book this evening. Others can and do influence us, but the individual alone experiences and must decide. I, an individual, have responsibility for my life. My decisions, and the consequences flowing from them, shape who I am.

But we are just as thoroughly social as we are individual. Individualists miss this basic fact.[7] Modern psychology tells us that we could not even become fully human persons if it were not for the contributions and influence of other people. Research on the development of infants indicates clearly that it is only in interaction with other persons, usually parents, that an infant learns to develop consciousness and learns to make sense out of the events of daily life. Even something as simple as the child's cry for help is learned from others. When an infant feels pain, its response instinctively includes crying (and many other reactions), but the cry can become a call for help only as the child learns that adults interpret the cry in that way and come to offer help in response.

But it is not just oral signals such as the baby's cry or the word "help!" whose meanings are "worked out" in human interaction. All our actions, our thoughts, and even our feelings have the meaning they do because of the interaction between ourselves and others and because of the human structures within which we live. A growing awareness of this seems to be causing, for example, a perceptible change even in psychological counseling, which traditionally has not often looked beyond the individual seeking help and a few other important persons in that individual's life. Now more often there is discussion of the various human "systems" that place demands and constraints on each individual living within them.[8]

This awareness of the communality of each of us is nothing new in the Judeo-Christian tradition. As we saw in Chapter 2, the people of God never thought of themselves as a group of individuals who came together out of a commonly held interest. Rather, each person became fully an individual out of belonging to the nation God chose. Strength of character and force of will were highly valued, but always with the awareness that rootedness in the community was the source and salvation of individuality.

What does all this have to do with justice? The popular meaning of justice as meaning only individual justice does not ask any questions beyond this individual person here and now. What is just treatment for this woman in this low-ranking job without chance for promotion? Individual justice demands the fulfilling of the agreements made between her and her employer at the time of hiring. Individualism tends to go no further in pursuit of justice because it overlooks the unconscious bias her superiors may have against women. Or it may overlook the cultural reasons why this woman may be different from the more assertive, active, or career-oriented men who fill the more responsible positions in that firm. The individualist view of the world tends to ignore the various forces that powerfully shape each of us. As a result, in taking such an individualist position we accept no moral responsibility for the way those forces mold and change us. Modern sociology can be of great assistance in helping us understand the way in which even the subtle forces of socialization are the work and the responsibility of human persons.

In their classic book *The Social Construction of Reality,* Peter Berger and Thomas Luckmann have articulated much of what sociologists now take for granted about human persons and society. They argue that we misunderstand either the human person or society or both if we do not grasp the truth of the following three statements:

1. Society is a human product.
2. Society is an objective reality.
3. The person is a social product.[9]

Individualism does not recognize the interrelated truth of these three, and it is especially naive about the third. But let us look at each in turn.

1. Society Is a Human Product.

Society is a vast amalgam of people and patterns within which we live. With the exception of a fairly small circle of friends whom we come to know quite well, we know most other people only by actions of theirs that influence our lives. We know very little about the motives, beliefs, or feelings of most people whom we hear about, depend on, or even come in contact with. We do not really get to know much about our U.S. Senator, our local police chief, or the clerk in the grocery store.

It is in the one-to-one situation that others are most available to us, although even there we usually experience the other not as immediate and unique but as one who falls into this or that social category: school teacher, fire fighter, college student. Even so, the face-to-face situation is flexible; experience shows that preconceived notions and prejudices are most easily changed in such a contact.[10] A racist individual, for example, is much more likely to change by meeting and coming to know a black co-worker than by reading a book on the inaccuracy of racist stereotypes.

Still, even in face-to-face situations we usually operate on the basis of expecting certain *types* of behavior from the other person. Automobile drivers expect certain behaviors from gas-station attendants, and the attendants expect certain behaviors from the customers. For example, the attendants expect a pattern to be repeated, namely, that drivers pay after the gas is pumped into the tank. They are surprised (not to mention angry!) when their expectations are not fulfilled and a driver leaves without paying. Society is made up of a myriad of such patterns, and it "works" only when most of those patterns go on unbroken. During a war or natural disaster, many such sets of expectations may go unfulfilled, and then we hear that society "has broken down."

Where do all these expectations come from? Clearly, from people. Some of these expectations have very long histories. Most were not chosen randomly as if any set of patterned behavior were as good as any other. Most of those patterns exist "for good reason."[11] Still, human beings were the ones to develop and sustain those expectations, and they might have done it differently. We are reminded of this fact every time we notice the differences between two countries in either something fundamental, such as freedom of speech, or something less significant, such as style of dress or forms of sports entertainment.

Not only the patterns of our action but even the things we know about our world are products of human effort. As Berger and Luckmann point out, society would not function without a "social stock of knowledge." The adult male in a hunting society knows how to stalk and kill an elk because he has entered into the group of hunters and has taken as his own the language and wisdom of the hunt, language and wisdom developed slowly and improved by many generations of hunters before him.

All of our language is dramatically social in its origin and its current effect. We often casually think of language simply as providing names for thoughts and perceptions we would have anyway even if there were no words. But the language we speak opens up possibilities (and closes off others) even with regard to what we perceive from our world. Eskimos have thirteen different words for snow, allowing and even requiring a member of that group to be aware of many differences in the various forms of snow that most of us do not notice and probably would not even be able to notice without further tutoring. "The facts" about freezing rain are not just some sort of objective set of ideas. "The facts" are always "the facts which we in this time and place consider important," and there is always some sort of communal assessment of what counts for a fact.[12]

If all expected patterns of behavior, if language and even knowledge are products of the interaction of humans with one another and with their "world," it is clear that their "world" is also *their* world and not the only possible world. That is, "the world" we live in is itself a product of human persons. To be sure, it is not completely a product; the Rocky Mountains and the pebble in the sand are not human creations. But the world we know, experience, and influence is a human product. The title of Berger and Luckmann's book captures this: *The Social Construction of Reality.* Society is a human product.

2. Society Is an Objective Reality.

As soon as we recognize that society is in a real sense a human product, we tend to see it as a kind of subjective, temporary thing that changes at the whim of the persons who make it up. After all, if patterns of behavior and language and even knowledge are social products, can we not change them? How could they also be "objective" and resistant to change? What happens, of course, is that these things become "institutionalized." Berger and Luckmann present us with the following revealing example.[13]

Imagine two men from very different cultures, each culture unknown to the other. Suppose that these two people are the sole survivors from two different shipwrecks and that by chance they are cast up on the same island and meet there. Having no common language, they can only watch each other, each attributing motives to the other's actions as each carries on with the chores necessary for daily life. One may be able to start a fire in a way unknown to the other. Yet as that person repeats the action, the other thinks, "Ah, there he goes again," and begins to expect that behavior in similar situations in the future. Eventually the two cooperate in their tasks, and each is aware that the other sees and expects various habitual behaviors. One gathers wood, and the other starts the fire. "Ah, there he goes again" becomes "Ah, there we go again." Up to this point these routines are easily changed by these very people who set them up. Habits exist, but they are flexible.

But if one of our two disaster victims is a female and one a male, they might have children. At this point a dramatic shift comes about in this small social world. Procedures and habits are passed on to a new generation. The awareness among the two, "This is how we're doing it," soon turns to "This is how it's done" when the children are instructed in making a fire or gathering wood. From the child's point of view, the procedure existed beforehand and confronts the child as an external fact.

Before there were children, routines were fairly accessible to change and were "transparent"; the adults could see through them to what they really were—mutually agreed upon patterns of behavior. There was some degree of objectivity even then, since any change required some effort to change the other as well as oneself. Yet with children

> the objectivity of the institutional world "thickens" and "hardens," not only for the children, but (by a mirror effect) for the parents as well. The "There we go again" now becomes "This is how these things are done." A world so regarded attains a firmness in consciousness; it becomes real in an ever more massive way and it can no longer be changed so readily. For the children, especially in the early phase of their socialization into it, it becomes *the* world.[14]

In fact, from the children's point of view, the social world has an objectivity rivaling that of the natural world. They do not perceive language or patterns of behavior or knowledge as having conventional origins at all. Ask any three-year-old to confirm this. That a tree is called a "tree" is just as natural and obviously true as the fact that the leaves on the tree are green. In fact, it would probably be less shocking for the child if the oak in the front yard sprouted blue leaves next spring than if people started denying it was really a tree after all. Society is an objective reality.

3. The Person Is a Social Product.
American individualism thinks of the ideal individual as "the self-made man." In addition to the use of sexist language, there are two errors here. The first is the mistaken belief that a person *should* live with minimal dependence on other people. The second is the erroneous presumption that it is even *possible* for a person to live and grow without a high degree of dependence on other people. The prevailing American attitude attributes both success and failure almost exclusively to the credit or blame of the particular individuals involved. This makes for ungrateful winners and depressed losers in the game of life. And it leads to bad economic policy.

All this is not to say that personal initiative and effort are unimportant. In fact, they are crucial. The point is that if we notice only these elements, we miss the equally important fact that the very capacity for initiative and effort is first formed in us independently of our doing. This is but one of the ways in which the human person is a social product.

Consider Berger and Luckmann's example of the difference between the children and the two adults who originally met on the island. Before there were any children, routines of behavior and language were understood by the adults as their *own* effects. From the children's point of view, however, the routines they grow up with existed before them. Their acting in those patterns or talking with those words is their doing but not by their choice. Their attitudes, behavior, language, and knowledge are shaped— we might even say created to a large extent—by the social network of prevailing attitudes, expected behaviors, common language, and taken-for-granted knowledge in which they grow up.

One of the most powerful influences on us is the one that most of us least note in our daily life: language. We ordinarily think of words as naming our preexisting experiences. Yet the very availability of linguistic "names" influences whether and how we become aware of the untold thousands of sense stimuli and responses in any minute of our lives. "As a sign system, language has the quality of objectivity. I encounter language as a facticity external to myself and it is coercive in its effect on me. Language forces me into its pattern."[15]

Take the example of two first-year college students, Mary and Tom. They are both doing poorly, each failing the same two courses and not doing very well in the others either. They have just gotten back the results of a biology test, and have both failed it. Both are coming to think that they are not strong students and that maybe they should drop out of college. In one last attempt to improve, they both attend a workshop on student skills given by the student services office, and each hears for the first time about the phenomenon of "test anxiety." Some students, they're told, know enough but get so nervous at tests that they cannot think straight.

Suppose that at this point Mary's eyes light up as she says, "Yes, *that's* what happens to me. I do well in the lab and I can answer the questions when the instructor asks them orally, but on a test I get nervous." Tom says, "Not me. I wish I could answer oral questions, but I have as much problem with them as with a written test." Before attending that workshop, the experiences of these two students were probably not identical, but they were most certainly much more similar than their experiences were afterward. Mary came to experience herself differently because she learned of a *new way* to think about her life. The idea contained in the name "test anxiety" led her to reconfigure her experience and to turn to addressing *that* problem and not just to spend more time on biology. This is not to say that language and the knowledge it summarizes creates her experience independently of what goes on nonverbally in her life. But who she is (which of course includes her perceptions of herself) and how she acts will be different from now on because of language.

In general, we categorize our own life experiences under types of experiences summarized by society in a common language. We understand, "make sense of," and shape our lives by language and by the social stock of knowledge codified in language. [16]

There is yet another way in which the human person is a social product. Sociologists call it "role." We each fill many different roles in life, and these roles are principal elements in the definition of who we are. When two people meet, they most often describe themselves by the roles they fill: "I'm a banker," "I'm a student," "I drive a truck."

We act out a role when we engage in a kind of activity typical of a particular group of persons we belong to. Personnel managers hire people for jobs in large firms. Parents read to their small children. Students take courses in college. Someone watching these people (and familiar with these roles) will recognize these activities as characteristic of personnel managers, parents, and students and will tend to think of these people as *holders* of these roles.

Those individuals will find that their self-apprehension is determined by the actions they are in the midst of doing ("I'm hiring a file clerk"). Afterwards the actors understand themselves in identification with the role ("I'm a personnel manager"). The definition of the role—what is expected of persons in this position—becomes a part of the actor's makeup.

Of course, it is only a partial identification: The person has other roles in other situations. But an entire sector of self-consciousness is organized in terms of these various roles. The person did not define the roles, yet to a significant extent the roles define the person. The person is a social product.

There is an important responsibility here. The individual has to weigh the rightness or wrongness of what is expected in any role, but it is precisely the fact that only a part of the self is identified with the role that allows all too many of us to justify irresponsible actions. We often hear, "I don't want to do this, but as a personnel manager (or parent or student, etc.) I must." Since the roles we play do to a large extent define us, our very values and instincts are slowly shaped in accordance with our roles. Not only do we find it hard to live out our "personal" values in our (social) roles, but the gap narrows between "personal" and role-based standards of action as our values tend to change. The person is a social product.

From Sociology Back to Ethics

Both scripture and social science demand that our understanding of justice rely on a vision of the human person as not just individual but also as thoroughly social. Our reality—reality as we know it—includes socially constructed elements (such as institutionalized patterns of action) as well as elements that exist independently of human activity (such as the trees and hills). The prevailing individualistic vision in the United States has, as a result, two basic defects in its approach to justice.

The first is its mistaken belief that the individual person is solely, or almost solely, responsible for success or failure. The highly paid executive is seen as successful because of individual efforts; the newly wealthy entrepreneur in home computers "did it himself"; the unemployed single parent just never did make the effort to learn marketable skills. It is true, of course, that in each case the individual's effort is a key element. Yet the individualist "description" of these situations leaves out the thousands of employees who work with and for the executive, the hundreds of scientists whose pathbreaking work made microcomputers a possibility, and the family and neighborhood setting that made it nearly impossible for a black teenager to get through high school.

If we look back to some of the problems we first discussed in Chapter 1, we are now in a better position to understand their origins. We saw there that many of the unsuccessful and the locked-out poor in the United States see themselves as failures. The reason for their attitude is the dominance of individualism—a dominance so strong that even those who have nothing whatever to gain by it fall under its illusions. The unemployed workers who struggle daily to find a job are led to believe that they are the problem. This problem is made worse by the fact that the successful in America have often learned to congratulate themselves too heartily for their accomplishments and as a result cannot become more sympathetic toward the unsuccessful without calling into question the character of their own success. The unsuccessful generally have less, and the successful more, than they justly deserve.

The second major defect of individualism is directly related to this shortsightedness about personal responsibility. Because individual effort takes up so much of the canvas, the picture painted makes institutional structures seem less important in discussions of economic ethics than they really are. Individualism tends to consider social structures important only as barriers to individual effort. It misses the importance of institutional structures in shaping strong creative individuals and in preventing the severe inequalities that develop in the play of luck and self-assertion in the free market.

The demands of justice are based both on our accomplishments and on our needs. These accomplishments and needs seem at first to be centered solely on the individual. Yet since both depend in part on the humanly created structures within which we live, and since our response as a society to the demands of justice must be embodied in social structures, the character of those structures is a question of justice as well. In the economic realm, the individualistic failure to recognize this most often results in sacrificing justice to so-called efficiency, as we will soon see.

Efficiency and Justice

Inefficiency is the sort of thing that no one defends. Even those who struggle for justice recognize how important it is to use our resources efficiently so that those resources can meet as many human needs as possible. To waste resources in a world of scarcity violates our charge of stewardship.

At the same time, though, people who object to policy proposals aimed at greater justice often do so on the grounds that they are inefficient. As we saw in Chapter 6, the "efficient" solution to a problem usually ignores many nonmonetary values. Now that we have examined justice more closely we can understand better the often hidden relationship between questions of efficiency and questions of justice.

The first thing to note is that economists and others have long recognized a significant tradeoff between efficiency and justice. In a now-famous study entitled *Equality and Efficiency: The Big Tradeoff,* Arthur M. Okun examines the ways in which greater economic efficiency often reduces equality in society and how most efforts to assist the poor (and increase equality) are detrimental to efficiency and the overall level of production in society. There are two recurring themes in his essay: "The market needs a place, and the market needs to be kept in its place."[17] He proposes to rely on the market for the things it does well but to employ other mechanisms at times since "the tyranny of the dollar" would, if given the chance, "sweep away all other values, and establish a vending-machine society."[18]

Okun and all defenders of the market are correct in recognizing the assets of the market. The concern for efficiency in the market is an essential part of our charge to use God's gifts wisely and to produce the means for a fulfilling life for all people. Thus, arguments for efficiency contain an insight that Christian stewards must live by. But this is not all they contain.

Arguments for efficiency often conceal an underlying value judgment in favor of individual justice and against social justice. While it is true that those interested in social justice, to be consistent, must be concerned about the efficient use of resources, not all those interested in efficiency are concerned about social justice. Take an example: government regulation.

In recent years we have heard a great deal about the importance of reducing government regulation of industry because of the tremendous inefficiency such controls cause. Federal Trade Commission rulings about unsafe consumer products, Federal Drug Administration decisions about unproven drugs, and Occupational Safety and Health Administration directions about work place safety have all been attacked for requiring individual firms to incur unnecessary costs. Some politicians have called for the abolition of such agencies. The implicit argument is often that such regulations increase the cost of doing business but do almost nothing to improve people's lives that would not be done anyway. Consumers, on their own, can buy more expensive but safer products if they wish, and workers, on their own, can include safety provisions in their contract negotiations if they consider them worthwhile. These goals, it is said, can be achieved more efficiently through the ordinary interaction of the market.

Such critics might honestly be objecting to government action *only* on the grounds of efficiency. If that were the case, the justice seekers who, after careful consideration of the costs and benefits, support such governmental activity can only respond that the critics have underestimated the good (or overestimated the harm) done by these federal agencies. However, this answer may not get very far because the charges of inefficiency often hide a deeper objection that is not openly admitted.

This deeper, hidden objection is that the government should make little or no effort to establish any sort of justice beyond individual justice—which is another way of saying that individual justice is the only sort of justice there is.

The free market, of course, is the organizational embodiment of individual justice. The rules of the market are the rules of individual justice. No one may coerce another person to enter into an agreement, but all voluntary agreements must be upheld. Individuals know, better than anyone else, what is in their own interest, and they enter into voluntary agreements—to buy this, or loan that, or work for a particular employer—because they estimate that they will be better off if they do so than if they do not.

In short, to argue in favor of the market is to argue in favor of individual justice, but *only* individual justice.

Individual justice is a crucial dimension of our common life, and anyone seeking to live out the Christian economic ethic must attend to it. Yet many persons who again and again turn to the market for the solution to a problem do so because they do not value or even recognize the equally important dimension of social justice. We saw in Chapter 6 how it is usually more accurate to replace the phrase "the efficient solution" by the phrase "the market solution" (since so many people exclude all nonmonetary costs and benefits from their calculations of efficiency). We can now see that in many cases "the efficient solution" is "the individualistic solution." But that solution may be a violation of the fundamental requirements of social justice.

Professional economists are usually in an ambiguous position when these issues are raised. On the one hand orthodox economic analysis requires that the shortcomings of the market be recognized and that economists admit that government can and should intercede at the request of the citizenry in cases such as externalities (where costs, such as pollution, are imposed on people *outside* the firm) and other universally recognized "market failures." To put this concretely, economists have little sympathy for the steel manufacturer who wants the right to pollute the atmosphere freely.

On the other hand, however, orthodox economic analysis still tends to limit solutions to those that do the very least to interfere with or distort market forces. Thus, one approach to pollution control that is popular among orthodox economists is to set an effluent charge or pollution tax. That is, the government weighs all costs and benefits, including those often ignored, such as health effects on people miles away from the smokestacks. After assessing the cost to the firm of reducing the pollution using existing technology (filters, scrubbers, etc.), the government sets a tax on pollution, and the firm is free either to buy equipment to reduce both its pollution and its pollution tax, or to do nothing about pollution and pay a higher pollution tax.[19]

This is economically more efficient than, say, setting maximum limits on pollution (for example, so many tons per year) for all firms, since reducing pollution to a maximum allowable limit will force some firms to spend more to reduce pollution than the benefits are worth. It will also lead some other firms to reduce pollution less than they would otherwise if there were a pollution tax.

The point is that while economists quickly recognize that the steel mill must pay for its polluting the air, they often have trouble understanding why most citizens are repelled by the idea that a profitable firm could be allowed to continue high levels of pollution if it chooses to pay the tax instead. Most citizens' sense of social justice is violated here. The option the economist offers the firm is roughly equivalent to saying that we as a society are willing to give people the option to be honest or to steal and pay the penalty of a jail term. But this is a misinterpretation of the moral glue that holds society together.

Penalties are assessed to deter and punish the irresponsible, but the vast majority of persons refrain from stealing because stealing is wrong, not just because the costs of being caught are high. Pollution cannot prudently be reduced to zero, since low levels of pollution do not cause much damage but are very costly to eliminate. Still, the communal decision about pollution standards should make it clear that each firm's debt to the common good entails meeting publicly held standards and that only irresponsible egoism would lead a firm willingly to violate them. The fact that so many orthodox economists fail to appreciate this widely held conviction is evidence that in spite of efforts to make efficiency a technical and non-normative tool of analysis, economists, in promoting efficiency, often promote one vision of justice over another without admitting or even noticing what they are doing.

In a wider sense, the insights into individualism examined earlier in this chapter lead us to realize that many other public policy debates allow efficiency concerns to mask deeper presumptions in favor of individual justice and against social justice. In debates about the rights (and duties) of owners of property, economic efficiency has become a greater and greater concern in recent years. A whole new intellectual field concentrating on the interplay of law and economics has been created out of this seminal concern that the courts should examine the efficiency effects of their legal judgments. [20]

Public policy debates over proposed laws to make it more difficult to close plants in the Snowbelt and move to the Sunbelt or the Far East are a good example. In the effort to secure justice many people have proposed laws that require longer advance notice of plant closings, or to require larger severance and relocation pay, or to require community or state approval prior to plant relocations. Proponents of these laws are frequently reminded that such a policy thwarts the efficient allocation of capital to its most productive use. And it does, if we do not consider the social costs external to the firm. Often, however, such an objection masks the more fundamental protest: that firms and stockholders have no social justice obligations to the workers and the community. This view presumes that firms are expected to fulfill all contracts and will, out of self-interest, attempt to maintain a good public-spirited image, but that they owe nothing beyond the demands of individual justice.

The Christian economic ethic will not support such an interpretation. While Christians, as stewards, must be careful to include efficiency as a central concern, they need to develop a critical sense of suspicion when efficiency arguments are raised against justice causes. The response to such objections must be twofold. The first approach to make is a determined effort to see the wisdom implicit in the concern for the efficient use of resources. The second is to question whether the proponent of efficiency has a well developed sense of the demands of social justice.

We should give our careful attention to an argument in favor of efficiency whether it comes from, say, a libertarian, who denies the importance of social justice, or from a person who is well known as a seeker of social justice. At the same time, we need to realize that we tend to believe a person who expresses concern with great vigor and conviction. Unfortunately, the ones who argue most vehemently for efficiency are often the very ones who have little concern for social justice. (This is not surprising, since a strong justice concern would temper such vehemence.) Thus justice seekers will need to assess not only the explicit arguments of proponents of efficiency but their implicit presumptions about justice as well.

Let us return to our earlier example of the rise in the price of energy. Social justice demands that the poor receive those elements basic to a life of hope and dignity. For instance, society must make some provision for the basic heat and transportation needs of the poor. Individual justice demands that the owners of energy resources be allowed to reap the benefits of higher energy prices. The concern for efficiency—making our existing energy reserves stretch to meet as many needs as possible—requires that consumers not receive the wrong "signal" of artificially low prices that will induce them to consume too freely.

We cannot propose here any detailed, concrete, policy demanded by the Christian economic ethic over all other possible policies. Yet the outlines of a just solution seem clear. The poor must be helped to meet rising energy costs. This could be accomplished through "life-line" rates, where a basic allotment of electricity or fuel oil per month is provided at a cost below the free market price, with additional units consumed being sold at the higher, market price. It might alternatively be accomplished through additional income tax rebates to low-income people or perhaps through "energy stamps" like food stamps. To fund such programs, energy companies—who benefit from the higher prices caused by the OPEC cartel—would have to contribute a disproportionate amount of the profits that individual justice in other circumstances might have left to them. The rest of us middle-income Americans will have to put up with higher energy prices in deference to the insight embodied in the concern for efficiency. We will use energy more frugally as a result.

We cite this as an example of a possible just solution to the problem. Several other identifiable policies designed to address this problem for the long term might also work. National programs to subsidize energy conservation investments— insulation, weather stripping, etc.—are already in place and should be expanded to assist low-income people more. Emphasis on various forms of renewable energy could work toward relieving the problem of resource depletion and could thereby give the nation greater flexibility in achieving both justice and efficiency. Longer-term solutions must move to a greater "democratization" of the economy in an effort to offset the narrower interests of the stockholders of large firms. Possibilities include worker cooperatives, consumer cooperatives, and greater government regulation, control, or even ownership of energy resources.

Such options are part of the questioning of economic structures that must involve Christians in analyzing the merits of whole economic systems. Some believe that capitalism can be transformed enough to be truly democratized; others are convinced that only a decentralized, democratic socialism will suffice.

Our point is twofold. On the one hand the Christian economic ethic does eliminate some inadequate proposals from consideration (such as a completely free market solution with little corresponding effort to help the poor, or a contrasting totalitarian socialism). On the other hand it cannot of itself create a blueprint for the one and only acceptable answer. Life is too complex and ambiguous for that.

Summary

In this chapter we began a more formal inquiry into justice. We found that both individual justice and social justice are crucial elements in human life, even though American individualism often misunderstands this. Individual justice is universally recognized by Americans. Yet once we see that individual justice is founded on the worth of the human person, we must recognize that this very worthwhileness of persons requires social justice as well. All people have a right to what it takes to meet their essential needs, those things "without which self-respect and hope could not endure."

We saw how sociological insight into the social construction of reality contradicts many naive individualistic descriptions of human life. And we examined the relation of social justice and efficiency. Social justice seekers must attend to efficiency, but many Americans who stress efficiency again and again do so as a covert way of promoting individual justice while obstructing social justice.

We turn now to Chapter 8, where we will delineate the particular elements of social justice and see how they might be applied to a number of concrete issues of economic policy.

8

Empowering Justice in Economic Life

Economic life in the United States needs fundamental change. Millions live in poverty and unemployment and are "locked out" of our system. Millions more are underemployed or have no employment opportunities other than deadening and dehumanizing ones. Even many who are "successful" believe they are little more than gears in a machine too large to influence. Christians, whether "locked out" or "successful," have the responsibility to establish a more just and humane network of economic relationships.

Our aim in this book is to assist persons striving for justice to relate the demands of the Christian ethic to economic life today. We outline a procedure by which any group of committed justice seekers could begin to have an effect on their world. By means of the Montgomery bus boycott example in Chapter 1, we have seen how a small but committed group of persons can have significant influence on existing economic structures by developing and empowering operative norms for action. In Chapter 6 we viewed several generally accepted tools of economic analysis from the perspective of the Christian ethic, and in Chapter 7 we examined the relationship between social justice and efficiency.

In these final chapters we need to do three things. The first is to bring together the elements essential to achieving justice. The second is to illustrate the movement from these general principles about justice to concrete operative norms that a small disciplined community might make actually effective. These two topics will be addressed in this chapter. The third is to analyze the life of such justice-seeking groups; it will be the focus of Chapter 9.

The Elements of Social Justice

From the point of view of the Christian economic ethic, social justice is best seen as a process that will never be fully completed in any nation or within any economic structure. Sin will always be present in human society. Love, of course, is absolutely essential in the life of the Christian, but it alone is not complete. The need for prophetic critique of both sinful structures and individual lives will always endure. No one can map out what the perfectly just society would look like. Still, much *can* be said, and we here outline six elements essential to that ongoing process we call justice. We do not claim this is the only possible list. Some of these could be broken into smaller parts, others could be combined, and a few additional elements might be proposed. Yet each of these, in some form or other, is crucial to the notion of justice to which the Judeo-Christian tradition points today.

1. The Just Entitlement of the Poor
In Chapter 2 we saw the attention that the Scriptures devote to the just treatment of widows, orphans, foreigners, and other poor persons. Zechariah proclaimed God's message:

> "Render true judgments, show kindness and mercy each to his
> brother, do not oppress the widow, the fatherless, the sojourner,
> or the poor; and let none of you devise evil against his brother in
> your heart."
>
> (Zech. 7:9-10)

The law provided that the grain at the edges of the fields was not to be harvested but was to be left for the poor. Any grapes that were missed or that fell to the ground were not to be gathered by a second trip through the vineyard but were to be left for foreigners, widows, and orphans (Lev. 19:9-10). We have recounted Jesus' ministry to the poor, the infirm, and the outcast.

When answering the disciples of John the Baptist who asked whether Jesus was the one who was to come, Jesus answered:

> "Go and tell John what you have seen and heard; the blind receive their sight, the lame walk, lepers are cleansed, and the deaf hear, the dead are raised up, the poor have good news preached to them."
>
> (Lk. 7:22)

And as clearly as the Scriptures speak of the importance of the treatment of the poor, the issue was even more clearly stated by the early church. Ambrose of Milan taught:

> God has ordered all things to be produced so that there should be food in common for all, and that the earth should be the common possession of all. Nature, therefore, has produced a common right for all, but greed has made it a right for a few.[1]

Like most of the Fathers of the early church, Ambrose held that the rich are no more than stewards for the things they own. "The rich are in the possession of the goods of the poor, even if they have acquired them honestly or inherited them legally."[2]

Using the language of Daniel Maguire, we can say that the poor—like all human beings—have worth simply because they are persons, and this worth entails a rightful claim to the essentials of life. Clearly we do not want to provide for such needs in a manner that will create a stultifying dependence, but providing those things necessary for self-respect and hope is our obligation nonetheless.

Thus we speak of the just entitlement of the poor. They have a valid claim on those goods possessed by the rich over and above the necessities of life. When we look not at the entitlement of the poor but the obligation of the well-to-do, we arrive at the second element in our understanding of social justice.

2. The Limited Rights of Property Ownership

Because the world was created by God, who intended it for the use of all people, any sense of "ownership" of the earth or its fruits has to be a limited one. The Judeo-Christian tradition has not generally opposed the idea of private ownership of property;

in fact it has upheld it as a fundamental aspect of its defense of the dignity and rights of the individual person. As we have seen, however, the rights of property ownership stop far short of the nearly absolute control that many persons today presume.

From the beginning, the Judeo-Christian tradition has stressed the dignity and worth of the individual person while at the same time recognizing that every individual finds personal identity as a member of a people. Treatment of the poor and foreigners is one area where this appreciation for the dignity of every person is evident. This sense is also evident in the recognition of the right of each individual to ownership of material things. It is true that believers called to be forgoers live with a minimum of possessions, but this has generally not been the case for most Christians. The goods of the earth have been created by God for the benefit of all, and individual ownership, rather than communal ownership, has been the most frequently employed relation between people and the things they use and consume.

However, the fact that all people and things have been created by God implies that the ownership of things by any one person entails only a limited control over those things. The bounds of that control have been understood in several different ways in the Christian tradition. In the language of the Covenant, Christians have recognized that humans have material things at their disposal only through the goodness of the Lord who has set obligations toward the poor for those who have possessions. Within the tradition of natural law, Christians have seen that those who own things must not violate the inherent end of natural things that God intended: No matter who "owns" them, material goods are to meet human requirements and may not be stockpiled in overabundance when others are in need. In the more modern stress on the inherent rights of persons, Christians have recognized that the right of persons to a basic level of sustenance in society constrains the right of ownership on the part of others.

In many ways, of course, this insight into the limits of ownership is recognized even in our individualistic society today. Ownership of real estate is subject to laws of eminent domain.

People are taxed to provide for services to the elderly, unemployed, disabled, and others. Still, we in our society have been brought up to think even of our own persons in terms of "ownership" and the authority to control. As we have seen, C. B. Macpherson referred to this as possessive individualism, where we think of ourselves as *owning* individual rights, abilities, and potential. When "ownership," an external relation between a person and a thing, is employed as the basic metaphor in our image of ourselves, it is no wonder that we have lost sight of the limits to which all ownership is subject.

Thus, private ownership of property has a complex relationship to the dignity of the individual. On the one hand, every individual has the right to own and consume what is needed for a basic standard of living. On the other hand, when the ownership of material things by someone stands in the way of the livelihood and flourishing of others, the owner has the obligation to alter or terminate that ownership. We have seen that in the realm of goods needed for sustenance this involves the redistribution of those goods. As we will see presently, when this involves the ownership of material things used to produce other goods and services—such as factories, mills, and transportation systems—there is a similar obligation to organize or control those enterprises in accord with values beyond the self-interest of the current owners.

3. The Reorientation of Personal Life

Christians pressing for social justice need to attend carefully to the implicit direction of their own lives. Much of this book is devoted to the importance of altering social structures, and Christians have most often failed in not doing just that. But it is equally clear that social change cannot occur and endure without individual personal change as well.

Here we find ourselves confronted by the option Jesus presented to his disciples: to be either forgoers or stewards. The demands of the economic ethic begin in our interpersonal lives. We who are well-off as citizens of a wealthy nation are living in a kind of complicity with a system that treats many people unjustly.

172 TOWARD A CHRISTIAN ECONOMIC ETHIC

We will find it quite difficult to transform and make more just the larger economic institution of society, but we can and must reorient our own lives in line with the stewardship to which we have been called. We will address this question in greater detail in the next chapter, but for now we can recognize the importance of achieving this reorientation not just individually but in community.

In Chapter 1 we saw the central importance of operative norms in the life of both individual and group. While each of us could by ourselves make lifestyle changes in consumption and other activities, our commitment to such changes will be more intense and secure if we are consciously part of a group whose members will expect such changes of one another. One of the most fundamental contributions of modern sociology to Christian ethics has been the understanding of the connection between the internal sense of obligation that a person feels and the possibilities for shaping that sense of obligation when each person in a community pays conscious attention to operative norms.

4. The Transformation of Social Structures

When we carry this modern insight into the possibilities for more ethically responsible group life on to society at large we recognize the importance of transforming social structures in accordance with the basic demands of social justice. This attention to institutional structures has been criticized and even condemned by some as foreign to the Christian message, but we must remind ourselves of its importance to a truly Christian economic ethic.

Individual persons have, of course, always been admonished to live responsibly in their economic relationships. Beyond this, however, the Judeo-Christian tradition has always stressed the *communal* responsibility for morally proper economic behavior. In the Old Testament, Zechariah recounts the obligation which the Lord set concerning "widows, orphans, foreigners who live among you, or anyone else in need" and reports the Lord's response:

> "As I called, and they would not hear, so they called, and I would not hear," says the LORD of hosts, "and I scattered them with a whirlwind among all the nations which they had not known. Thus

the land they left was desolate, so that no one went to and fro, and the pleasant land was made desolate."

(Zech. 7:13-14)

In early Christianity, local church leaders recognized this communal responsibility and created structures within the Christian community for assisting the poor. This important effort was not left to the choice of private charity alone.

While it is true that the early Christians did not spend their time trying to influence the secular authorities to alter the social structures, it is an error of anachronism to argue that therefore Christians today should not do so. It was also the case that just about no one in those early centuries thought there should or even could be an election to choose the next Roman emperor. Yet today we all agree that it is important that we elect the president of the nation by democratic means. What has happened in the intervening centuries?

As we saw earlier, the modern historical consciousness and a sense of the rights of the individual have constituted a new mindset or world view. We have chosen to structure our political system as a democracy because it fits the most basic of human values better than a monarchy or dictatorship. Similarly, citizens of the modern world have an obligation to form and reshape economic structures according to fundamental human values. The economic realm must be subject to political decision. If a totalitarian structure leads—as it has, for example, in Poland in this decade—to a nation violating the right to organization by workers, then those economic structures must be radically altered.

The demands of morality confront us in both our individual and communal life. Significant change is always slow, particularly change in economic structures and public expectations. We must be realistic and not naive in pushing for the transformation of social structures, but push we must.

5. The Use of Countervailing Power
Because the Judeo-Christian tradition has always possessed a clear vision of the close relation between faith and moral activity,

it has always recognized the demands of the moral life. Because it has likewise possessed just as clear a vision of the power of sin, especially the sin of powerful people, it has also given a place of great importance to the prophetic stance. Out of this tradition of prophetic denunciation of evil comes the fifth element in a Christian understanding of social justice, the use of countervailing power against the powers that preserve unjust social structures.

Contrary to the situation in other Mideastern societies of the day, ancient Israel was able to retain and value the tradition of prophecy that time and again criticized the prevailing leaders and customs of the nation. This is truly remarkable in an era when despotism rather than democracy typified the political climate of nearly all societies. Though the strident message of the prophets was undoubtedly resented by those at whom it was directed, the prophets became an important part of the tradition inherited by the Christian church.

We saw in Chapter 6 how the premodern effort of Christians in moral exhortation and in creating justice structures within the church led in the modern era to efforts at transforming societal structures in the wider community within which the church exists. The difference was brought about by modern insight into the transformation of those structures. Similarly, the personal prophetic denunciation of evil, which was directed at the wealthy and powerful in premodern times, now entails in the modern era the marshaling of public effort and influence—countervailing power—to offset the might of the powerful in order to create a more just and humane world.

James Luther Adams has pointed out that this sense of the prophetic tradition in Christianity had a significant influence on the political structures of the United States, in the incorporation of a separation of countervailing powers in the three branches of government outlined in the Constitution.[3] But if this aspect of Christianity has influenced the modern world, the influence just as clearly runs in the opposite direction as well.

In Chapter 1 we cited the Montgomery bus boycott as an example of effective social change in the interests of social justice. People had long been denouncing the evil of prejudice and discrimination, but it was not until a countervailing power was marshaled, in the form of economic losses for the bus company, that real change took place. This process began with the moral conviction of a small group whose efforts were directed at a specific, relatively small change in the operative norms of the city: that blacks should be able to sit anywhere on a public bus. To achieve this goal, however, there was required a tremendous effort by a large number of poor people willing to endure the day-to-day hardships of getting to work and to other activities without the public transport on which they almost totally depended. But such countervailing power was required.

Similarly now, if Christians are effectively to confront unjust economic institutions, they will have to employ countervailing social and economic power against the vested interests that support the status quo. This will not be easy or neat. And as in the bus boycott, people on both sides of the struggle will be claiming the Christian heritage. But of course this is not new. The prophet Micah found that the response of the powerful to prophetic confrontation is often a sense of self-confident surprise that anyone would think them deserving of God's anger: "Surely his words are words of kindness for his people Israel" (Mic. 2:7). Countervailing power will be needed because the powerful will not willingly recognize and give up their advantage.

6. Reliance on Democratic Decision Making

This sixth and last element of social justice springs from the same awareness that those in power tend to be blind. Since the leaders of any group, even one striving for social justice, can confuse their own goals with the demands of justice, the counterbalance of democratic process should act as a structural safeguard.

The history of Christianity depicts an ambiguous relation between the institutional churches and the democratic movements that have come to prevail in Western societies. Historians often point to the Reformation as one of the wellsprings of the sense of the dignity of the individual that led to the demand for democratic political structures. Yet when actual democratic movements developed in the seventeenth through the nineteenth centuries, many churches found themselves in alliance with the older, aristocratic classes in society. From the churches' point of view, those political movements were too often self-consciously atheistic and violent. Many churches had a similar reaction, for similar reasons, to the efforts in the nineteenth and twentieth centuries by workers' organizations to humanize and democratize the economic realm. History has shown that it is all too easy for religion to become allied with those in power.

But another fundamental problem was one that still exists and that will always be an ambiguous dimension of democracy. For all the evils of monarchic or dictatorial rule, a simple move to decision by majority rule will not guarantee that the right laws and policies will be adopted. The Christian ethic, including its economic ethic, is based on values essential to human life whether or not the majority in a group recognizes them. The Christian community must continue to resist those who propound the fallacious idea that relying on the preferences of a majority will solve all ethical questions.

Christian churches were at first skeptical about the modern movement toward democracy in politics, largely because many of democracy's early advocates were atheists. Still, the communal sense of human life inherent in the Judeo-Christian tradition has made for a strong appreciation of democratic values by Christians today. Within disciplined Christian communities that are striving for social justice, democratic processes and the concomitant stress on civil rights and liberties must be incorporated into both their method and the ultimate goal they envision for society. This reliance on democracy as a method and safeguard occurs with the presumption that, while the outcome of a democratic process might itself run counter to the standards of justice, the prophetic stance is a safeguard against the excesses of democracy. A robust and democratic communal life is both a goal and the primary means of implementing an economic ethic.

These, then, are six elements crucial to any Christian notion of social justice:
1. the just entitlement of the poor;

2. the limited right of property ownership;
3. the reorientation of individual personal life;
4. the transformation of social structures;
5. the use of countervailing power;
6. the reliance on democratic decision making.

While these principles are not specific enough to render solutions to particular questions, they represent the framework within which Christian communities can strive for social justice with hope.

From General Principles to Operative Norms

Once we have in hand these six general principles essential to social justice, we must survey the terrain on which our striving for justice will take place. Our efforts could be applied to a tremendous number of different "places": assisting the unemployed and the elderly in our congregation in getting food and shelter, working to pass a citywide referendum for more local and responsive representation on the city council, actively supporting efforts to end the arms race, opposing U.S. aid to military governments in Latin America—the list goes on. The needs in all directions are great, and no individual or group can address very many of them at once. So where do we start?

We can think of this vast array of pressing needs in three separate sections or arenas. First, efforts within our own small disciplined Christian community; second, efforts to create greater cooperation and discipline within a wider network of groups moving toward social justice; and third, strivings aimed explicitly at transforming larger social, political, and economic structures. Let us look at each of these separately.

Christians working for justice must do so in community, the first arena, since communal accountability is both the means to justice and the essence of justice. In most cases, the small disciplined community will be a subgroup of a larger congregation not all of whose members will participate in justice efforts. In some cases the small disciplined community will be part of a

religious order or other large Christian group. We can consider
three distinct actions that are important in the small community.

The first is self-conscious reflection, prayer, and discussion
aimed at strengthening the operative moral norms prevailing in
the group. Included here would be empowering others in my
community to expect me to increase my financial contributions to
justice causes or to increase the amount of time I spend in
working for social change. The second sort of action is work at
implementing justice within our local church—for instance,
assisting elderly church members in getting meals, lodging, or
transportation to medical services. The third kind of activity in
this first arena is effort expended to raise the operative norm in
the whole worshipping congregation of which our justice striving
community is a part. Here both good example and explicit policy
proposals to the church board or parish council are important. We
will look more intently at the life of the small disciplined community in the next chapter.

The second major arena for efforts aimed at greater justice is
the developing of a network of organizations working for justice,
with cooperation centering on specific justice issues. Included in
such a network will likely be other Christian communities. But
just as importantly there will also be groups with little or no
explicit relation to Christianity or religion at all: neighborhood
organizations, community action groups, senior citizens' associations, groups of various ethnic minorities, labor unions, local
organizations of larger political parties, and so on.

Alliances with others whose beliefs and philosophical under-
pinnings differ sharply from theirs are sometimes threatening to a
small group (Christian or otherwise) whose own beliefs are
crucial to the group's existence. The question inevitably arises:
What if through a network we are forced to compromise our
convictions or become identified publicly with events or outcomes that we did not endorse? These are very real risks, but the
alternative to accepting such risks is failing to cooperate with
other justice groups and consequently having no impact on the
structures responsible for so much misery and harm. Our social
structures are the way they are not just by coincidence; rather,

they are sustained and preserved by certain groups that benefit from them. The only way that such structures will change is if significant social power is exerted, and this will happen only if large numbers of people push in one direction together. Without alliances this is impossible.

In fact, those striving for justice need to realize that focusing too narrowly on only some kinds of injustice tends to splinter the overall effort. Blacks see injustice done to them but can refuse to recognize their own injustice to Hispanics. Hispanics recognize this but can oppress women in their midst. Middle-class whites may strive for more adequate welfare payments to the poor but may fail to see their own racism, sexism, or their own place of privilege in the economic system. Thus networks with varying groups tend to help the community be critical about its own vision.

Ordinarily, then, a basic procedural step is for the Christian community to associate itself with other groups around specific justice issues. These issues will entail raising the level of operative moral norms in the society, sometimes at the local level and sometimes at the national or international level. The intention always is to end the pattern of injustice.

This brings us to the third arena where justice striving must operate: actual transformation of dominant social structures. Whether injustice occurs at the local, national, or international level, it is rarely simply an interpersonal event between the victim and a malicious perpetrator. Injustice nearly always entails a sustained pattern of abuse of one group by another and is nearly always legitimated as an unfortunate side effect of social structures designed to support other, more important human values. Thus, reducing already minimal support to the poor is often justified on the grounds that this will reduce the federal deficit, which will in turn lessen inflation. Or similarly, governments in Latin America appeal to the need for a rising gross national product as a justification for concessions made to multinational firms or local elites who perpetuate nearly feudal conditions on the great agricultural plantations.

Once we have these three arenas in mind, we must face the question: How do we move from our convictions and general principles about social justice to concrete operative norms capable of bringing about a real change in each of the three arenas of concern? Every small disciplined community will be unique, with a history and context different from all others. No two justice issues are identical, and the empirical situation of each neighborhood or city where an issue arises will be unlike every other. Still, by viewing several issues briefly we will be able to exemplify a process for relating religious and social scientific approaches in a way that leads to the development of operative norms. For the remainder of this chapter we will examine five crucial issues to which Christians need to respond.

1. Welfare Programs for the Poor in America

Our common sense tells us that the locked-out and deprived face material scarcity every day. The undernourished children of the poor, the unemployed workers who futilely seek unavailable jobs, and the shoddy health care sporadically provided to many of the underemployed are instances where the poor experience scarcity as *objective poverty*. Millions of Americans, not to mention two billion other people in the world, simply do not have the resources required to provide for themselves the necessities of life.

This form of scarcity experienced as objective poverty needs to be placed alongside another sort. Many "successful" career people experience scarcity because they inordinately desire a wide range of unneeded, costly status and luxury goods. Too often they are utterly absorbed in acquiring more ostentatious estates, boats, stereos, exotic travel, job promotions. Their experience of scarcity issues entirely from their own *subjective covetousness*, which they display as conspicuous consumption.

This inquiry now discloses the extent to which a distorted reality permeates the experience of scarcity as interpreted by the affluent. As we noted in Chapter 6, scarcity as the gap between unlimited wants and what is available is a sign of human greed. Most of these well-off feel no powerful urge to respond to the needs of the poor, and most of their efforts on behalf of the poor are but crumbs. This leaves it to defenders of social justice to propose specific claims or obligations that will establish principles and policies for just entitlements belonging to every needy person.

The opposition to income supplements for low-income people often comes in the form of claims that they are economically inefficient, that they give the wrong "signals" to poor people, rewarding them for not working. Generally speaking, this is faulty reasoning, for it ranks a lower goal (increasing production by a slightly greater economic efficiency) over a higher goal (respecting the fundamental just entitlement of all persons). It actually represents a morally inefficient means to the social welfare of the nation.

This is not to say that efficiency has no bearing whatever in matters of justice. In proper perspective, orthodox economic analysis is quite helpful. Without proper precautions, well-intentioned efforts to help the poor can make them overly dependent on such assistance and can in fact be structured so as to discourage those who are looking for employment and self-respect. Currently in the United States, almost all welfare programs are structured so that there are significant reductions in benefits when the recipient gets a low-paying job and begins to earn money in the marketplace. Because any poor family receives benefits from more than one program—e.g., Aid to Families with Dependent Children, food stamps, Medicaid—the partial cutback in each program offsets much of the new earned income. Often the poor person gets to keep only 20 to 40% of the money earned. Whereas the wealthy pay at most about a 50% income tax, a poor person may face implicit marginal rates of "taxation" of 60 to 80% or more. This undercuts the person's interest in finding work. It leaves us with demoralized people and fewer productive hours worked, in addition to higher welfare costs. While space does not permit us to investigate this in detail, the proposal to remedy this problem by distributing substantial income supplements through a "negative income tax" is promising.[4]

The principle of the just entitlement of the poor demands that we structure a more significant transfer of income from the "successful" to the poor. Some in the nation have tried to spread the idea that welfare programs help primarily those who do not really need assistance. However, all serious studies of persons on welfare have found that nearly all of them either cannot work (are too old, too young, disabled), cannot work without adequate daycare (single parents of small children), or cannot find work (are unemployed). The image of vast numbers of welfare cheaters is a right-wing illusion.

The importance of democratic decision making and the need for using countervailing power means that welfare recipients themselves must be involved in all efforts to alter the current welfare system. Small disciplined communities will need to ensure that their alliances include some of the many groups formed by low-income people in their areas. Since it is a just act for the poor to claim public assistance as an entitlement upon the abundance of the well-off, any effort to assist them should be coordinated with the efforts of the poor themselves.

It remains for us to translate this analysis into sharply focused operative norms. Christian stewards should assume major responsibilities to work on this project with welfare recipients so that, together, they may strengthen democratic decision making.

Christian disciples, especially those who are better off financially, ought to join with other justice contenders to expect one another to build political power to advance a specific set of social justice projects with welfare recipients; each project should be focused upon concrete local or state needs of recipients; primary leadership for projects should be in the hands of welfare recipients; supportive leadership should be provided by nonrecipients. Concrete examples of possible projects:

(a) developing political power to remove the sales taxes on food, prescribed medicine, and clothing (at least children's clothing) in states where such taxes are still in effect;

(b) providing educational experiences in our congregations for disciples to prepare family budgets based upon existing monthly family welfare grants for one, four, and six persons;

(c) cooperating with any local welfare-justice seeking group, led by welfare recipients and supported by justice

*contenders, to obtain information or more substantive
assistance from welfare offices.*

We would want to submit these operative norms to a small
disciplined community of disciples for consultative sharing until a
final norm emerges.

In deciding upon (and eventually acting upon) the operative
norms suggested above, stewards would need to be thorough in
using helpful sources of information and creative in preparing
themselves for their efforts. Thus, project (a) would require a
careful study of tax inequities and a look at what other states are
doing, especially in the arena of sales taxes. A good resource is
the publication *People and Taxes*.[5]

In considering project (b), members of the concerned community should for a few months keep a record of their own monetary
expenditures so as to identify the costs required for an *adequate*
food diet and other *absolute* needs. If the group then prepares
family budgets for at least three imaginary families—poverty-,
middle-, and upper-income levels— this will help the participants
to identify the difference between scarcity as *absolute needs* and
scarcity as *social wants*.

These proposals only begin to address the dire need for more
long-range welfare reform. We should remember, however, that
the operative norm in Montgomery first centered upon the
practical issue of bus seating. We believe that such focused
operative norms as the above can pass the reality test: They are
comprehensible, immediately goal-oriented, and realizable.

2. Income Effects of Energy Policy

There are, of course, many issues in national economic policy
that affect the distribution of income in the nation. One of them is
the energy policy that we saw in the last chapter. The choice
between price controls (to keep energy cheaper) and allowing
energy prices to rise to the free market level (reducing the
demand and increasing the long-term supply) carries some
obvious implications for the economic well-being of the poor.

The poorest 10% of Americans spend about 34% of their
income on energy, by direct and indirect consumption. The

wealthiest 10%, while they spend more actual dollars on energy than the poorest, spend only about 5% of their income that way. When the price of energy rises by 100% (that is, when prices double) over a certain time period (and the price of oil has done so several times since 1973), the real income of all Americans falls, when we consider the effect of higher prices for all kinds of things that take energy to produce and transport to the consumer. But note that while the real income of the richest 10% of Americans falls by about 5%, the real income of the poorest 10% falls by 34%.[6]

But this is not the whole of the problem. When higher prices are charged, that money goes into *someone's* pocket. While some of those billions of dollars go into exploration for new energy, the whole amount accrues to owners of energy sources. Most energy resources are owned by corporations, and since the wealthiest 10% of all households own over 90% of all corporate stock, the best estimates are that the rise in incomes for that top 10% would be about five times larger than the fall in their income caused by the higher energy costs.[7] The doubling of energy prices causes a decrease in income for the poor and an increase in income for the rich. Relying simply on a "free market" in energy would severely *increase* the income inequality in the nation.

Considering these facts and the inquiry into energy policy of the last chapter, we must ask, How then might a small Christian community formulate operative norms for itself in preparation for promoting a more explicit operative norm for American energy policy?

Christian disciples ought to investigate carefully the debate surrounding a national energy policy and ought to join with other groups striving for justice to expect one another to build actual political and economic power to advance a specific set of proposals. Concrete examples include:

(a) empowering the entitlement claims of low-income people to the basic necessities either by keeping the price of energy low for them (for example, through regulations for "life-line" rates) or by reimbursing them for any rises in that price;

(b) supporting a reduction in the use of nonrenewable energy by subsidizing renewable energy alternatives and conservation technology and by charging a higher energy price for at least middle- and upper-income classes;

(c) developing standards within the local church for a simpler lifestyle that is more frugal in our individual use of energy.

As before, we would want to submit these norms to the reflection and discussion of both the small disciplined community and the wider network of justice-seeking organizations. The final form of operative norms for the nation can be developed only in the actual situation.

3. Competition

We need to examine a whole cluster of issues surrounding competition: Some problems are caused when it does not exist and some others even when it does. As we have just seen, capitalism relies on competition among firms to ensure that no firm will abuse the consumer's interests; even according to the defenders of capitalism, monopoly is dangerous. But our question has to do not with monopoly—strictly defined as the existence of *only one* firm in the industry serving a particular market. There are few examples of pure economic monopolies (telephone or electricity service in a town, for example), and these are generally regulated by government agencies. Rather, our concern is with the problems and injustices created where a few or even several large firms operate in an industry.

Economists recognize that in such a situation firms tend toward collusion to reduce supply and set prices. If the firms get together, they can increase their profits by agreeing to set a higher price for the product they make. For this scheme to work, all the firms making the agreement must be willing to reduce the quantity of the product they produce per year and must not undercut the agreed-upon price. Such agreements forming "cartels" are, of course, illegal under U.S. antitrust laws; this is one reason why economists consider such collusion less likely to occur. But in the view of most mainstream economists there is an even stronger reason why such agreements are unlikely to occur and last very long. That reason is self-interest. After such a collusive pact is made, it is in the self-interest of each of the firms to cheat on the agreement. Once the price is artificially raised, any one firm can increase its *own* profits if it sells more than the amount designated by the cartel. But if all the firms start doing this, we have competition again, and the price will fall back to the pre-agreement level. As introductory economics textbooks often say, such collusive agreements "tend to be unstable."[8]

Critics charge, however, that such optimism is naive. In Chapter 6 we saw some examples of the failure of competition. Let us consider one other—one that illustrates well how both justice and efficiency can be violated by the institutional structures of production.

The oil industry is, by technical economic standards, fairly competitive. Of course, the largest oil companies are huge; Exxon is the largest single firm in the world. But the largest three or five or seven oil companies do not together make up nearly as great a percentage of the oil market as do the largest three firms in steel or automobile or cigarette manufacturing. Economists see this as significant because even if the big seven oil companies colluded, they would have a lot of competition from other oil companies not part of their agreement.

A number of recent studies, however, have found that in spite of an apparently competitive structure, the oil industry—both before and after OPEC—has behaved in remarkably noncompetitive ways.[9] We cannot go into great detail here, but we can review at least a few of the findings.

John Blair, in his book *The Control of Oil,* traces the long fifty-year history of international agreement and "cooperation" among the major oil firms. In the early decades of the century the pacts were bold and explicit. In 1928 the three dominant international oil firms (the companies now known as Mobil, Shell, and British Petroleum) worked out the "As Is Agreement." Included among its provisions were the acceptance of the share of the market that each of the three held and an agreement not to allow a glut of oil in one part of the world to upset the stability of prices in any other area. This is but one example of a number of similar agreements involving most of the major oil companies.

In more recent decades, the major oil companies have employed more subtle procedures, but the result has been the same: Up to 1973 when OPEC quadrupled the price of oil, the price structure was kept fairly stable, with overall production growing just about as fast as consumer demand and with prices remaining constant or falling slowly. The key to such coordination of supply was the procedures for allocating production among the partners of a consortium—the cooperative undertaking of a number of oil companies to develop the resources of a particular nation. The procedures are intricate, and we will not reproduce Blair's explanation here. But suffice it to say that in spite of great variations in the year-to-year oil production of each of the countries now part of OPEC—these variations being caused by natural and political upheavals—the overall production of these countries *as a group* rose at a remarkably consistent rate between 1950 and 1972.[10] Rather than competition for greater profits that would pit the oil companies against each other, Blair argues that a concern for their own security and for the certainty of their *current* profits led the firms to price stability in the world of oil.

In 1973 and again in 1979, OPEC raised the price of oil dramatically. It did so by the means that cartels always employ: cutting back production and setting an artificially high price. At first, many economists doubted that OPEC could remain an effective cartel for long. Milton Friedman, for example, estimated that the tendency to cheat on the agreement would bring an end to OPEC in twelve to eighteen months' time. But this has not happened in spite of the fact that OPEC itself has only a weak structure internally and almost no means for monitoring compliance of its members—not to mention no means whatsoever for disciplining those who cheat on the cartel. Then how has the agreement lasted so long?

The answer according to industry critics like Blair seems to lie in the oil industry's decades-old practice of stabilizing the market. A representative bit of evidence indicating exactly this was inadvertently supplied by the chairman of the board of Exxon on national television in 1975. When asked to explain a recent dramatic cutback in oil production in the Middle East, the executive replied that Europe was having a recession and "our estimates of what the oil demand was going to be just didn't materialize, so we had to cut back."[11] According to orthodox economic theory, no competing oil company would act in this way; only a firm or group of firms that had the power to coordinate supply to equal demand at the going market price would do so. If Exxon were engaged in economic competition with other firms, cutting production would have done them no good and gasoline prices would have fallen during the recession. Prices did not fall. Blair contends that Exxon and the other oil companies prevented a glut and "stabilized" the market. Without the oil companies to coordinate output, he asserts, OPEC itself would collapse.[12]

The point of this whole discussion for our purposes is twofold. The first is that the structure of the production process—how firms are organized and how they relate to one another—is very significant for the overall attainment of justice and efficiency in the economy. Without such efforts at "stabilizing" oil markets, energy and almost everything else might be considerably less expensive; for the poor in particular the difference is enormous.

Second, we can see the important role that power plays in the economy. Economists tend to recognize and worry about political power and the ways that government influence is abused. But orthodox economists generally suffer from an advanced astigmatism that blurs the reality of economic power in situations where profit-maximizing competition conflicts with security-maximizing cooperation. Competition—the guarantor against injustice in capitalism—is less prevalent than the theory of free markets would indicate.

But if excesses of power entail injustice where competition breaks down, they can also do so—in a very different way—where competition works well. Consider a second example, where the free market and an unequal distribution of income *can* lead to starvation.

As we have seen, competition among agents in production—firms in an industry—is crucial to the capitalist vision of justice.

Without competition one firm or a few together will likely exploit consumers. With competition, it is said, we will have not only justice but, since the free operation of the price system accompanies competition, efficiency also. Why is this so according to the usual interpretation, and why must a moral assessment at points object?

When markets operate freely, valuable productive resources—such as steel for office buildings or machinery—are sold to the highest bidder. That buyer is able to bid that much for, let us say, a certain building because he or she can use that building in production, sell the product to consumers, and receive a return on his or her investment, a profit. There may be other producers who could also put that building to good use, but looking at consumer demand for *their* products, they must have decided it was not economically feasible for them to pay such a high price for the building. Instead, they purchase some less expensive structure.

Economists describe this process as the market allocation of resources (the building, in our example) *to their most productive employment.* Consumers, by the difference in their willingness to pay for the products of firms, determine how and where a multitude of different resources will actually be employed. The market system transmits that information to all participants by means of price. Similarly, when the cost of producing a product falls (as with calculators and computers in recent years) or rises (as with electricity), the changing prices transmit this new information to consumers, who make some adjustments in their buying patterns.

Consumers know how much it costs to produce each product not by doing research on the technological details of production but just by seeing the price of the product. Then employing their own value systems, consumers, it is said, set the values for the whole economic system by the choices they make in the market.

But what happens if some consumers are more wealthy than others? What if some, say Americans and Europeans, are much, much wealthier than others, say peasant farmers in Africa or Latin America? The answer is that consumers by their purchases still set the values for the whole economic system, but the wealthier the members of any one group are, the more effect they have on what will be produced. As we explained in Chapter 1, in this book we are generally limiting ourselves to examining economic life in the United States, as we are convinced that most debates about economics in the Third World are unresolvable without a prior analysis of the U.S. economy. Still, an understanding in the United States of the injustice caused by competition among consumers of vastly different incomes requires that for the moment we focus on life elsewhere.

From 1969 to 1974 a terrible drought occurred in the Sahel, that huge expanse of land cutting across several nations on the southern border of Africa's Sahara desert. Television reporters and journalists gave us vivid images of the dry creek beds, barren land, and starving people. The United Nations and other relief agencies sent hundreds of millions of dollars worth of grain to prevent massive starvation. Most Americans were rightly appalled at the extent of human suffering that afflicted these poorest of the world's poor. What was not made known was that during the height of the famine the Sahel exported far more agricultural products than were imported as food aid. Between 1970 and 1974, these countries were able to export $1.5 billion worth of food—three times the value of the grain imports to the region. How can this be?

When a farmer, whether in Iowa or Upper Volta, makes a decision about what to grow on a plot of land, the market gives him signals based on which crops will bring the most money. During the last several decades, parcel after parcel of land in the Third World has been shifted away from the production of local staple crops and into the production of crops for export to the wealthy nations of the world. This has happened in the Sahel.[13]

Long before the drought, the lure of greater income from cotton and peanuts reduced not only the acreage in grain crops but also the acreage that was traditionally left fallow for enrichment through crop rotation. Along with deeper plowing, this reduction impoverished the soil and made it more vulnerable to drought. During the drought, those farm lands still able to produce were used largely to produce export crops. The world market, operating as it was supposed to, allocated that farmland to its "most productive" use—measured, of course, by the "willingness" of consumers to pay. In effect, our ability to pay empowered us in the developed world to dictate the use of that land to help produce cotton clothing and peanut butter for us, rather than to grow millet and legumes to feed the local citizens in Africa.

The market mechanism, of course, is not the only cause for the malnutrition and death of so many in the Sahel. There *was* a drought, and the national governments did tax rural people heavily in supporting urban growth. It is also true that *some* citizens of the Sahelian nations profited greatly by those exports of agricultural products. But from the point of view of a Christian economic ethic, there is something fundamentally wrong when the ships that bring "relief" food depart with cargoes of peanuts, cotton, vegetables, frozen fish, and meat destined for other nations. Such economic "efficiency" is a terribly inefficient way to meet fundamental human needs.

We should note that in this case the market is working competitively. No single monopolist is twisting the system for his or her own selfish reward. The problem is one that economists have long recognized but little addressed: inequities in the distribution of income. The market system gains its appeal in situations where there are no grave disparities in economic power. But that is not the usual case. Even in the United States this problem is exhibited, for instance, in the systematic preference of building contractors for constructing middle- and upper-income houses rather than simpler housing for low-income people. On the world scale, our interest in having bananas on our breakfast cereal has the effect of keeping farmland in Guatemala from producing more food for local consumption. None of us intends any of these negative effects. No one wanted children of the Sahel to starve, but the market regularly does lead to such effects. Defenders of a worldwide free market simply do not see these outcomes as very significant in light of the good effects of the system's efficiency.

The Christian economic ethic, however, demands that the just entitlement of the poor be respected regardless of the benefits the rich may have to forgo.

We have seen then that the free market system, for all its benefits, can and does lead to injustice both when competition among producers fails and at times when competition brings about the allocation of resources as it is "supposed" to. We can now formulate an operative norm that might serve as a basis for reflection and action in the small Christian community attempting to strive for justice.

Christian disciples ought to join with other justice contenders to design specific justice projects to investigate and work against injustice in the production process. These projects might include:

(a) research and education in the ways large firms are not competing, and support for active enforcement of antitrust laws;

(b) study of the ways multinational firms act as agents for the wealthy of the world in allocating the resources of the Third World;

(c) resistance to U.S. government efforts to preserve a simple free market system internationally, and active support of Third World efforts toward establishing a new world order.

In each case, a small disciplined Christian community would need to shape a final and more concrete norm in the context of their local situation and in coordination with other groups supporting national and international efforts.

4. The Influence of Firms on Government
Another cluster of issues involving the structure of the economy in the process of production is the effect that producers can have on government in order to shape and condition the production process itself through governmental action. It is here that the tremendous growth in the size of firms has one of its most dramatic effects.

Adam Smith and others who were early promoters of free market economies understood the economy to be made up of a large number of relatively small firms. No one firm was thought to be crucial to the economy as a whole. But much has happened in two centuries, and one of the most fundamental changes has been the growth in the absolute size of firms. In nearly all fields, whether industry, trade, finance, or transportation, there is a trend toward larger and larger firms, often with a few giant corporations at the top and a larger number of smaller (yet often huge) firms below. As a result, both their importance to and their influence on government have changed.

Ever since the Great Depression, with the rising awareness that the government has to be actively involved in the economy, the growth in the size of firms has led to the conclusion that major firms cannot be allowed to go bankrupt. Congresses, both conservative and liberal, and presidents, both Democratic and Republican, have advocated government "bail-outs" of firms such as Lockheed and Chrysler as well as countless subsidies and legislative concessions to firms and industries whose health was judged to be crucial to the nation's economic well-being. No small firm could be so esteemed, but employers of hundreds of thousands of workers are viewed as too important to be allowed to fail. Even the market-minded Reagan administration granted billions of dollars in subsidies to firms unable to make a profit.[14]

The growth in the size of firms has also had a more direct effect on government. Very large firms (and other large organizations such as labor unions and trade and professional associations) can have a significant impact on the formation of policy through lobbying at the time a bill is being drawn up. Each year hundreds of millions of dollars are spent in this effort. Economists refer to this as "the special interest effect."

A small group with a lot to gain for each of its members is willing to spend a large amount of money to influence government. A very large group—usually consumers or taxpayers— may stand to lose the whole amount gained by the special interests just mentioned, but since each one of those consumers or taxpayers will not be losing very much, there is not much incentive for those individuals to resist the efforts of the special interests. For example, if ten firms in an industry would each year gain $1 million by some change in the law, they will be willing to spend large amounts of money to get it. If, say, ten million consumers are each likely to lose $1 from the scheme, probably not one of them would bother to go to the legislature or even to write a letter to fight it, since it would cost more to fight it than would be lost by ignoring it. In fact, since just getting the information on the scheme is costly in time and effort, very few of those consumers would even know about the plan in the first place.

We all hope, of course, that our elected representatives will possess the wisdom not to promote narrow, special-interest legislation that will actually treat consumers or taxpayers unjustly. But there are two major reasons why our hopes might be in vain. The first is based on the requirements for being elected and reelected to office. It takes money, lots of money. In many election races, the size of the campaign budget determines the winner. In almost every race, either candidate can be assured of victory by raising twice as much money as the opponent does. Contributions come from the widely successful political action committees (PACs) and directly from individuals, including lobbyists themselves. As long as big money has such influence, special interests tend to dominate.

The second reason why legislators may succumb to the pressures of special interest groups is the same reason why the general public might do so. Narrow interests can at times appear less narrow when wrapped with the cloak of wider national concerns. Consider two examples from the realm of energy again.

The Alaskan oil pipeline was justified by the oil companies on the grounds that the United States should not be so dependent on foreign sources of oil. But just as opponents predicted, no sooner was the pipeline completed than the glut of oil on the West coast led oil companies to petition Congress for the right to sell Alaskan oil to Japan. A second, similar confusion between the interest of the firm and the interest of the nation is apparent in the argument by the major oil companies that they needed full decontrol of oil

and gasoline prices to attain higher profits to finance more exploration. Some expansion in exploration has occurred, but since
then we have seen several oil companies use their profits instead
to buy other firms. The firms purchased ranged from newspapers to retail chains. Mobil, probably the biggest culprit in this
regard, bought Montgomery Ward, tried to buy Conoco, and
tried, again unsuccessfully, to buy Marathon oil, offering over $6
billion—almost *twice* the amount it budgeted for capital and
exploration the year before![15] Marathon, we might note, was in
the end bought by U.S. Steel, a firm that got a good share of its
profits through government protection from foreign steel—a
policy justified before Congress on the grounds that the American
steel companies needed higher profits to replace aging steel
plants.

Is the democratic process then being violated by the vicious
intents of the wealthy and powerful? Not exactly. There need be
no viciousness or malice involved. Rather, what we have is an
economic system that clashes with our political ideals of democracy as rule by the people for the people. We authorize self-
interested and rational business firms (and other well-heeled
organizations) to lobby Congress to attain what they want. As
Randall Bartlett puts it, the system, and not the motives of the
participants, is the key.

> The world is an imperfect place, and the systems which operate in
> it suffer this same fate of imperfection. This is not the result of evil
> conspiracies or radical alterations in the assumed nature of the
> agents in an economic system. Yet we must conclude that when
> we turn our self-interested, rational individuals loose in a world of
> uncertainty their behavior will impart a degree of partial paralysis
> to Adam Smith's famed invisible hand.[16]

A major flaw emerges whenever big business publicly or
secretly organizes to wield power over the political process. Such
business power usually is not held accountable because wielders
of power seldom acknowledge their ability to influence, to persuade, and to offer rewards or deprivations. Direct and indirect
uses of funds are available for many forms of stringpulling and

manipulation. Organized big business is unquestionably a center of enormous power. What is an efficient use of funds from the point of view of the firm leads to significant injustice within the economy as a whole.

What can any of us do about this? Here as elsewhere, there is no magic wand. Some people, including such free-market advocates as Milton Friedman, have argued that since the powers of government are twisted to support narrow interests, the powers of government should be severely reduced. Of course, it is no coincidence that these people, including Friedman, generally hold that individual freedom is the single most important element in human life. This overemphasis on individual freedom is a misunderstanding both of what psychology and sociology have taught us about the way human life is and of what the Judeo-Christian tradition has held about the way human life ought to be. It is our conviction that Christians and others in America must strive to eliminate these abuses of influence so as to enable the American people to resolve their disagreements and form national policy with the fewest possible distortions caused by narrow special interests.

We can now formulate an operative norm for justice-seekers addressing the influence exerted on government by agents in the production process.

Committed disciples and other justice contenders ought to expect one another to undertake specific projects to understand better and limit the influence exerted on government by large economic interests. Specifically this might entail any or all of the following sorts of efforts:

(a) research into the self-interested efforts of big business and other large economic actors that conflict with the public interest;

(b) support for full public disclosure of the budgets and activities of all lobbyists at the national and state levels;

(c) support for stronger campaign financing laws at all levels of government to reduce the influence of wealthy interests;

(d) active participation in widespread public action or citizens'-lobby organizations that press legislators for democratizing reforms in their election and legislation procedures.

Each small disciplined community will have to decide for itself which resources and existing organizations to rely on. A number of publications can help in their research efforts—for example, *The Corporate Examiner* and *Multinational Monitor.* Many areas have "good government" organizations locally; Common Cause is an example of a group pushing for election and legislative reform on the national and state level.

Only the naively optimistic will think that such reforms as we have just suggested will end *all* problems of special interests in politics. Even if persons with greater wealth, and small groups with much to gain, were to be prevented from making large financial contributions to political campaigns, narrow special interests could still have a somewhat disproportionate effect on the political process by contributing, say, volunteer time to one candidate's campaign rather than another's. A labor union, for example, could provide such volunteer services in exchange for a candidate's support of a bill that would increase the demand for union labor. Still, it is clear that reducing the influence of financial contributions to campaigns would greatly reduce the current abuses whereby small groups of citizens can have an effect vastly disproportionate to their numbers.

5. The Internal Operation of the Firm

The third and last group of issues involving the organization of the production process centers on the internal life of the firm. A business firm is an organization of persons working together in the production of goods and/or services. While each person in the firm has certain instrumental goals in mind—making a living being the principal one—the firm is more than just an instrument. It is a network of human relationships. And since most Americans, for about forty years of their life, spend about half of their waking hours from Monday to Friday *living within* that network of human relationships, the firm plays an immensely influential role in shaping the character of the citizens of the nation.

Sociologists have amply demonstrated how each of us is influenced and changed by the social setting we find ourselves in. When we move our residence to a different state or city we slowly pick up habits or preferences or at times even an accent to our speech that would have been quite foreign to us previously. Some of the most important ways in which we are shaped, however, are not so obvious as these. We can notice these because we can compare two living situations where "the way we do things" differs from one situation to the other. The most important shaping of us as persons usually occurs through taken-for-granted procedures that are the same no matter which city or town we have lived in. And because we are not aware of places or situations where things are done differently, we tend to presume that "the way we do things" is "the way things are done." To take one example, North Americans are often struck by Latin Americans' different sense of time. For most of us, a two o'clock meeting might get started twenty minutes late because some people failed to get there "on time," but it is incredible to us that it might began an hour and a half or even two hours late. In traditional Latin American culture, not an eyebrow would be raised.

We have already seen, in Chapter 1, the single most important element in the shaping of behavior and attitudes that the social setting effects: the norms that are operative in a group of people. We can enumerate the ways that business firms shape the people who are a part of them by listing the norms that are operative there (i.e., that the members of that group expect one another to live up to). Employees are expected to be punctual; they are expected to be civil in their dealings with one another; they are expected to work diligently. Of course, the boss will always expect a subordinate to do these things, but our point is that if all or most of the people in the work situation do *not* expect one another to do these things, they probably will not be done.

If, then, the firm is a major influence on the character of the lives of most people, what can the Christian ethic say about the way these organizations operate? Let us first look at the question of the *size* of the firms and then turn our attention to their *goals*.

As firms, or any other social organizations, grow in size, there develops a corresponding growth in the sense of irresponsibility on the part of the people who make up the firm. It is not that people in large firms are untrustworthy, but rather that in larger organizations people tend to define their responsibilities more narrowly and are less likely to expect one another to be at all involved in matters not specifically assigned to them.

John Lachs has analyzed this development by considering the more basic phenomenon of "mediation," which he defines as the performance of an action by one person on behalf of another. Society is made possible by such mediation. I expect my newspaper to be delivered, and I pay the mechanic to fix my car. Depending on others who specialize in the performance of certain types of action is an example of "the division of labor" that Adam Smith and others have recognized as a crucial element in the growth of the wealth of any nation. But Lachs reminds us that mediation also has three major negative effects, and these tend to worsen as an organization grows.[17]

The first effect is the manipulation of people. If I want to have someone else do something for me, that person all too easily can come to have only an instrumental value to me. Such persons will help me get what I want, but I may not even reflect on the fact that they are persons who are valuable *apart* from what they do. If I am a middle or upper-middle manager, I may not ever even *see* the people who ultimately carry out my decisions. If people below me feel used, they in turn often treat others as means to be manipulated for their own ends.

The second result is passivity. As the chain of mediated action gets longer and longer in a large organization, people's jobs get defined more and more in terms of doing this or that action. Employees may be very busy, so they are not passive in the sense that they are not doing anything. Rather, since the initial motives for a particular activity come from outside (from someone higher up the chain of mediated action), workers feel detached from the action they perform. They learn to do what their jobs require. They learn to put their own creativity on hold. They learn to be passive.

The last result of mediation is "psychic distance." Only those who finally perform the action see its immediate consequences. Those who initiated the chain of mediation are interested in the particular consequence that was the *purpose* of the activity, yet attaining this purpose will not be its only effect. The board of directors or president of a firm may make a decision that has unintended negative consequences (for employees or for people living near the plant or for consumers) that do not appear to the decision makers to be as severe as they actually are. In fact, the psychic distance may be so great that the decision makers may not even notice the hardships imposed. When a corporate headquarters in California decides to close a plant in the Northeast and move it to the Sunbelt, the very size of the firm makes it less likely that the policy makers are even aware of the costs they are imposing on others by the move. With the rapid growth of firms that we have observed in the recent past, this problem is getting more and more severe.

Thus, the increase in the size of the firm has had crucially important effects on the ways the people who make up the firm are shaped. Superiors tend more and more to treat those under them as instruments rather than persons. Subordinates at any level tend to become more passive and tend to take less and less responsibility for events outside their own job description. Those at the top level of control, the board of directors, become more and more distant from and uninformed about the actual consequences of their decisions. Unless these tendencies are counteracted by some concrete transformation of the structure of the firm, the people making up the organization become less fully human and the external effects of the firm become more inhumane. We will present shortly an operative norm that will address this problem, but first we will turn to the second part of the problem.

We have been looking at the effects that *size* has on the internal operation of the firm, but we must also consider the effects of the *goals* and *charter* of the firm in the first place. We have seen how the modern understanding of property—coming primarily from John Locke—presumes nearly absolute control by the owner over the object possessed. Following this conception of ownership, American law has chartered the business corporation, granting it the status of legal person before the law. As the initial Lockean understanding of property was flawed, so too is the form of the corporation that exists today.

The firm, of course, is not just the stockholders or their representative on the board of directors. The firm includes all the persons who make their livelihood in that social organization. Yet only those who own the buildings and tools (the stockholders) are recognized as having a right to decide on company policy. Excluding employees from any direct part in decision making led in the early industrialization of England and the United States to extreme abuses of workers of all ages. Still today many employees in dangerous situations must struggle to force companies to increase safety, and workers everywhere have only indirect influence on the behavior of the firm.

The public, too, is excluded from a share in control of the firm, in spite of the fact that huge modern firms have dramatic impacts on their environments. This is true whether the issue is the pollution that may poison lakes hundreds of miles away or a plant closing that devastates a community when the firm moves its operation to an area with lower taxes and lower wages. Since the ownership of property should be seen to include a responsibility to others and should recognize the just entitlement claims of the poor, the firm acts unjustly when it ignores the costs of lakes killed by acid rain and towns and cities withering away as capital flees.

What can the Christian disciple do in response? We can now formulate an operative norm for striving for justice in the internal operation of big businesses.

Committed disciples should join with other justice contenders to expect one another to undertake specific projects designed to transform the internal operation of one business firm in their area. Specifically, this might entail any of the following kinds of efforts:

(a) support to unions or un-unionized workers' groups in their efforts to improve physical and psychological health and safety of the workplace;

(b) participation in stockholder resolutions aimed at increasing the firm's operative level of responsibility toward workers and the public;

(c) active support in the political process for laws requiring worker and public representation on boards of directors. This might follow the example of West Germany, where "codetermination" is a legal requirement; that is, firms must have representatives of labor on their boards;

(d) political advocacy of public purchase and ownership of firms in crucial industries that cannot be responsibly run by other means.

Once again, each disciplined community will have to develop its own operative norm in its own context. In many areas, efforts are already going on that disciples can assist. In other situations, a community may initiate a project and find others to assist. In all cases, careful analysis and the development of the power to make norms operative is the key. The process begins within the small disciplined community and is repeated in successively larger groups within the society.

Summary

In this chapter we have been examining the interplay of social justice and economic efficiency. We began by outlining six elements essential to the Christian notion of social justice:
1. the just entitlement of the poor;
2. the limited right of property ownership;
3. the reorientation of personal life;
4. the transformation of social structure;
5. the use of countervailing power;
6. the reliance on democratic decision making.
We then addressed a number of concrete problems where narrow economic efficiency clashes with justice. We saw these under five

headings: welfare programs, the income effects of energy policy, competition, influence on government, and the internal operation of the firm.

The problems we addressed are found within larger social structures that require transformation. We called this situation the third arena where the effort for justice must take place. In moving toward that very wide and resistant set of social structures, we spoke of the need for work with other justice-seeking groups, whether specifically Christian or not. We referred to this as the second arena for our working for justice. Such alignment with other groups in shaping wider social structures is essential.

Yet the first efforts that Christian disciples must make in their seeking of justice are those within the small disciplined Christian community. We have not yet systematically addressed this crucially important first arena, and it is that topic to which we now turn.

9

Empowerment Through Small Disciplined Communities

There is an old children's story about a group of mice who were deliberating about how to solve the problem of the local cat who regularly caught and ate members of their clan. After considerable discussion and much hemming and hawing, one young mouse proposed the perfect solution. Since the problem was that the cat would sneak up on unsuspecting mice, the whole matter could be resolved by making the cat more conspicuous: Simply tie a bell around the cat's neck, and everyone would hear him coming from far away. The whole group rejoiced to hear such a brilliant solution to their problem. No longer would mice have to live in fear. At that point, however, an elderly member of the group asked a question that put an end to the celebrating: "Who will bell the cat?" Knowing that no mouse could tie a bell on the cat before encountering an untimely demise, the mice agreed that the basic problems in life cannot be solved, and they adjourned their meeting.

Christians and others attending to issues of economic justice face a similar problem. How can any one person or small group of persons have any effect on national and international problems? Having spent the bulk of this book looking into what the Christian economic ethic calls for in economic life, we must now face this question, How do we put these aims into practice?

We have already seen the basic outline of an answer in Chapter 1. In this final chapter we will outline in more detail how a small group of justice seekers can begin to relate to one another and to their world in ways that make a difference. No one small group will alter national economic structures by itself, of course, but in coordination with a few other such groups, local patterns can begin to change. And when a large enough number of groups press for fundamental change, even national expectations and structures are altered. The Montgomery bus boycott and the civil rights movement have demonstrated this.

In this book we address ourselves primarily to Christians seeking to live a life of faith according to the challenge Christ has put before us. Many others in this country and the rest of the world who are not practicing Christians are also struggling for greater justice. While we center on what Christians can and must do, we do not want to create the impression that it is likely that justice-seeking Christians alone will be able to transform the nation. In fact, without "networking" with all sorts of other groups that are also working for economic justice, it is doubtful that basic change could come about. Even *with* such cooperation the task is monumentally difficult.

We will address the issue of networking later in this chapter. For now we will examine the life of the "small disciplined community," a group of Christians working for social justice. First we should review what we have already learned about how social change comes about in society, by returning to the analysis of operative norms begun in Chapter 1.

Operative Norms and Social Change

Most social change occurs without much thought about it. Whether we look at the historic changes brought about by the industrial revolution in the eighteenth century or at the influence on American life caused by the invention of television in the twentieth, the life patterns of individuals and nations most often shift without people exercising much control over the process. There are two major reasons for this.

The first is that most changes in our lives come gradually. There are, of course, abrupt and dramatic changes in life—as when an agricultural family loses its farm in hard times and must move to the city, or when a long-time employee is laid off in a recession. These and similar occurrences have been all too common, even in the past few years, and we do not mean to make light of the terrible hardship these events cause. Still, most change is slower and less visible from close range.

Any clear vision of a major social change usually requires a perspective that only is possible many years later when the cumulative effects of small changes are visible. For all the influence of television on our culture, none of us believes it is a monumental decision whether we will watch this or that program, or whether we will not watch television at all on a particular night. Yet our nation has a far different character now that the average family watches four hours of television each day. Patterns of recreation, of reading, and of family interaction are very different because of the influence of television, even though no one set out to change those patterns and even though few people have been conscious of the changes brought about by television in their own lives. Similarly gradual changes have occurred in work patterns at the place of employment, in the procedures for election to political office, and in a myriad of other phases of life.

The second reason why people exercise so little control over social change is that current patterns of interaction and current trends in a particular direction are difficult to alter. Even when we are conscious of developments that are unhealthy or inhumane, we are usually at a loss to find a remedy. Anyone who has objected to the operating procedures at the local auto dealer's service department or at the offices of local government knows that even on a relatively small scale, change is hard to accomplish. When we consider patterns of interaction that have been going on for decades or centuries in a nation, it is no wonder that change is not easy. And in addition to the force of habit and tradition, there is what we might call the force of history: Certain new conditions exist and cannot be ignored or turned back. For example, with the industrial revolution came the development of remarkably productive factory systems that could produce far more from the same amount of labor and raw materials than had ever before been possible. There was a kind of inevitable force to the changes brought about by the industrial factory. It was not impossible to continue spinning and weaving in the traditional manner; it was just that the cloth produced that way was now so much more costly than factory-produced textiles that consumers would not pay more for homespun even though it was harder to produce.

Thus when we ask why people ordinarily have so little control over social change, the answer is that they are at times unaware of the changes taking place and even when they are aware and try to stop or influence such change, it is terribly difficult to do so.

We can draw three lessons from this. The first is that it is a major job just to "keep up" with the developments in our societal life. Reading newspapers and periodicals critically and staying aware of current events and conditions is essential to living responsibly in our age. The second is that we need to address very carefully the task of empowering ourselves and others to bring about structured change in our institutional lives. The third is that whether or not we strive to shape our institutions, their very existence depends on our accepting and internalizing their operative norms. Social change, whether for better or for worse, cannot occur without the majority of participants in the group coming to think differently about what they should be doing.

Thus, our stress in this book on the importance of operative norms is not foreign to the way even strong individualist non-believers and fundamentalist Christians live their lives. They too live out of operative norms that are the cement of every institution they inhabit. The difference is that those who ignore social ethics are inadvertently legitimating whatever institutional patterns happen to exist at the time. This is irresponsible.

As we outlined in Chapter 1, any group of Christians who want to live according to the demands of the gospel will have to be attentive to the elements required for shaping sound moral structures. Let us return briefly to the diagram we used there.

FIGURE 1
Building Sound Moral Structures

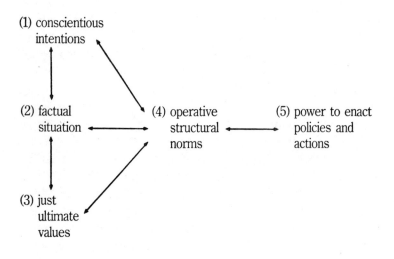

   In Chapter 1 we recounted the events of the Montgomery bus boycott, that crucial step in the civil rights movement. While the boycott, by itself, did not directly affect blacks outside the city, it became a focus of national and even international attention and empowerment. A sound new moral structure began to arise from inner critical moral consciences (1) and from roots in the ultimate values of the gospel (2). Mrs. Parks' action became a trigger that set in motion a new operative norm, with its expectations of new boycotting, especially on the part of blacks (3). Almost of one accord blacks, with some white participation, began their "walk for freedom," catalyzed by Mrs. Parks.
   This operative norm can be expressed verbally as follows:

Responsible citizens should expect one another to refuse to ride buses until unjust seating arrangements are abolished (4).

This produced a crescendo of power that mobilized new policies and actions (5). Soon the civil rights movement enlarged the norms in order to challenge other forms of segregation and discrimination.

Any persons experiencing God's call to greater justice and wanting to generate the power necessary for shaping social structures will need to develop appropriate operative norms. For those struggling for economic justice in society, these norms must be based, first of all, on conscientious intentions. Without this crucial element of individual honesty and faithfulness, even just ultimate values will be subverted by the self-serving interests of manipulative social activists. What is needed is a solid spirituality and a strong personal integrity in the pursuit of justice.

At the same time, without sound ultimate values even the best-intentioned Christians can legitimate tragically unjust burdens simply by ignoring them. For example, the leaders of the so-called Moral Majority have demonstrated a thorough misunderstanding of the justice demands of the Christian tradition. In order to grasp just ultimate values, Christian stewards must engage the historical tradition of Christianity with theological integrity and must be willing to be open to secular criticism of that tradition. Such criticism is required because of the effects of both sin and finitude in Christians, who, after all, are human like everyone else. For example, Christians in the last century learned much from secular critics of church stances on slavery, and we have much to learn from secular sources today on such topics as feminism and the role of women in church life. This is not to say that non-Christians have little to learn from the Christian tradition, but rather that Christians must be open to prophetic critique from any source in their efforts to act out of sound ultimate values.

Equally important is careful attention to the factual situation. Here we include both the insights of psychology, economics, political science, and sociology, as well as good old-fashioned "savvy" about how groups operate and about what is possible within this particular grouping at this time. When a group does not attend to the empirical situation, it often sets unrealistic goals and eventually dissolves in discouragement in the face of recurrent failure.

Studying the Christian tradition and discovering the just ultimate values there is no easy task. We have spent much of this book doing simply that. Still, the shortcoming most prevalent among Christians who begin with the minimal belief that we need a more just society is naivete about the practical possibilities in a particular situation. Any norm the group proposes for its own life or for the life of a larger network of groups must be a feasible next step for those involved.

If the norm requires too much, the majority will find it too difficult and will not believe it ought to be lived out. Recall Harry M. Johnson's definition of an *operative* norm as distinct from an impotently abstract norm:

> An "operative" norm is one that is not merely entertained in the mind but is considered worthy of following in actual behavior; thus, one feels that one ought to conform to it.[1]

Operative norms create in their users a feeling that the norms are "worthy" of being followed in actual behavior; hence obedience is not an unpleasant experience. In addition, such norms depend upon an inner sense of "ought" to motivate public conformity. Thus, black leaders in Montgomery did not propose that black people stop paying their rent (and risk eviction) or go on strike (and face indiscriminate firings and violence in a racist economic situation). This would be asking too much of people. Good stewards have responsibilities to kin and friends that restrain them from sacrificing too much even in a good cause. (Forgoers in the group may be willing to make such sacrifices for the greater good. This sort of remarkable generosity is a grace to the group, but it should not be preached as a rigid norm for all Christians.)

At the same time, the norm proposed should not ask too little of people. In the short run, people may prefer not to face the difficulties entailed in a challenging norm, but in the longer term such efforts to "bring along" everyone (by not asking too much) risk losing the participation of those who know that more has to be done to secure just social structures.

We have, then, a general outline for building sound moral structures. We can now look more closely at the basic group that takes for its task this effort of beginning to restructure institutional life toward greater justice.

The Small Disciplined Community

None of us is going to change social structures alone. We all know that if any such change is to take place, very large numbers of people need to be working together. This was (and is) clearly true of the civil rights movement. It is true of the efforts to overcome the sexism so deeply ingrained in our society. It has been true in the labor movement from the beginning. Coordinated effort is required.

We address this volume to those who seek to live out the Christian economic ethic in their lives. This is not to ignore those who approach economic morality from other perspectives, whether religious or secular; in fact, these others are essential to the efforts Christians put forth. However, we will center on the process within a Christian context, presuming that the reader will be situated within the Christian tradition and will be working most directly with others who share the calling of Christ.

We propose to call the basic justice-seeking group within the Christian framework "the small disciplined community." We call it a *community* because its success depends on the willingness of its participants not just to share a series of public activities but also to share in a real way their faith and vision and to be open to altering their own way of life through interaction with the others in the group. We call it a *small* community because it will usually not have more than fifteen or twenty members, and sometimes may start with only four or five. Most often the group will likely be a subgroup of a larger congregation, perhaps a standing committee on social issues or social justice. Sometimes it will simply be a group of people who band together because of an interest in living out the justice demands of the gospel more fully. Sometimes the group will be the institutional leadership of a religious order of sisters, priests, or brothers. (While we address ourselves primarily to "stewards" and not principally to "forgoers" in religious orders, the analysis we present concerning the small disciplined community can apply to the justice-seeking efforts of all Christians.)

We refer to this group as a small *disciplined* community because of the absolute need for carefully attending to the requirements for changing institutionalized patterns. "Disciplined" here does not mean that there must be a long list of rules for the group to live by, but it does mean that the group members must agree to empower the others in the group to expect certain behavior of them. In the language of the Hebrew scriptures the group must strike a covenant. The key is the difference between individual and structured action that we detailed in Chapter 1.

Even within a group it is possible to engage in merely individual action. If each person intends to do only what he or she wants, then individual action is the predominant element in the group. (However, even a very loosely defined group gathered around, say, a common hobby or interest must engage in some sorts of structured action or it would not be a group at all.)

Structured action occurs when members of any group expect or require one another to enact certain patterns of behavior. Anyone who is not willing to allow a group to define at least *some* behaviors (e.g., time of meetings, procedures at meetings) has no real reason for joining any group. In fact, in nearly all groups that are of any importance to their members, patterns of expected behavior predominate. (This fact is far more visible to outsiders than to group members.)

The difference in a small disciplined community is that the group members are critically conscious of the patterns of action expected. They self-consciously discuss just what they will expect of one another. This may entail an agreement that each member will do a certain amount of reading in preparation for an issue to be discussed at the next meeting. It may involve the decision that each member will ask the others to expect him or her to arrive on time for each meeting. The group will certainly need to be careful not to legislate minor details, but most existing groups have little problem with this. The most difficult thing for most people is getting used to the idea of belonging to a group that so self-consciously sets out to define what its internal expectations will be.

To some, all this may seem like just too much rule-setting. However, as we saw in earlier chapters, social life is possible only because of the patterned expectations people have of one another. In most circumstances, though, we are not conscious of the expectations we live out (because as operative norms, those expectations seem like reasonable ones that any person should be willing to follow and that do not seem so hard to follow anyway). Whether part of a national movement to restrict armaments and military aid or part of an attempt to raise the level of consciousness in our own congregation over the plight of the unemployed in our neighborhood, the small disciplined community must attend to the question: What prevailing norms are we challenging, and what better norms do we want to empower in their place?

Since this is the aim, even group life within the small community needs to be attuned to the question of which norms are operative and which are not. Individualism finds such accountability within the group to be a threat to its vision of freedom of the individual. A healthier understanding of both the individual and social dimensions of the human person helps us realize that empowering others to expect certain things of us (and vice versa) increases human freedom and opens up the possibility for greater and more humane influence over the socially expected patterns that make up what are more technically called "social structures."

One very creative approach to developing a small intentional community has been provided by The Center for the Ministry of the Laity. In what Dick Broholm and others in the Boston area call *"covenanted support for ministry,"* we find a helpful set of guidelines for developing vibrant Christian communities whose life is directed out into the larger world. Let us look at each of the three terms individually.

The group forms and periodically redrafts a *covenant* for itself.

> To covenant is to promise, to commit to, to become obligated; it means that come what may, we are "in this together." To covenant with one another reflects the covenant that God has made with us; to covenant with one another says "the Word did become flesh and dwell among us and continues to dwell among us as we gather together."[2]

What is happening here, of course, is what we have called empowering operative norms. And while the terminology used in this book is borrowed from the modern discipline of sociology, the idea itself is based on the fundamental dynamic of covenanting that has been the basis of the whole Judeo-Christian tradition: God's covenant with Israel. The insights of the modern era into the workings of group life lead us to realize that all groups have an implicit covenant among the group members. The covenanting process within the small disciplined community merely makes explicit (and improves) what goes on at an unconscious level in every group.

The group members work at providing *support* for one another.

> There are really two essential ingredients, two essential gifts that come in support. The first, which we often think of, is the gift of *communion,* which means nurture or encouragement, to uphold or to comfort.
>
> The second, which is less often recalled, is the gift of *agency,* which means to enable or move to action. It means to get unstuck, to discover alternatives for acting and to move on them.[3]

The two effects of communion and agency are crucial. Through the group's prayer and reflection the members ground themselves in the faith they share. Through open discussion and mutual challenge the members solidify their personal lives and support each other to act hopefully in what are often discouraging situations.

In gathering, the group members are aware that their lives participate in the *ministry* of Christ and his church.

> We gather together for a specific purpose—to encourage and enable one another's struggle to be faithful in the midst of confusing and ambiguous choices and actions, on the job, at home, in the community, and as global citizens. It is where we reflect on the meaning we give to our actions, relationships and work. It is a base from which we plan and move into actions that result from the inner meanings that are important to us.[4]

Each member of the group is involved in a number of different settings in life: work, home, church, clubs, other organizations. As the laity center makes clear, Christians can minister in each of these situations. The center itself is designed to encourage groups created to support this diversity of ministry.

This kind of support is a key part of the life of the small disciplined community as well, although the main focus of the latter is communion and agency for social ministry. That is, since it aims at transforming structures, the group will often engage in endeavors that are shared by most or all its members—something not necessarily true when a support group aims principally to provide encouragement to the work that people are already doing in a wide variety of occupational and social settings.

Each small disciplined community is unique, but most find that the group centers its outreach efforts on only two or three projects (or perhaps even one) at a time. Thus while the group does provide support for transformative activity in the many different work and social settings members live within, it also goes beyond support and becomes the place where members study and actually plan and bring about common efforts aimed at transforming the world within which the small disciplined community exists.

As The Center for the Ministry of the Laity and other groups have developed materials that are helpful in forming such a group and developing the relationship-building skills necessary to sustain such a group, we will not develop here many of the elements of group life with which the reader will want to become familiar.

But it should be clear that careful attention and hard work are needed.[5]

The Work of the Small Disciplined Community

We have spoken in this chapter in more general terms about the mutual accountability that the small disciplined community must generate in its midst. We need now to look at two topics in particular that the group will normally address in its own midst. These are the need for a careful self-education on all issues addressed and a discussion of the consumption patterns of group members as stewards of God's gifts in a world where poverty is the normal lot in life for the majority of people on the earth. We will then look at a typical "issue" that the small disciplined community might take on in each of the three arenas outside the group: the local congregation, the network of justice-seeking groups in that geographic area, and the national and international economic realm.

1. Self-education: Study and Involvement

Each small disciplined community needs to provide for its self-education. This problem should be addressed in the group whether or not it is also done in a larger network of which the smaller group of stewards is a part. In many cases self-education occurs very effectively in cooperation with other justice-seeking groups that also aim to learn more about the issues. Still, in most cases the small disciplined community will feel the need to begin its education internally in a careful manner.

Assume, as an example, that a small disciplined community was formed in 1983 in a particular congregation and that during the first two meetings it became clear that one strong interest of the group was the plight of the many unemployed and under-employed in the area. The members decide to become better informed about the issues, and each takes on a task prior to the next meeting.

Some will visit the local institutions that serve the poor and unemployed in the area, including a visit to a labor union considering the purchase of a plant that has been shut down, and another to a group in a nearby church that one of the members has heard is planning to open a soup kitchen. Others set out to find and become familiar with some articles in thoughtful periodicals on the same problem in the nation as a whole.

As a part of the next meeting, a young computer programmer named Sarah proposes to the group that everyone read an article entitled "Revising the Budget: Bad News for the Poor" by Robert Greenstein, which appeared in *Christianity and Crisis*, a periodical to which Sarah subscribes. She regards this essay as required study for all who are to be trained to understand that, while the President is claiming that the really impoverished are still being helped by his "safety net," large budget reductions definitely mean a decrease in federal support for the poor.

At that point Jim, an insurance agent, and Mary, a homemaker, both question Sarah's polarizing the issue politically. Isn't the problem, they ask, just that the nation is going through a recession, which has, of course, been particularly hard on those laid off from their jobs? Accusing the President of lying is not, they believe, the way to start off.

Sarah responds that lying may not be the problem but that she believes the Administration is being misleading. Then she begins to explain the Greenstein "story." First, she summarizes Greenstein, who began his report with a quote from President Reagan. On April 13, 1982, the President addressed 100 national religious leaders. In his speech Reagan said: "Overall social spending on the part of the government is up. . . . (W)e're maintaining our fundamental commitment to the poor." Greenstein then stressed that all of us need to ". . . avoid concluding that because overall spending on what the Administration calls 'social programs' is up, therefore the basic support programs for the poor share in this growth. . . . Spending for these programs would in fact be reduced."[6]

Mary answers that she believes greater justice means that social programs were the part of the budget that needed increasing. Sarah outlines Greenstein's description of two types of "social programs" run by the federal government:

(a) Those available to all persons regardless of their income; namely, Social Security, Medicare, civil service retirement, and military retirement. These four programs comprise the vast bulk of federal spending for "social programs." . . . The incomes of most of these recipients, including about 85% of all persons on Social Security and Medicare, are above the poverty line.

Now to the second set of "social programs" provided largely by federal and state governments. Here we find:

(b) "social programs" targeted for *low income* people. Here is the complex of welfare services for the poor.

We look next to the dollar costs of both the (a) and (b) "social programs." In the four category (a) programs—Social Security, Medicare, civil service retirement, and military retirement—the 1983 budget called for more than $275 billion. These clearly constitute the vast bulk of all federal spending for so-called "social programs." Turning to the category (b) "social programs" we encounter the popular assumption that these services consume huge proportions of the federal budget. In truth, their combined cost amounts to only ten percent of it. Dollar figures for the most costly category (b) programs show that costs will run about $8 billion in 1983 for Aid to Dependent Children and $11.5 billion for food stamps. In contrast, allocations for category (a) show about $15 billion for military retirement, about $20 billion for federal civil service retirement, about $50 billion for Medicare, and about $150 billion for Social Security.[7] Sarah goes on to quote Greenstein:

Under the Reagan budget, appropriations for the low income programs would fall *from about $100 billion in fiscal 1981* (the last pre-Reagan budget year) *to about $62 billion in fiscal 1983.* . . . Despite his words to the contrary, President Reagan has *not* proposed simply to "slow the rate of growth" of these programs.[8]

Another group member then says he believes that although military and civil service pensions are clearly *not* for the poor, at least some of the social security payments are going to the poor and that part of this program should be counted under the category (b) programs. Others, including Sarah, agree. Still, she responds, the poor are definitely worse off in spite of the President's statements that implied they were not.

Our basic point here is that this group is off to a good start at educating itself on the issue. Group members must be willing to dig into an issue and to say openly what is on their minds, even when (or especially when) there is significant disagreement. Throwing chairs at one another is out, but a healthy debate can only help in the group's knowledge of the factual situation prior to developing operative norms.

A second major part of the self-education process is involvement—involvement in the struggles for justice in society. People usually think of participation in justice activities as the end result, the outcome, of a process of study, reflection and decision. And it is. But it is also a crucial *part* of the study and reflection that goes into the process in the first place.

The point, of course, is that our reflection is based on our lived experience, and the experience of struggling for justice will affect how we later think about and act within justice movements. Joe Holland and Peter Henriot, in their *Social Analysis: Linking Faith and Justice,* use the term "insertion" to refer to this "being involved," and they name it as the first moment of the process of responding to injustice. If a small disciplined community is to develop and empower an operative norm for a situation, the questions that Holland and Henriot suggest concerning insertion are a helpful part of the group's self-education:

> Where and with whom are we locating ourselves as we begin our process? Whose experience is being considered? Are there groups that are "left out" when experience is discussed? Does the experience of the poor and oppressed have a privileged role to play in the process?[9]

These are important questions for anyone who wants to work for justice, but they are particularly important for stewards who are among the "successful" in our economy. The reason is that economically successful stewards have most or all of their interpersonal contacts with other "successful" Americans. As a result the "successful" generally have little or no direct experience whatever of the injustice of our economic system or of the people on whose shoulders the weight of that injustice falls. It is only through involvement with persons who suffer from and struggle against injustice that economically successful stewards can really come to know this crucial part of the "factual situation." This, of course, takes us on to networking with other groups (something we will address in more detail shortly), but it is necessary to recognize the central role that involvement plays in the education process that the small disciplined community must develop for itself.

2. Consumption

The question of the consumption style of Christians bring us back to the issues of Chapter 2. There we saw how Jesus has called his followers to one of two lifestyles—as either forgoers or stewards. Some in the Christian community have felt the more radical call to forgo nearly all wealth and to live with a minimum of possessions. Most Christians have recognized a different call, one that better allows the believer to take on direct economic responsibilities for others, as in a family. This second lifestyle, that of the Christian steward, is based on the goodness that material possessions can bring to human life, but it is just as thoroughly attuned to the dangers that material possessions present to even the most dedicated Christian.

Genesis tells us that when God created the world, "he saw that it was good." This basic fact about creation itself has been taken throughout the tradition to mean that the material world is not an evil against which the spiritual part of the human person must struggle. Jesus himself was a forgoer, but he enjoyed the fruits of the earth and pointed to their use not only for physical sustenance but also as an integral part of human thriving and celebration, as at the marriage feast at Cana. While responsible stewards restrict their consumption of material goods, it is definitely *not* because material things are bad for humanity.

There are, however, three central reasons for Christians and others to monitor their consumption carefully. The first is one that, as we saw in Chapter 2, the early church leaders pointed out. To allow material possessions too large a part in our lives leads inevitably to a hardening of our hearts and a deadening of our sensibilities for the more subtle realities of personal interaction and a life of faith. In spite of our own sense that we will not be changed just because we are buying this or that particular thing, our consumption pattern has undeniable effects in our life and on who we are.

The second reason for careful attention to our consumption is the fact that the vast majority of people in the world live in poverty. To continue spending on ourselves all the money we make without any limit ignores this fact. It says that the poor have no claim on us. It says that we have complete control over whatever we earn. In short, it contradicts a basic Christian conviction about human life. We have only provisional control over the goods of the earth; God alone has absolute "ownership." The poor have a just entitlement to the necessities of life, and our ignoring this just claim denies them their due.

Uncontrolled consumption leaves us oblivious to the intense pain of starvation felt by children too young to speak, oblivious to the tragic effects of brain damage caused by malnutrition in childhood, oblivious to the heart-rending choice forced upon many adults in many Third World nations either to live in silence and watch their children suffer needlessly or to speak out against injustice and risk kidnapping, torture, and finally execution that would make their children orphans. While stewards have an additional obligation to work for greater justice, their care in limiting consumption is a sign of identification with the poor of the world and a witness to the injustice whereby a small minority of the world's population is consuming far too large a portion of the fruits of the earth.

The third reason for limiting consumption is that by doing so, stewards will have a portion of their income to spend in the pursuit of justice. Each steward should be conscious of dividing his or her income into a use fund and a surplus fund. The use fund is meant to cover the necessary expenses of daily life—including both physical and cultural expenditures—with a modest savings for long-term planning and retirement.

The surplus fund is, on the other hand, that portion of an authentic steward's possessions that is not needed for use functions. This surplus can be shared with others in need or disbursed to religious movements, community agencies, and justice causes. The surplus is to be channeled into policies and actions that structure greater justice and efficiency into the economy. Stewards are morally forbidden to shift surplus funds into satisfying individual and family wants and felt needs. The surplus of stewards will be either committed to new policies and programs to strengthen justice and efficiency or corrupted into self-centered advantage.

When considering *surplus* and *use funds*, it is important to alert ourselves to a consumerism that threatens to engulf the U.S. economy. What is the significance, for example, of the flood tide of home video games and electronic appliances, often costing hundreds of dollars? There is an imperative need for a new breed of Christian consumers who discipline themselves to practice the *principle of mutuality in consumer spending*. That is, stewards must become ever more conscious that, as an integral part of their right to spend in providing for themselves and their families, there is the obligation to expend personal income for those in the nation and the world who live without the means for hope and dignity. Two guidelines can help Christians to enact a new *structural operative norm*. This norm can be stated in two parts:

> *(a) Christian stewards ought to expect one another to consume according to their own authentic blend of material, social, cultural, and spiritual needs.*
>
> *(b) Stewards ought to expect one another to affirm the principle of mutuality, where as they spend for their own needs they spend proportionally to support the right of all others to meet their needs as well.*

The total task is to mold these basic needs and rights into a more just economy that undergirds equitable consumption for all people—this with the greatest possible economic efficiency and justice.

Obviously, the crucial question here is just how a person or family is to divide income between the two funds. The truth of the matter is that there is no one answer to the question. Each person and family is unique, and each small disciplined community will find a different set of decisions made by its members on this issue of consumption lifestyle. It is neither necessary nor advisable for the whole group to arrive at some common position. Two different families may well decide to set aside a different proportion of their incomes for the surplus fund. What is important is that each steward reflect seriously on the requirement that Jesus placed on all his followers and that this reflection be shared among the group.

3. Work Within the Larger Congregation

In most cases the small disciplined community will be made up of members from a particular congregation who have come together to seek better ways to live out the call of Jesus in their daily lives. As a result, the congregation, or other larger body to which the group belongs, is itself often a locus of significant interest and a logical place to begin the group's efforts to shape expectations outside its own membership. Even where a small disciplined community consists of stewards from two or more local congregations (and perhaps even two or more denominations) most members will feel a particular responsibility to challenge their own worshipping communities to greater awareness and economic accountability. Most justice-seeking stewards find that their congregations have given almost no serious thought to the part they play in the national and international economy.

The approach to the larger congregation must be made thoughtfully. Any holier-than-thou attitude will not only alienate the others and thwart success but will also violate the requirement of conscientious intentions that are needed as a guard against insensitive manipulation of others by Christians ostensibly striving for greater justice.

Each congregation will have its own history and its own norms that structure the way discussion and change come about within it. The small disciplined community will need to pay careful attention to the factual situation there, reading the expectations of church leaders and estimating what next step in greater accountability might be possible for the congregation. Recall from our diagram on building sound moral structures that the choice of a norm to empower is crucial. To aim for too much will lead to failure; to aim for too little will dissipate energy to no effect.

One small disciplined community in Schenectady, New York, has decided to press the church board to examine the investment of endowment funds to see what sorts of corporations are benefiting from the stocks and bonds owned by the congregation and to support stockholder resolutions aimed at greater justice in the life of those firms in the world. Of course, any small disciplined community taking on this issue will need to do some careful self-education on the topic of investment responsibility. Books such as *People/Profits: The Ethics of Investment,* edited by Charles Powers, and *The Ethical Investor* by Simon, Powers and Gunnemann, as well as materials from the Interfaith Center on Corporate Responsibility, would be requisite.[10] Direct contact with church people, the pastor or rector, and other church leaders must be combined with a well-prepared presentation at a formal board meeting. The goal is a structured oversight of the moral dimension of investment, parallel to the function of a portfolio manager, whose usual responsibility is to oversee the financial profitability of the investments.

Other issues that the small disciplined community might press within the larger congregation include assistance in providing meals to disabled or elderly persons in the neighborhood or presenting a series of workshops for the wider congregation on topics of economic justice. The talents and interests of the members of the small disciplined community will indicate which directions are most promising.

4. Participation in Local Networks

While a small disciplined community will likely expend a portion of its energy in transforming the expectations within the larger congregation, its thrust to alter the patterns of economic activity in society requires efforts beyond the Christian community itself. One of the most important and most promising arenas for activity is the local area: the neighborhood, town, or city where the group is located.

In almost every case, the small disciplined community will find that it is not the first group in the area to seek greater economic justice. In many cases, we Christians are Johnny-come-latelies to these efforts. This says quite a bit about the history of the Christian churches, but at this point the group is well advised simply to understand that while their efforts stand on their own merits, they may be perceived by other justice seekers as representatives of a primarily conservative institution (a church) that has often been aligned with the forces of resistance to change. Whether or not this is a fair presumption on the part of other justice seekers, it is a sobering and humbling awareness for Christians and will press the small disciplined community not to be presumptuous in its efforts.

Since there will usually be a number of other groups seeking social change in the local area, one of the first steps for members of the small community will be learning more about what is already happening. Group members will probably already be participating in these efforts before the small disciplined community is formed, so there will be a foundation already laid. It is important for the group to begin with participation in ongoing efforts for two reasons. The first is that involvement in the struggle for justice is a requisite part of the group's self-education, and becoming part of already-existing movements is the primary way to be involved. In those other grass-roots efforts are many who have been striving for greater justice for many years. Of particular importance to small disciplined communities made up of middle- or upper-income members is the fact that some of the justice efforts will be led by the poor themselves, and contact with these people will be essential if the group is to understand the problems of our economy well and be part of a solution that is not just imposed from above. The second reason for joining existing efforts is that the group will have a greater likelihood of success early in its history.

Thus, for example, small groups of committed Christians around the nation have joined forces with others in organizing to stop redlining—the practice by some urban banks of designating (in red ink on a map) some areas of the city that seem to be deteriorating and to authorize no further loans or mortgages in that area, regardless of the credit-worthiness of the borrower. (Redlining has had the effect of accelerating deterioration and of thwarting popular efforts to reverse such a trend.) When the small disciplined community addresses such an issue, it consciously becomes part of a network of groups working on that same issue. Included in the network may well be neighborhood associations, a senior-citizen group from the area, local organizations of one of the political parties active in the area, several other church-based groups, and a few other local organizations interested in preventing the neighborhood from deteriorating. As with many issues, the small disciplined community plays a crucial role as link between the local congregation and the larger network.

Middle-class Christian churches can play an important part in the efforts of poor people to save their neighborhoods, since one of the central tactics employed to marshal the power necessary to alter bank policy is organizing large numbers of persons with money in that bank to threaten to withdraw their funds if the policy is not changed. These people need not be very rich, but there needs to be a large number who are willing to act. Here lies the importance of networking. No one group, not even a whole congregation, would likely be able to get enough people to make a significant difference to a large bank. Yet if many organizations in the city work to get many of their constituent members to participate, banks can be (and in fact have been) forced to alter their policy and provide greater justice to the previously redlined area.

The small disciplined community, then, would be cooperating in empowering a new norm for people's private banking patterns:

*Responsible stewards should expect one another to do their
banking only at financial institutions that incorporate just
lending policies in their daily practices.*

Whether through direct appeal and preaching within the larger
congregation or through public campaigns with demonstrations
and bumper stickers, the small disciplined community can have
an important effect in such an effort to raise the level of justice in
the community.

There are a myriad of other justice issues facing the local civic
community. Many of these are already being addressed, but
some may not be unless the small disciplined community
organizes the network to do so. In any case, participation in a
network of groups aiming at the same or similar goals is an
essential step in marshaling the power to effect a change in
publicly operative norms. As we mentioned in Chapter 1, there is
always a danger in networking for any relatively small group
whose own philosophical or religious convictions are the primary
rationale for their participation. It is possible that other groups or
the network as a whole could take a step that appears to compromise a basic value of the smaller group. For this reason most
networks center on practical actions aimed at change and do not
spend much time discussing the underlying reasons for taking the
actions. Not only does it make sense strategically for Christians
to work with other groups; it is also important theologically, since
God's action in history is not limited to the work of those who
profess his name explicitly.

To some Christians this seems to depreciate the importance of
intentions, of explicitly striving to change the "hearts" of all with
whom they come in contact. It is for some a difficult lesson to
learn, but the whole point of the network is that groups with
differing rationales can work together, if not on each and every
issue, at least on the one that the network has been created to
address. This approach does not belittle intentions and the reasons behind convictions; rather it recognizes that even though
not all will agree on the underlying philosophical or religious

reasons, Jesus' stress on the poor and outcasts can be embodied in our day and in our economy.

5. Confronting Injustice
on a National or International Level

While the issues at the national or international level are different from those at the local level, the procedures for confronting them are similar. The reason for this is imbedded in the basic structure of societal change. At any level, the primary method for altering social structures is altering the operative norms of the social grouping involved. Whether that social grouping is a congregation, a city, or a nation, basic change in expected patterns of behavior comes from changes that began in the local setting. Whether the target is a bank's redlining policy or the nation's armament policy, fundamental change must begin with the norms that average citizens consider worthy to be followed.

Networking is the only way to overcome the distance between the small disciplined community and the vast, far-reaching social structures and policies to be altered. In dealing with national or international issues the networks must be much larger, and thus they will involve less face-to-face interaction and will rely more on the printed word. Consider three examples of issues that differing groups, Christian and secular, have taken on in the past decade: world hunger, the marketing of infant formula in the Third World, and disarmament.

Our first example begins with a small church in metropolitan Atlanta, where occasionally at a Sunday morning worship service a "call to mission" is presented. Any member of the congregation may sound a call by sharing a concern and asking others to join. If there is a response, the group meets regularly, establishes its own guidelines and expectations as it tries to develop a greater understanding of the problem, and to some degree becomes involved in working toward change.

In this way, several years ago a group was formed to focus on the problem of world hunger. As their study deepened, so did their concern, especially for two young couples in the group. The two men, both with seminary training, vowed to give two years of voluntary service in the field, and their wives volunteered to continue their employment to support the households. Their church continued its commitment to the project, so when the emphasis became educational, space in the church basement was provided, the church printing facilities were made available, and other members volunteered to assist. This was the birth of *Seeds*, a magazine, and *Sprouts*, a newsletter, published twelve times a year.

In 1982 *Seeds* received national attention when it was awarded the first annual World Hunger Media Award as the best U.S. periodical dealing with the hunger problem. The *Seeds* project has grown to include six full-time staff members. They write, teach, speak, provide leadership for conferences and workshops, and research hunger needs.

Seeds is action oriented and can make printed material available (upon request) in the "How to" category; for example:
• how to form a hunger committee;
• how to start a food pantry;
• how to start a hospitality ministry for homeless, hungry people, especially during the winter months;
• how to run a church garden project;
• how to write your Congressperson about hunger;
• how to celebrate an alternative Christmas;
• how to teach children about hunger with games.
All of these projects have been done in the church where the *Seeds* staff persons are members.

This is a telling example of what grass-roots organizations can accomplish with limited resources, but with an abundance of creativity, commitment, and group support. We can follow their progression from the small disciplined group, into the larger congregation, to cooperative endeavors with neighborhood churches and community groups, into national church conventions, national secular and political organizations, and finally into international situations. Not every small disciplined community will be involved so thoroughly in all these arenas, but the *Seeds* project is clear evidence that it can occur.[11]

Our second example concerns nutrition in the Third World. The World Health Organization, at its 34th Assembly in Geneva, Switzerland, was concerned over the impact of infant formula upon the health of mothers and babies, when artificial formula feeding was compared with breast-feeding. The best available evidence indicated that five million infant deaths each year were due to diarrheal disease and/or malnutrition, and one million of these deaths were associated with artificial-formula feeding. On May, 1981, the Assembly, after years of preparatory work, took a final vote that recommended a code supporting breast-feeding and set controls upon formula feeding. One hundred eighteen nations supported the code, three nations abstained, thirty nations were absent, and only the United States voted against the code![12]

For many years before the World Health Organization vote, groups in this country and abroad worked to marshal public support for a more responsible set of guidelines for infant-formula manufacturers. Publications such as *The Corporate Examiner* and a number of newsletters have provided the information linkage necessary to keep large numbers of low-budget organizations informed on recent developments. Although primarily designed to assist in responsible stock ownership, the *Examiner* provides some of the resources that allow small disciplined communities to take on giants in a two-billion-dollar-a-year market.

We saw earlier the advantage of participating in already-existing efforts within local networks. When issues at a national level are addressed, this is practically a requirement. Most small groups do not have the time, experience, and contacts around the nation necessary to launch a successful national effort. In addition, the assessment of the factual situation that goes into formulating a new operative norm includes an estimate of what additional normative expectation is actually feasible. Thus it is necessary to be attuned to the movements for positive change that are currently touching the lives of large numbers of people. This does not, however, leave the small disciplined community as merely a rubber stamp of existing national trends. Often it will be necessary to sharpen the analysis and widen the focus of ongoing efforts. Take, for example, the movement for a nuclear freeze.

Our third example concerns militarism, a topic that many do not at first think of as an issue of economic justice. The fact of the matter is that in addition to the alarming set of issues surrounding disarmament and simple survival as a civilization in the face of increasingly destructive weapons, the immense investment of human and material resources in the military has had a staggering effect on the number of the poor and unemployed and on their ability to cope. Matching huge increases in military spending have been severe cutbacks in federal expenditures for programs for those below the poverty level. Even orthodox economics reminds us that the issue is one of national priority in the face of scarcity.

Many "hawks" in Congress and in the executive branch talk as if there is no trade-off between military expenditures and the rest of the federal budget. Not only is there a trade-off, but the reasons behind the push to expand U.S. military presence in the world are directly tied to the reasons why such "hawks" are willing to cut expenditures for programs such as food stamps, research into solar energy, Aid to Families with Dependent Children (AFDC), and funds for education. Tying these together is the phenomenon we saw in Chapter 5: an individualistic Lockean vision being employed to legitimate national security capitalism. While professing a sort of rugged individualism (which leads to fewer publicly funded services such as job-training, quality secondary and postsecondary education, etc.), the national leaders provide more financial and military support to multinational firms (which results in immense tax breaks for the wealthy and creates "friendly" military governments in Third World countries).

The details of all this are lengthy, of course, but we refer to it here to indicate the sort of role that the small disciplined community can play in an existing national network such as the nuclear freeze movement. Laying bare the true dynamics of the American public's expectations for "a strong defense" is a crucial part of any effort to alter the public norms currently fueling the arms race. In this issue and in many others, the small disciplined community has much to contribute, even if its justice efforts are only a small part of a national endeavor.

The Christian Economic Ethic and a "Secular" World

As we consider the influence of the small disciplined community on justice issues in either the local civic community or the nation as a whole, we are faced with a particular question that does not arise either within the small disciplined community or within efforts to alter the life of the local congregation. This question is one whose answer we have taken for granted since page one of this book. It does not arise within the small disciplined community or the local congregation because both of these are expressly Christian. But it does arise in wider contexts precisely because not everyone there *is* a Christian. The question might even be posed by our critics with a mild taunt in their voices: Even if there is such a thing as a Christian economic ethic, what relevance does religious belief have to public life in a secular society? Since this question can have three distinctly different meanings, we will answer it in three parts.

1. Public Discourse and Arguments "from Authority"

In its first (and fairly naive) meaning, the question might be rephrased: "In a secular world, what good are arguments and conclusions based on the Scriptures and on theologians who lived in the third century? Are you going to quote the New Testament to the city council?" At the core of this question is a confusion between the kind of reasons why any one person or homogeneous group holds a particular conviction and the kind of reasons that "make sense" to a pluralistic community where many different religious or philosophical positions are represented. To understand this confusion we need better to understand "arguments from authority."

When any group with a history has to settle a disagreement or vote on a controversial proposal, the group members on each side of the issue employ as part of their arguments the views of widely respected leaders of the group in the past and other "authorities" whose wisdom and vision are taken for granted within the group. Thus, for example, where in a Christian group people might quote Jesus or Paul, discussions at a conservative "think-tank" might refer to John Locke or Abraham Lincoln, and in a Marxist gathering one would hear references to Lenin and Marx. There may, of course, be a disagreement within the group about which side a particular "authority" would really take in a disagreement, but the point is that every group does appeal to some "authorities."

However, even though a group or individual comes to a conclusion based on such authorities, it may be necessary to defend that conclusion in a still larger social grouping—as when Christians, Republicans, or Marxists try to influence national or even local policy. No matter how influential St. Paul, John Locke, or Karl Marx was in arriving at those conclusions, it is highly unlikely that anyone will refer to any of them at a Congressional hearing or a city council meeting. Why? Because in the nation and city they are not universally recognized as "authorities," and so the response to quoting them may be "So what?" This fact of life does not mean that they are unimportant or wrong. It simply reminds us that in public discourse between individuals or groups that do not share respect for a particular authority, references to that authority will not be at all persuasive.

Recognition of this basic element of social life leads "dovish" Democrats to appeal to Republican president Dwight Eisenhower's warnings about the military industrial complex and leads Republicans such as Ronald Reagan to quote Democratic "authorities" such as Franklin D. Roosevelt in presenting arguments on national issues.

We can now see the confusion implicit in the first meaning of the question about the relevance of a Christian economic ethic to a secular society. From the point of view of the steward, it is not only possible but completely reasonable for Christians to come to their own ethical stances employing Christian (as well as "secular") sources even if religious formulations are not later used in discussions in society at large. From the point of view of citizens who are not Christians, since nearly every group or individual in society respects certain "authorities" who are not looked up to in society generally, they need feel no surprise—nor threat—when Christian stewards do likewise. The issue at stake in our original question about the role of religious belief in public life is not the difference in the authorities appealed to in religion and in secular society. We must look elsewhere.

2. The Charge of Idiosyncratic Minority Politics

The second possible meaning of the question of the relevance of the Christian economic ethic to a secular society centers on a different issue. According to this complaint, the basic values of this ethic are not widely shared in the United States, and the basic insights into how individual and social life works are founded only on religious vision and are not sound descriptions of the human situation that nonbelievers could agree with. This sort of stance respects the right of Christian stewards to live their lives as they wish but laments the negative effects this minority has when its idiosyncratic convictions are pressed into national or even local politics.

It is a fundamental premise of this book, however, that the wisdom implicit in the Christian economic ethic is not the sole possession of a group of eccentric visionaries. In every age, proponents of this ethic have been thoroughly immersed in the problems of the "real" world and have proposed solutions appropriate to the everyday realities of economic and social life. Look at Amos as he responded to the wealth and hypocrisy of the leaders of his day; look at Ambrose as he brought the acumen of a civil administrator to his new position as bishop; look at Calvin as he set out to restructure the life of the community in many of its dimensions.

As we have argued in Chapter 7, the descriptions of the human person and social life that are implicit in the Christian tradition correspond closely to the insights of contemporary psychology and sociology. In fact, it is individualism (and in particular the orthodox economic interpretation of human life) that misunderstands many of these realities of life and ignores the scientific insights available on the issue. The individualist description of human life is far too individualistic to be accurate.

When it comes to the basic values in the Christian economic ethic, these too are neither idiosyncratic nor foreign to American life. The strong sense of the rights of the individual (which requires both respect for individual initiative and support for democratic decision making in economic life) is widely held. The equally important sense that there must be economic cooperation and communally determined limits to individual assertion is also widely recognized and is evident in events ranging from cooperative barn-raisings to American populist movements to child labor laws and anti-pollution ordinances.

Of course, many of us Americans have become quite comfortable with the wealth that our current, highly productive, and yet unjust economic system enables us to attain. Thus it is no surprise that most middle- and upper-income Americans will resist many changes in our economy that justice requires. But this says only that there is a lot of work to be done; it does not imply that the Christian economic ethic is un-American or a purely religious utopian dream.

3. Public Norms, Civil Legislation, and Religious Belief

The third meaning to the inquiry about the relevance of the Christian economic ethic to secular life arises out of a more general question that requires thoughtful response from Christians. The larger query is this: How should Christians distinguish between those standards for living that should be legislated in societal life (such as prohibitions against murder and guarantees of basic standards of justice) and those that individual believers may live out but that should not be made mandatory in society?

The first thing for us all to recall here is that, historically, Christian communities have taken a number of different stances toward the "secular" world around them.[13] Many early Christian communities and later Christian sects resisted contact with and corruption by the non-Christian world around them. For centuries after the Roman emperor Constantine legalized Christianity, it was taken for granted as an essential part of society. A multitude of Christian standards *were* at various times mandated in civil society at large. There has been no single answer to our question within the Christian tradition, and we Christians in our nation in this era will have to develop an answer appropriate to our situation, just as Christians in other times and places have done.

This is no easy task, but it is made a bit less difficult within a pluralistic political democracy like ours by applying two basic "tests" to any proposals for public implementation (such as ours aimed at greater economic justice).

The first test is directed to the tradition: Are the basic values at stake ones that most scholars and thoughtful believers agree have been held fairly consistently in the Christian tradition as standards for responsible communal living (even if they may not always have been implemented as well as they might have been)? The second test concerns respect for contemporary pluralism: Are the basic values at stake ones that many (even if not all) other thoughtful citizens, operating out of other philosophical or religious positions, also hold as standards for responsible community life, or are those values unique to our own religious convictions?

Clearly, these two "tests" will not solve all problems. There will be debates among Christians as to whether certain values *have* been consistently held. And, of course, not *all* other philosophical and religious positions will agree with us; otherwise there would be no public disagreement! Practically speaking, unless a policy proposal passes the first test, only a small portion of Christians and Christian churches will make an effort to implement any proposal. Unless it passes the second test, Christians will not muster the political clout to make a difference. Fundamental respect for the individual (including one's self) implies that each person must act in accord with his or her conscience (even as a "minority of one" on a particular issue). Still, when a norm passes these two "tests," there is at least corroboration of one's convictions and an assurance that they are not idiosyncratic within either the Christian or the civic communities.

There is an additional meaning of our original question on the relevance of the Christian ethic to economic life that falls under this third section. It represents a significant confusion on the part of many well-meaning Christians who believe that the churches go too far in trying to influence economic structures. It is one of the major charges made by Michael Novak in his influential book, *The Spirit of Democratic Capitalism.* In Novak's words, "No intelligent human order . . . can be run according to the counsels of Christianity. . . . To run an economy by the highest Christian principles is certainly to destroy both the economy and the reputation of Christianity."[14]

At the heart of this rebuke is a misunderstanding of the difference between "highest" and "most basic" ethical principles. *No one* is proposing that the "highest" Christian principles be made mandatory. Selling all you have and giving the money to the poor, giving your tunic also to the thief who would take your cloak, giving up your life for your friends—*these* are the "highest" Christian principles. But these are and always have been *counsels* for *individual life,* not *laws* for *society.*

Rather than these, the Christian economic ethic requires the public implementation of the *most basic* ethical principles. While such principles do put limits on the behavior of the wealthy and powerful, they guarantee not wealth and power for all people but the basic elements for a life of dignity and hope for even the poorest and least respected members of society. Guarantees of adequate diet at home and due process in the factory and office are crucial. Relief from sexual harassment and racial discrimination are basic rights. Active governmental support of workplace democracy and corporate social responsibility must replace resistance to reform and accommodation to the status quo.

It is quite instructive to look to the debate over related economic reforms over the past century. As each and every humanizing reform was proposed, the defenders of a less restricted capitalism claimed that such high-minded, idealistic reform would derail the train of progress and keep it from its ultimate destination of wealth for all people. We now take for granted child labor laws, the forty-hour workweek, worker safety ordinances, workman's compensation laws, Social Security, labor unions, and a host of other changes. Yet every one of these was attacked as foolish moralism and was attained only by long and deliberate struggle by low- and middle-income workers. Basic justice has always appeared to the privileged as unrealistic perfectionism. It is not.

Summary and the Task Ahead

As we respond to the question about the relevance of the Christian economic ethic to the secular world we find ourselves back at the point where this book began. The relevance comes not from the fact that this ethic is Christian. Our belief in Jesus, the Christ, is specifically Christian, but we do not try to legislate that for all. Rather, the problems of injustice in economic life cry out for redress; the victims of injustice struggle daily for survival, dignity, and hope. The Christian economic ethic is built upon insights into human life and values critical for it and calls Christians to develop a structured response.

In this book we have traced the basic outlines of that ethic from its Hebrew roots to the modern period, where the Christian churches have all too often neglected its implications outside of the individual realm. We have looked briefly at some of the basic ideas of economic science and have urged that Christians must not only learn to learn from economics but that they must learn to use economics with care, being aware of its proclivities and biases. We have examined, in particular, the relation of efficiency to justice and have addressed several concrete economic policy issues currently being debated in the nation. In addition, we have investigated how social change comes about and have proposed a framework for effecting change—a framework that can be employed by the small disciplined community, a group of Christian stewards striving to live out Jesus' challenge more fully.

Each of these elements in this book is of necessity only an introduction for the reader. Much more work and study is required. Above all, only a conscientious living-out of the steward ethic by a multitude of Christians in small disciplined communities will bring the experience, wisdom, and power required to transform local and national patterns of interaction.

No one of us has to attempt this alone. Many, many people are already engaged in the struggle for justice. On a worldwide scale the numbers are immense, and the most hopeful sign is the number of places where the victims of injustice are providing the leadership in this effort. We economically successful Christians of the United States must be open to such leadership from others within and outside our nation as we strive continuously to transform our economic life.

If we take Jesus' parable of the last judgment at all seriously, everything depends on it.

Notes

Chapter 1 (pp. 1-24)
1. Frances Moore Lappé and Joseph Collins, *Food First: Beyond the Myth of Scarcity* (New York: Ballantine Books, 1977), pp. 19-23.
2. Gustavo Gutiérrez, *A Theology of Liberation* (Maryknoll, N.Y.: Orbis Books, 1973). See, for example, ch. 2.
3. Michael Novak, *The Spirit of Democratic Capitalism* (New York: Simon and Schuster, 1982). See especially ch. 16.
4. Robert K. Merton, *Social Theory and Social Structures,* revised edition (Glencoe, Ill.: Free Press, 1959), p. 167. Merton here is citing Irving Wylie's *The Self-made Man in America* (New York: Free Press, 1954), pp. 3-4.
5. Ibid., p. 163.
6. Ibid., pp. 168-69. The "unsuccess" of the welfare system visits the tragedy of parents upon their children into future generations. The parents, locked into the frustrations of this poverty cycle, often are simply unable to provide the education and training that might boost their children into successful careers. In 1977, for example, some 7,836,000 children were recipients of the welfare program Aid for Families with Dependent Children (AFDC).
7. U.S. Bureau of the Census, Current Population Reports, Series P-60, No. 140, *Money, Income and Poverty Status of Families and Persons in the United States: 1982 (Advance Data from the March 1983 Current Population Survey)* (Washington, D.C.: U.S. Government Printing Office, 1983), pp. 21, 24. Data on 125% of the poverty level for 1959-1979 comes from the 1981 report (No. 134, p. 25).
8. Arthur I. Blaustein, Report to the President, National Advisory Council on Economic Opportunity, October 1980.
9. U.S. Bureau of the Census, p. 31.
10. See W. K. Frankena, *Ethics,* 2nd ed. (Englewood Cliffs, N.J.: Prentice-Hall, 1973), p. 113.

11. Harry M. Johnson, *Sociology* (New York: Harcourt, Brace and World, 1960), p. 8.

12. Amitai Etzioni has developed a discriminating analysis of social power in his *The Active Society* (New York: Free Press, 1968), chs. 8, 12, 13-15. Warren Breed has published, with Etzioni's approval, a much briefer synopsis of *The Active Society* in his *The Self-guiding Society* (New York: Free Press, 1971). His chapters 10-13 deal directly with the interpretations of power developed by Etzioni. Those who do not care to tackle the 698 pages in Etzioni can gain a simplified approach to power in the relevant chapters in Breed's abridgement.

13. A careful inquiry into Jewish ethics in reference to public policy is provided by Martin Fox, "Reflections on the Foundation of Jewish Ethics and Their Relation to Public Policy" in *Selected Papers, 1980, of the Society of Christian Ethics* (Waterloo, Ontario, Canada: Willfred Laurier University Press, 1980).

Chapter 2 (pp. 26-52)

1. John R. Donahue, S.J., "Biblical Perspectives on Justice," *The Faith That Does Justice* (New York: Paulist, 1977), p. 76.

2. Gerd Theissen lists this sort of rejection of material goods as one of several characteristics of Jesus and of other wandering charismatics of the time. See Gerd Theissen, *Sociology of Early Palestinian Christianity,* trans. John Bowden (Philadelphia: Fortress, 1978), ch. 2.

3. Richard J. Cassidy, *Jesus, Politics, and Society: A Study of Luke's Gospel* (Maryknoll, N.Y.: Orbis Books, 1978), p. 31.

4. Ibid.

5. Martin Hengel, *Property and Riches in the Early Church* (Philadelphia: Fortress, 1974), p. 30. Another helpful source is J. L. Houlden, *Ethics and the New Testament* (London: Penguin, 1973); see index for "possessions."

6. Quoted by William Walsh, S.J., and John P. Langan, S.J., "Patristic Social Consciousness: The Church and the Poor," in *The Faith That Does Justice,* ed. John C. Haughey (New York: Paulist, 1977), p. 127. The authors are indebted to this excellent overview of patristic writings on the subject of economic ethics.

7. *Liber Regulae Pastoralis,* pt. III, 129.

8. Thomas Aquinas, *Summa Theologica,* II-II, q. 66, aa. 2 and 7.

9. A. J. Carlyle, "The Theory of Property in Medieval Theology,"
quoted in C. H. McIlwain, *The Growth of Political Thought in the
West* (New York: Macmillan, 1957), pp. 162, 163.
10. *Didache* 1.4.8: *Early Christian Writings,* trans. M. Staniforth (London: Penguin, 1972), p. 229.
11. Cf. Gregory of Nyssa, *Love of the Poor* and Ambrose, *On the Duties
of the Clergy.*
12. Gerhard von Rad, *The Message of the Prophets* (New York: Harper &
Row, 1962), p. 83.
13. Ibid., p. 89.
14. This has had tremendous significance in areas outside of ethics as
well. Many historians of culture attribute the development of science, technology, and industry in the West largely to this historical
sense of the Christian vision. See, for example, Langdon Gilkey,
Reaping the Whirlwind: A Christian Interpretation of History (New
York: Seabury, 1981).
15. Stephen Charles Mott, "Biblical Faith and the Reality of Social Evil,"
Christian Scholar's Review, vol. 9, no. 3, 1980.
16. Aquinas, *S.T.,* II-II, q. 58, a. 8.
17. Aquinas, *S.T.,* II-II, q. 84, a. 1.
18. Robert Heilbronner, *The Making of Economic Society* (Englewood
Cliffs, N.J.: Prentice-Hall, 1975), pp. 40-41.
19. Heilbronner, p. 42.

Chapter 3 (pp. 53-66)
1. Ernest Troeltsch, *The Social Teaching of the Christian Churches,*
trans. Olive Wyon, 2 vols. (London: George Allen & Unwin, 1931;
reprint ed., Chicago: University of Chicago Press, 1981), II:555-56.
2. Ibid., II:554, 557.
3. Karl Holl, *The Cultural Significance of the Reformation,* trans. Karl
and Barbara Hertz and John H. Lichtblau (New York: Meridian
Books, 1959), p. 63.
4. Ibid., p. 30.
5. Troeltsch, II:610.
6. Ibid., II:591.
7. Ibid., II:610-611, 621, 642-49.
8. Ibid., II:642.
9. Max Weber, *The Protestant Ethic and the Spirit of Capitalism* (New
York: Scribner's, 1956), pp. 50-56.
10. Ibid., p. 175.

11. Alfred North Whitehead, *Science and the Modern World* (New York: Macmillan, 1935), p. 57.

12. Thomas Mun, *England's Treasure by Forraign Trade: Or the Ballance of our Forraign Trade is the Rule of our Treasure* (London: Thomas Clark, 1664; reprint ed., Oxford: Basil Blackwell, 1949), p. 88.

13. Harry M. Johnson, *Sociology* (New York: Harcourt, Brace & World, 1960), p. 8.

Chapter 4 (pp. 67-82)

1. In order to avoid unnecessary confusion over such phrases or such a term as "classical or Lockean liberalism," or "liberalism," let us at the outset of this chapter differentiate them from present-day liberalism or conservatism. Lockean or classical liberalism in the seventeenth and eighteenth centuries represented an individualistic, capitalistic political movement initiated by the emerging commercial, financial, and industrial leaders and oriented towards personal liberty. In 1680 this liberal movement represented the values which are held by "conservative" economic and political forces today. "Conservatives" today want to conserve individual liberty the dominant individualistic and capitalistic values which liberals of the seventeenth, eighteenth and nineteenth centuries fought hard to bring into force. (In the terminology of sociology, they helped to empower new operative norms.) "Liberals" today are also fighting to bring into force new values, but these tend to be more communal and are aimed at reducing individualism. In this chapter we will use the term "liberal" and "liberalism" to refer only to the *older* meaning of the term: a person or movement stressing strong individual liberty in politics and economics.

2. John Locke, "Second Treatise on Government" in *Of Civil Government,* Everyman's Library edition (London: Dent and Sons, 1943), ch. 2, sections 4-5 and 13.

3. Ibid., ch. 9, sec. 123.

4. Ibid., ch. 8, sec. 95; ch. 9, sec. 127, 137, 138.

5. Ibid., ch. 5, sec. 25.

6. Ibid., ch. 5, sec. 26.

7. Ibid., ch. 5, sec. 30 (italics ours).

8. Ibid., ch. 5, sec. 36.

9. Ibid., ch. 5, sec. 46.

10. C. B. Macpherson, *The Political Theory of Possessive Individualism* (Oxford: Oxford University Press, 1972), p. 275.
11. Ibid., p. 3.
12. William T. Bluhm, *Theories of the Political System* (Englewood Cliffs, N.J.: Prentice-Hall, 1965), p. 321.
13. Macpherson, p. 228.
14. Ibid., p. 231.
15. Locke, ch. 2, sec. 4.
16. T. V. Smith and Eduard C. Lindeman, *The Democratic Way of Life* (New York: New American Library, 1951), p. 9.
17. Seymour Martin Lipset and Earl Raab, *The Politics of Unreason* (New York: Harper & Row, 1970), p. 5.
18. Smith and Lindeman, p. 91.
19. *The New York Times,* March 18, 1978, C. 23.
20. Ibid.
21. Ibid.
22. Warren Breed, *The Self-Guiding Society* (New York: Free Press, 1971), p. 198.
23. Ibid., p. 199.
24. Ibid.

Chapter 5 (pp. 83-113)

1. Adam Smith, *An Inquiry into the Nature and Causes of the Wealth of Nations,* ed. Edwin Cannan (New York: Random House, Modern Library edition, 1937), p. 3.
2. Ibid., pp. 7-9.
3. Ibid., p. 13.
4. Ibid., p. 14.
5. Smith's major work on morality—less known today than his work on economics—is *The Theory of Moral Sentiments.*
6. While this book does not allow sufficient space to treat the history of economic thought in any detail, the reader may wish to refer to any of a number of good nontechnical overviews— for example, Robert Heilbronner, *The Worldly Philosophers* (New York: Simon and Schuster, 1980); Robert Lekachman, *A History of Economic Ideas* (New York: McGraw-Hill, 1959).
7. A brief introduction to Marxian economics is Ernest Mandel's *An Introduction to Marxist Economic Theory* (New York: Pathfinder Press, 1970).

8. Veblen is probably best known for his *The Theory of the Leisure Class*, but his *The Theory of Business Enterprise* (New York: New American Library, 1958) is a perceptive analysis of some of the tensions within industrial capitalism.
9. John Maynard Keynes, *The General Theory of Employment, Interest, and Money* (New York: Harcourt, Brace & World, 1965), p. 372.
10. Lester Thurow, *The Zero Sum Society* (New York: Penguin Books, 1981), p. 96.
11. See, for example, David M. Gordon, *The Working Poor: Towards a State Agenda* (Washington, D.C.: Council of State Planning Agencies, 1979), especially ch. 3.
12. M. Mesarovic and E. Pestel, *Mankind at the Turning Point* (New York: Dutton/Readers' Digest, 1974), p. 1.
13. Donella H. Meadows et al, *The Limits to Growth: A Report for the Club of Rome's Project on the Predicament of Mankind* (New York: Universe Books, 1972), p. 58.
14. Fred Hirsch, *Social Limits to Growth* (Cambridge: Harvard University Press, 1976), p. 27.
15. Roger Shinn, *Christianity and Crisis*, March 16, 1981, p. 55.
16. Ibid., p. 56.
17. Hirsch, p. 189.
18. Ibid.
19. *The Economic Report of the President*, 1981, Table B-29, p. 267.
20. Ibid., Table B-28, p. 266.
21. Ibid., Table B-29, p. 267.
22. The Business-Higher Education Forum, *America's Competitive Challenge: The Need for a National Response* (Washington, D.C.: 1983).
23. Thurow, pp. 85-91.
24. See Olson's *The Rise and Decline of Nations: Economic Growth, Stagflation, and Social Rigidities* (New Haven: Yale University Press, 1983).
25. Thurow, p. 90.

Chapter 6 (pp. 116-138)

1. M. Douglas Meeks, "The Holy Spirit and Human Needs," *Christianity and Crisis* 40, no. 18 (Nov. 10, 1980), 307-16.
2. Orthodox economists, as citizens and not as scientists, have at times provided an additional argument in favor of the market: that it promotes democracy in the political realm. For a classic statement

of this position, see Milton Friedman's *Capitalism and Freedom* (Chicago: University of Chicago Press, 1962), pp. 7-21.

3. See, for example, Robert A. Goldwin, "Locke and the Law of the Sea," *Commentary,* June 1981, pp. 46-50.

4. For a helpful discussion of "psychological egoism" and its relation to ethical reflection, see Peter A. Facione, Donald Sherer, and Thomas Attig, *Values and Society: An Introduction to Ethics and Social Philosophy* (Englewood Cliffs, N.J.: Prentice-Hall, 1978), pp. 55-56.

5. Using the terminology of orthodox economics, when the economist says the individual acts out of self-interest, it is assumed that each individual has a utility function that includes all the possible things and events in life that affect that person's happiness or satisfaction. Thus, even if an individual values altruistic or charitable actions, such actions are grouped along with eating a fine meal or enjoying a good book. All are seen as actions that bring satisfaction to the self and are in this sense "self-interested."

We might note, however, that any economist who judges capitalism to be more feasible than socialism on the grounds just stated in the text is making some assumption about the content (and not just the form) of the utility functions of most people. The assumption is that among the elements in the utility function, the "selfish" ones outweigh the "altruistic" ones.

6. Randall Bartlett, *Economic Foundations of Political Power* (New York: Free Press, 1973), p. 198.

Chapter 7 (pp. 139-166)

1. We refer to a rise in "relative price" of oil in comparison to other goods and not to a rise in price due to inflation. If the price of oil, the price of oil drilling equipment, of labor and of nearly everything else rose about equally (as in a general inflation), no more oil fields would be tapped.

2. Lester Thurow, *The Zero Sum Society* (New York: Basic Books, 1980), pp. 188-89.

3. C. B. Macpherson, *The Political Theory of Possessive Individualism,* p. 3.

4. Daniel C. Maguire, *A New American Justice* (New York: Doubleday, 1980), p. 60. We should note that Maguire makes apologies for the sexist language in the traditional (and succinct) formulation of justice. We should also note that Maguire, following Josef Pieper,

speaks of three kinds of justice: individual, social, and distributive. Our use includes these latter two under the single term "social justice."

5. Maguire, p. 62.
6. Ibid.
7. One of the extreme forms of individualism in social scientific description goes so far as to deny the existence of social wholes. "Methodological individualism" denies the existence of an entity called "society" or a process called a "war." Rather, they would say, these are only shorthand ways of referring to relationships among individuals. Needless to say, most social scientists find this position naive. For a classic defense of methodological individualism see Karl Popper, *The Poverty of Historicism* (New York: Harper & Row, 1964), pp. 149-52.
8. See, for example, Gerard Egan and Michael Cowan, *People in Systems: A Model for Development in the Human Service Professions and Education* (Monterey, Calif.: Brooks/Cole, 1979), chs. 1 and 10.
9. Peter L. Berger and Thomas Luckmann, *The Social Construction of Reality* (Garden City, N.Y.: Doubleday, 1966), p. 61.
10. Berger and Luckmann, pp. 28-30.
11. On this issue Berger and Luckmann have been taken to task by some of their sociological colleagues. The authors tend to overplay the significance of human decision in choosing a pattern of action and tend to underplay the influence of nonhuman elements on the issue of which behaviors are most appropriate in a particular type of situation.
12. There was a time earlier in this century when philosophers of science hoped to establish that the confirmation or contradiction of scientific theories depended solely on the factual outcomes of experiments, separate from the scientist's convictions and interpretations. This hope has been dashed on the rocks of realism, and nearly all philosophers of science acknowledge that "the scientific community" of a discipline or subdiscipline plays a crucial role in deciding what counts as "factual" scientific evidence as well as what counts as an interesting scientific problem in the first place. For one of the basic statements of such a perspective, see Thomas Kuhn, *The Structure of Scientific Revolutions* (Chicago: University of Chicago Press, 1970).
13. Berger and Luckmann, pp. 56-59.
14. Ibid., p. 59.

15. Ibid., p. 38.

16. Ibid., p. 39.

17. Arthur M. Okun, *Equality and Efficiency: The Big Tradeoff* (Washington, D.C.: Brookings Institute, 1975), p. 119.

18. Ibid.

19. For a more complete discussion, see any introductory economics textbook—for example, James Gwartney and Richard Stroup, *Economics: Private and Public Choice,* 2nd ed. (New York: Academic Press, 1980), p. 692.

20. The *Journal of Law and Economics* is an illustration of these recent developments.

Chapter 8 (pp. 167-203)

1. Ambrose of Milan, "Duties of the Clergy," quoted in W. Walsh, S.J., and J. Langen, S.J., "Patristic Social Consciousness: The Church and the Poor" in John C. Haughey, S.J., ed., *The Faith That Does Justice* (New York: Paulist, 1977), p. 127.

2. Ambrose of Milan, "On Lazarus," quoted in Walsh and Langen, p. 129.

3. James Luther Adams, "Mediating Structures and the Separation of Powers," in *Democracy and Mediating Structures,* ed. Michael Novak (Washington, D.C.: American Enterprise Institute, 1980), pp. 1-33.

4. A negative income tax is a device that works like an income tax in reverse. An income tax begins with a certain minimum income that is tax-free and then taxes a percentage of all income above that minimum level. A negative income tax also begins with a certain income level (for convenience, let us say $7,000). The government then *pays the individual* a certain percentage (say, 50%) of the dollar amount by which that person's income for the year falls short of the $7,000. Thus if a woman earned $4,000 at a part-time job, she would, in our example, get $1,500 from the government (50% of the difference between $4,000 and $7,000). The negative income tax also establishes a guaranteed minimum income for all citizens— which would be $3,500 in our example (since even if a person made zero dollars, 50% of the difference between $0 and $7,000 is $3,500). For a more complete treatment of the negative income tax, see any introductory economics text—for example, *Economics: Private and Public Choice,* by J. D. Gwartney and R. Stroup (New York: Academic Press, 1980), pp. 623-24.

5. *People and Taxes* is available by yearly subscription (215 Pennsylvania Ave. S.E., Washington, D.C. 20003).
6. Lester Thurow, *The Zero Sum Society*, p. 29.
7. Ibid., p. 31.
8. For a standard treatment, see, for example, Gwartney and Stroup, pp. 486-88.
9. Among these are John M. Blair, *The Control of Oil* (New York: Pantheon Books, 1976), and Anthony Sampson, *The Seven Sisters: The Great Oil Companies and the World They Shaped* (New York: Viking, 1975).
10. Putting Blair's findings more precisely, the average annual percentage increase in the output of the eleven countries from 1950 to 1972 comes out to be 9.55% with a "coefficient of determination" (r^2) of .999, an amazingly close "fit" of the hypothesis to the data.
11. Blair, pp. 291-92.
12. In an unpublished and unattributed review of Blair's book circulated by the American Petroleum Institute, the oil industry argues that the drop in production was due to refiners' anticipation of a price rise. In addition, the review asserts that only the Saudi government (and not Exxon) had sufficient market clout to stimulate increased demand by lowering prices. The arguments get more technical at this point (and beyond the level of economic expertise expected of the reader), but suffice it to say that the issue is not clearly resolved and that standard economic theory has had some difficulty in explaining how such a loosely organized (and at times internally belligerent) group as OPEC has held so well together for more than a decade.
13. See Frances Moore Lappé and Joseph Collins, *Food First: Beyond the Myth of Scarcity* (New York: Ballantine, 1978), especially ch. 11.
14. The Economic Recovery Tax Act of 1981 allowed firms losing money to cash in on investment tax credits from which formerly only profit-making firms could benefit. See, for example, the *Wall Street Journal*, August 27, 1981, p. 1.
15. *Wall Street Journal*, November 12, 1981.
16. Bartlett, *Economic Foundations of Political Power*, p. 79.
17. John Lachs, "I Only Work Here: Mediation and Irresponsibility," in R. DeGeorge and J. Pitchler, eds., *Ethics, Free Enterprise and Public Policy* (New York: Oxford University Press, 1978), pp. 201-13.

Chapter 9 (pp. 204-239)

1. Harry M. Johnson, *Sociology* (New York: Harcourt, Brace & World, 1960), p. 8.
2. The Center for the Ministry of the Laity, *Covenanted Support for Ministry: A Guide for Beginning Groups* (Newton Centre, Mass.: The Center for the Ministry of the Laity, 1981), p. i.
3. Ibid.
4. Ibid.
5. Materials from The Center for the Ministry of the Laity can be obtained from its office at 210 Herrick Road, Newton Centre, Mass. 02159. Also very helpful are *The Prophetic Parish* by Dennis J. Geaney (Minneapolis: Winston, 1983) and *Handbook to Mission Support Groups* by Gordon Cosby (available from Church of the Savior, Washington, D.C.). For a thoughtful integration of spirituality, the Scriptures, group work, and the demands of justice, see Paul Roy, S.J., *Building Christian Communities for Justice: The Faith Experience Book* (New York: Paulist, 1981). For a helpful treatment of many of the procedures required in work for justice, see Harry Fagan, *Empowerment: Skills for Parish Social Action* (New York: Paulist, 1979). For an interesting set of proposals for bringing justice issues from the small disciplined community into the home, see Michael True, *Homemade Social Justice: Teaching Peace and Justice in the Home* (Chicago: Fides/Claretian, 1982).
6. Robert Greenstein, "Revising the Budget: Bad News for the Poor," *Christianity and Crisis*, June 21, 1982, p. 180.
7. Ibid., p. 181.
8. Ibid.
9. Joe Holland and Peter Henriot, S.J., *Social Analysis: Linking Faith and Justice* (Maryknoll, N.Y.: Orbis Books in collaboration with the Center of Concern, 1983), p. 9.
10. See Charles W. Powers, ed., *People/Profits: The Ethics of Investment* (New York: Council on Religion and International Affairs, 1972); John G. Simon, Charles W. Powers, Jon P. Gunnemann, *The Ethical Investor: Universities and Corporate Responsibility* (New Haven: Yale University Press, 1972). This latter book is definitely *not* just for universities, in spite of the subtitle. The Interfaith Center on Corporate Responsibility, which publishes *The Corporate Examiner*, is located at 475 Riverside Drive, Room 566, New York, N.Y. 10027. The *Examiner* studies a wide range of data and problems where justice issues are confronted.

11. Subscriptions are available from *Seeds,* 222 East Lake Drive, Decatur, Ga. 30030 at $10 per year.
12. *The Corporate Examiner,* September 1981.
13. For a thorough investigation of the relation of Christianity and the secular world, see H. Richard Niebuhr's famous *Christ and Culture* (New York: Harper, 1951).
14. Michael Novak, *The Spirit of Democratic Capitalism* (New York: American Enterprise Institute/Simon and Schuster, 1982), p. 352.

Index

A

Action, individual and structured, 13, 212
Adams, James Luther, 174, 248
Affirmative action, 143
Alaskan oil pipeline, 194
Alienation, 81
Allocation of resources, 125, 189
Ambrose of Milan, 37, 41, 169, 234, 248
American Petroleum Institute, 249
Andover Newton Laity Project, 213, 215, 251
Aquinas, Thomas, 38-39, 41, 44, 48, 241

B

Bartlett, Randall, 135, 195, 246
Berger, Peter, and Thomas Luckmann, 149, 247
Blacks, 18, 98

Blair, John M., 249
Breed, Warren, 81, 241, 244
Broholm, Dick, 213
Business climate, debate concerning, 97

C

Calvin, John, 58, 63, 234
Campaign contributions, 118, 193
Capitalism, 86-96, 134, 185
Carlyle, A. J., 39, 242
Cash crops, 4, 190
Cassidy, Richard J., 33, 241
Center for the Ministry of the Laity, 213-15, 250
Christian ethics and social science, 120-22, 147
Civil rights movement, 18, 208
Co-determination, 133, 202
Community, small disciplined: see small disciplined community
Competition, 89, 185-92

Conservativism and
  liberalism, 243
Consumer communism of
  love, 30
Consumerism, 222
Consumption patterns, 216,
  220
Corporate Examiner, The,
  230, 252
Corporation, influence on
  government, 192-97
Corporation, internal
  operation, 197-202
Corporations: *see* firm
Countervailing power, 173-75
Covenanted support for
  ministry, 213
Covetousness, 48, 125
Cowan, Michael, 247
Creation, and doctrine of
  property, 40-42, 169-71

D

Democratic decision-making,
  73, 163, 175-76
Didache, 37, 41
Disarmament, 228
Discrimination, 143
Division of labor, 199; in
  Adam Smith, 87
Donahue, John R., S. J., 27,
  241

E

Economic science and
  justice, 160
Economics, 85, 94-96, 100,
  117, 122-36
Efficiency, 129-30, 157-58
Egan, Gerard, 247
Energy policy, 139, 163, 183
Etzioni, Amitai, 81, 241
Exchange, in Adam Smith,
  88
Externalities, 130

F

Fact/value distinction, 122
Firm, the, 95, 133, 192
Forgoers and stewards,
  30-31, 45, 55, 171-72, 220
Free market, 126, 159, 190
Freedom, 44, 75
Friedman, Milton, 99, 187,
  196, 245

G

Gilkey, Langdon, 242
Goldwin, Robert A., 246
Gordon, David M., 99, 245
Government, role of, 139,
  158
Greenstein, Robert, 217, 251
Gutiérrez, Gustavo, 5, 240

H

Haughey, John C., 241
Heilbronner, Robert, 48, 242
Hengel, Martin, 34, 241
Hirsch, Fred, 102, 245
Hispanics, 98
Hobbes, Thomas, 67
Holl, Karl, 57, 242
Holland, Joe, and Peter
    Henriot, 86, 219, 251
Human nature, 42, 134-35
Hunger, 190

I

Indians: see Native American
    Indians
Individual justice, 142, 144,
    158-61
Individualism, 141-47, 156,
    213, 235
Injustice, and social
    structures, 179
Institutionalism, 93
Interfaith Center on
    Corporate Responsibility,
    252

J

Johnson, Harry M., 210, 241
Just entitlement of the poor,
    37, 45, 145, 168

Justice, 27, 38, 98, 141-48,
    168

K

Keynes, John Maynard, 93,
    245
King, Martin Luther, Jr., 18,
    22

L

Labor unions, 91, 94
Lachs, John, 199, 249
Langan, John P., S. J., 241
Language, as social, 150-53
Lappé, Frances Moore, and
    Joseph Collins, 240, 249
Law of the sea treaty, 132
Liberalism, 72-79, 243
Limits to growth, physical,
    100-02
Lobbying, 118, 193
Locke, John, 41, 67, 131,
    200, 243
Luther, Martin, 54-58

M

Macpherson, C. B., 71, 144,
    243, 246
Maguire, Daniel C., 246

Market, 125-29, 159
Marx, Karl, 90, 93
Meeks, M. Douglas, 125, 245
Merton, Robert K., 7, 240
Militarism, 231, 232
Ministry, 215
Montgomery bus boycott, 18, 208
Mott, Stephen Charles, 43, 242
Multinational firms, 5
Mutuality, in consumer spending, 222

N

Native American Indians, 98
Natural law, 38, 44, 170
Needs and entitlement, 145-46
Negative income tax, 181, 248
Networks, 178, 179, 224-27
Norms, operative: *see* operative norms
Novak, Michael, 237, 240, 248, 252

O

Oil crisis, 139
Okun, Arthur M., 158, 248
OPEC, 139, 249

Operative norms, 16-17, 21, 47, 49, 205-13
Original sin, 136
Ownership, 169, 201

P

Plant closings, 161
Pluralism, 236
Pollution, 129, 132
Possessive individualism, 71, 85, 144, 171
Poverty, 8, 125, 221
Power, 3, 12-13, 17-22, 43, 46, 188, 209
Powers, Charles W., 251
Price controls, 139, 140
Productivity, 87, 105, 109, 110
Property, 28, 37-40, 68, 70, 76, 117, 131-33, 140-42, 169
Prophetic critique, 44, 174
Proportional sharing, 33, 222

R

Redistribution, 126, 134
Redlining, 226
Reverse discrimination, 143
Reward/deprivation, 23
Roles, 155

S

Scarcity, 101-04, 123-25
Seeds, 229, 252
Self-interest, 88-92, 134-35,
　246
Shinn, Roger, 103, 245
Sin, 43, 44, 135, 168, 174
Slavery, 77, 119
Small disciplined community,
　177, 211-32
Smith, Adam, 85-87, 199,
　244
Social change, 205, 206
Social construction of reality,
　147-58
Social justice, 139-66, 167-77
Social structures, 2, 172, 213
Socialism, 134
Socialization, 154-57
Sociology and ethics, 156
Sociology and individualism,
　149
Soviet Union, 12, 91
Special interests, 193, 194
Stewards, 30-34, 45, 60,
　140, 157-58, 172, 204-39
Stockholders' rights, 140
Structured action, 14, 212
Supply, effect of prices upon,
　140
Surplus fund, 35, 221, 222

T

Third World, 4, 97

U

Thurow, Lester, 99, 109, 111,
　143, 245, 246, 249
Totalitarian communism, 91
Troeltsch, Ernst, 30, 54, 242

U

Unemployment, 105, 106
Unions, 91, 94, 202
Use fund, 35, 222

V

Veblen, Thorstein, 93, 244
Vickery, William S., 104
Von Rad, Gerhard, 42, 242

W

Wealth, 2, 4, 28, 37
Weber, Max, 61, 242
Welfare programs, 94, 180
Wesley, John, 61
Windfall profits tax, 142
Women, 98, 105
World hunger, 190, 228

Z

Zacchaeus, 31-32